THE
SUPREME
COURT
AND
THE
PRESIDENCY

THE SUPREME COURT IN AMERICAN LIFE

SAMUEL KRISLOV, *General Editor*

The

Supreme Court

and

the

Presidency

ROBERT SCIGLIANO

THE FREE PRESS, New York

Collier-Macmillan Limited, London

The Free Press
A Division of The Macmillan Company
886 Third Avenue, New York, New York 10022

Collier-Macmillan Canada Ltd., Toronto, Ontario

Library of Congress Catalog Card Number: 76-128475

printing number
1   2   3   4   5   6   7   8   9   10

Preface

This is a study of relations between the Supreme Court and the Presidency. Its thesis is that these two institutions were intended by the framers of the Constitution to act, for certain purposes, as an informal and limited alliance against Congress, and that they have in fact done so. The purposes of the alliance were to counterbalance the power of Congress, particularly that of the House of Representatives, and, to a lesser extent, to counterbalance the political principles and class interests which Congress was seen to embody. These purposes were achieved by strengthening the judicial and executive branches and by weakening the legislative branch, and by the arrangements for selecting government officers. And at least some of the framers perceived a special affinity between the judicial and executive powers. Probably the great change in the relations among the governmental branches over the years has not been between the Supreme Court and the Presidency but between these two institutions and Congress, brought about by the growth of Presidential power and the democratization of American political life.

The framers did not, of course, intend the Supreme Court and the Presidency to act as a single unit or for one of them to be subservient to the other. Separation of powers requires all branches to be independent, while checks and balances require each to have a jealous regard for its prerogatives.

This study examines basic aspects of the Supreme Court's relations with the Presidency across the entire span of American history, although not, generally speaking, in a chronological fashion. Each chapter treats a separate aspect of these relations, sometimes by historical periods but more often not. The table of contents adequately indicates what is covered. Judicial decisions on the Presidency are considered only insofar as they bear directly on Court–Presidential relations, for the case-law of the Presidency is not within our purview. The history of the Court has been divided into the following periods: 1789–1829, the Federalist Court; 1829–1861, the Jacksonian Court; 1861–1897, the Republican Court; 1897–1937, the (more or less) Conservative Court; 1937–1969, the Liberal Court.

Special appreciation must be expressed to those persons who helped me with their comments on the manuscript: David R. Manwaring, of Boston College (all chapters); Phillip Hassman, of the State College of New York at Geneseo (Chapters 1–6); Samuel Krislov, of the University of Minnesota (Chapters 1–6); Robert H. Stern, of the State University of New York at Buffalo (Chapters 3, 5); Daniel M. Friedman, Office of the Solicitor General of the United States (Chapter 6); and to those persons who performed various research labors for me: Alan F. Arcuri, Robert Bishop, Shelah Gilbert Leader, and Linda Vogler.

Contents

THE
SUPREME
COURT
AND
THE
PRESIDENCY

Separation of Powers

The Supreme Court and the Presidency act within a system of separation of powers. It is proper, therefore, to begin this study of their relations by examining the principle which underlies that system. The principle of separation of powers was formulated in the seventeenth and eighteenth centuries and is based upon a distrust of political institutions. Hence its primary purpose is to organize government power in such a way as to safeguard popular liberty against the actions of public officials. Only in a secondary way does it seek to balance the power of different classes in society by giving each one dominant influence in some part of government. Thus, the principle differs decisively from the ancient Greek and Roman principle of balance of powers, which was mainly concerned with the political influence of different classes and only secondarily concerned with the organization of government power.

As it has been applied in the United States, the principle

of separation of powers has three features. First, it groups governmental functions under three general powers: legislative, executive, and judicial; second, it allocates the three powers, with some intermixing, to separate departments, or branches, of government; and, third, it provides for a coordinate status among the three branches. These three components of the principle of separation of powers will constitute a framework for our examination of the relationship between the Supreme Court and the Presidency.

THE THREE POWERS

The principle of separation of powers first took form in the writings of the English philosopher Locke in the late seventeenth century and the French philosopher Montesquieu in the middle of the eighteenth century. Both Locke and Montesquieu admired the British Constitution of their time and extracted their ideas about separation of powers from its institutional arrangements; Montesquieu was cited by *The Federalist* as the source of American thinking on the subject.[1] Neither Locke nor Montesquieu regarded judicial power as distinct from the other powers of government but rather as part of executive power. In this respect, they were following the general British understanding, for the British monarch was considered the source of all judicial power and the head of all the courts of the law; the judges were his agents to whom he had delegated his whole judicial power.[2]

For Locke there were three main governmental powers: legislative, concerned with lawmaking; federative, relating to war, peace, and other external matters; and executive, relating

---

[1] Alexander Hamilton, John Jay, and James Madison, *The Federalist*, ed. by Max Beloff (Oxford: Basil Blackwell, 1948), No. 47, p. 246: "If he be not the author of this invaluable precept in the science of politics, he has the merit of at least displaying and recommending it most effectually to the attention of mankind."

[2] See J. L. DeLolme, *The Rise and Progress of the English Constitution* (London: John W. Parker, 1838), Vol. II, pp. 566–567, 569.

to the execution of domestic laws. It is not important to our inquiry that Locke gave the name of federative power to what we would call part of the executive power, but it is important that his executive power included the power to decide disputes between private individuals and to punish persons for offenses established by law: what we would call judicial power. In short, Locke considered both executive and judicial power, as we understand these terms, to be part of the function of enforcing the laws.[3] Like Locke, Montesquieu wrote of three governmental powers: the legislative power, concerned with lawmaking; the executive power relating to the law of nations which, like Locke's federative power, was concerned with war, peace, and other external matters; and the executive power relating to civil law, concerned with the punishment of crimes and the adjudication of disputes between private individuals. Montesquieu proceeded to call the last power, which corresponds to what we think of as judicial power, by just that name, and he shortened the name of the second power to, simply, the executive power. His scheme seems to omit what to us is the main element of executive power: the execution of domestic laws, but Montesquieu proceeds to incorporate this element into his discussion of executive power.[4]

In the American adaptation of the principle of separation of powers, the three powers of government are more clearly distinguished than in the writings of Locke and Montesquieu. The best theoretical discussion of the doctrine in its American setting comes from the writings of Alexander Hamilton and James Madison under the title of *The Federalist*, in which the authors had the American and not the British Constitution for their reference. In their view, legislative power consisted of the enacting of laws and appropriations, laws being defined as "rules for the regulation of the society." Executive power

[3] John Locke, *Two Treatises on Civil Government* (London: George Routledge and Sons, 1884), Book II, chs. 7, 9, 11–14. It might be noted that Locke did not limit government power to three species, but he felt no need to discuss the "other ministerial and subordinate powers." (*Ibid.*, para. 152.)
[4] Montesquieu, *The Spirit of the Laws*, trans. by Thomas Nugent (New York: Hafner Publ. Co., 1949), Book XI, esp. chs. 6, 19.

consisted of carrying out the laws, disbursing appropriated
moneys, and employing the nation's strength in relations, peaceful or otherwise, with other states. Judicial power consisted of
expounding the law and settling disputes under it.[5] In its tasks
the judicial power, although now clearly differentiated from the
executive power, still retains an affinity to part of that power.
Madison's comments on this affinity at the Constitutional
Convention are worth quoting.

> There was an analogy between the Executive and Judici-
> ary departments in several respects. The latter executed
> the laws in certain cases as the former did in others. The
> former expounded and applied them for certain purposes,
> as the latter did for others. The difference between them
> seemed to consist chiefly in two circumstances: 1. the collec-
> tive interest and security were much more in the power
> belonging to the Executive than to the Judiciary depart-
> ment. 2. in the administration of the former, much greater
> latitude is left to opinion and discretion than in the ad-
> ministration of the latter.[6]

For other early American views of the judicial–executive
relationship, one might cite Thomas Paine's observation that
"so far as regards the execution of the laws, that which is
called the judicial power is strictly and properly the executive
power of every country," or John Adams's assertion that only
the legislative and executive powers were "naturally distinct"
in the system of three separate powers.[7]

Judicial and executive power thus appear to be similar in
nature and closer to each other than either is to legislative
power. They differ, as *Federalist 78*, which treats the judiciary,
tells us, in that the judicial power rests upon judgment while the

---

[5] *The Federalist*, Nos. 47 (Madison); 48 (Madison); 75, from which the quotation is
      taken (Hamilton); and 78 (Hamilton).
[6] Max Farrand, ed., *Records of the Federal Convention of 1787*; rev. ed. (New Haven:
      Yale University Press, 1937), Vol. II, p. 34.
[7] Thomas Paine, *Rights of Man* (London: Everyman, 1944), Pt. II, p. 199; John
      Adams, *Defence of the Constitutions of Government of the United States of America*, in
      John Adams, *Works*, ed. by Charles Francis Adams (Boston: Little, Brown,
      1851), Vol. IV, p. 579. For an opposing viewpoint, see James Wilson, *Works*
      (Philadelphia: Bronson and Chauncey, 1804), Vol. I, p. 405.

executive power rests upon force, which is to say that the one depends upon the rightness of its actions and the other upon might. They differ in that the judicial power is reflective and the executive power energetic.

THE SEPARATE DEPARTMENTS

The second component of the principle of separation of powers relates to the distribution of governmental power. Each power is, for the most part, given to a separate department or branch of government; some mixing of power is not only allowed but required in order to keep the parts of government in balance. While the federal Constitution appears to make broad grants of executive and judicial power to those branches, it limits the amount of legislative power granted to Congress. The opening clause of Article II States that "The executive power shall be vested in a President of the United States," and Article III that "The judicial power of the United States shall be vested in one Supreme Court, and in such inferior courts as the Congress may from time to time ordain and establish," while Article I opens with the words, "All legislative powers *herein granted* shall be vested in a Congress of the United States." (Emphasis supplied.) The difference in wording suggests that the framers of the Constitution dealt more generously with the President and judiciary than with Congress. The first two branches need show only that a power is executive or judicial and not prohibited by the Constitution to justify their exercise of it, while Congress must find an affirmative grant of power or must show that a power is necessary and proper for carrying out a grant to justify its exercise of it.[8]

---

[8] An impressive, if not undisputed, body of literature supports the view that the Constitution, through the vesting clauses of Articles I and II, conveyed different amplitudes of power to the legislative and executive branches. See, for example, Chief Justice Taft's opinion in *Myers* v. *United States*, 272 U.S. 52 (1926), and the historical evidence and arguments it reproduces. But almost never is the vesting-clause argument extended to the power given the judicial branch. A notable exception is the Supreme Court's opinion in *Kansas* v. *Colorado*, 206 U.S. 46 (1907), at 81–82, where Justice Brewer

In mixing the powers, the Constitution spreads more legislative power than executive or judicial among the other branches. The President, for example, is empowered to recommend measures to Congress, to veto legislative enactments, and to call Congress into session on extraordinary sessions; while the Senate is given a part in appointments and treaties. The judiciary is given the power to invalidate legislative (and executive) acts, while the Senate on important occasions may act as a court of impeachment. Both houses of Congress are made the judges of the elections of their members.[9]

The actual blending of power in the American political system greatly exceeds what is directly authorized in the Constitution. First, Congress has delegated extensive functions to the other branches and has thus further bolstered them in relation to itself. Perhaps 155 federal agencies have been authorized to adjudicate disputes between specific parties or to promulgate rules—that is, legislate—within bounds set by Congress.[10] The Chief Justice of the United States and, in their circuits, the senior court of appeals judges, exercise executive power when they, under Congressional grant, assign federal district judges to courts other than their own to help reduce case backlogs. The Supreme Court as a whole exercises legislative power when, also under grant, it develops and revises rules of procedure for all federal constitutional courts.

The blending of governmental power exceeds the constitutional authorization, in the second place, because each branch exercises implied powers as well as those explicitly given it, and blended powers also have their implications. The House

observed that "the first article, treating of legislative powers, does not make a general grant of legislative power," but that, "on the other hand, in Article III, which treats of the judicial department . . . we find . . . granted the entire judicial power of the nation."

[9] Congress was fortunate to get this much judicial power, for the Virginia and New Jersey plans, as well as the plans submitted by Hamilton and Charles Pinckney, all provided in one form or another for the judicial trial of impeachments. To the very end, Madison was opposed to allowing the Senate to try Presidential impeachments. See Farrand, *Records of the Federal Convention*, Vol. I, pp. 22, 244, 292–293; Vol. II, pp. 136, 427, 551.

[10] Kenneth C. Davis, *Administrative Law and Government* (St. Paul: West Publ. Co., 1960), pp. 14, 16.

of Representatives may impeach: this power implies the judicial-type power to inquire into the conduct of civil officers for the possible purpose of impeachment.[11] The President may recommend legislation: this power implies the authority to engage in activity in support of recommendations. Finally, we simply cannot fully separate legislative, executive, and judicial activities, for each activity tends to merge with or to be transformed into the others.[12] In executing a law, for example, an official must often ask whether the law applies to particular persons, and the decisions made will tend to add a gloss, however thin, to it. Strictly speaking, we can characterize the powers of government only as being more-or-less executive or judicial or legislative.

THE COORDINATE BRANCHES

The distribution of power in the Constitution is intended to maintain a coordinate status among the three branches. The framers viewed the legislative branch as posing the greatest threat to this status, since they considered legislative power to be the most extensive and the least easily defined. Moreover, the legislative branch controlled the public purse and hence the salaries of judicial and executive officials.[13] In distributing governmental power in the way they did, the framers strengthened the judiciary and Presidency at the expense of Congress. They also strengthened the Senate in relation to the House of

[11] See President Jackson's "'Protest,' April 15, 1834, against the Resolution of the Senate Condemning the President for His Action 'in Relation to the Public Revenues,'" in *A Compilation of the Messages and Papers of the Presidents, 1789–1897*, ed. by James D. Richardson (Washington: Bureau of National Literature and Art, 1901), Vol. III, pp. 72–73.

[12] See Thomas R. Powell, "Separation of Powers: Administrative Exercise of Legislative and Judicial Power," *Political Science Quarterly*, 27 (June, 1912), 237: "No classification of powers can furnish mutually exclusive kinds of power, capable of differentiation by reason of their intrinsic qualities." See also Reginald Parker, "The Historic Basis of Administrative Law: Separation of Powers and Judicial Supremacy," *Rutgers Law Review*, 12 (Spring, 1958), 464–465.

[13] See, for example, *Federalist No. 48*, pp. 322–323.

Representatives, inasmuch as it alone was given several executive and judicial functions (the trial of impeachments, participation in appointments, and making treaties), and longer
tenure for its members. As the only part of the system selected
directly by the people, the House was considered the more
dangerous legislative chamber and hence most in need of
restraints.[14]

The framers used other means to counter what they viewed
as a natural imbalance among the three powers of government.
They took the selection of the President from Congress, where
they had initially placed it, and gave it to an electoral college.
They similarly reversed an initial decision placing the appointment of judges exclusively in the Senate. Judges were given
permanent tenure and the term of the President was fixed at four
years with indefinite eligibility (a change from the original plan
to limit him to a single term), all subject, of course, to the
exercise of the impeachment power. Finally, Congress was
instructed by the Constitution that it could not change the
President's salary during his term and could not lower but could
(because of the length of their terms) raise the salaries of judges.

We are led to suggest that the Constitution intended that
the Supreme Court and the President would be not infrequently
aligned against Congress. There is, as we have seen, a natural
affinity between the judicial and executive powers, and the
leading framers so regarded them. Both branches are involved
in executing the law, in expounding it, and in applying it to
specific cases. Secondly, as we have also seen, the Supreme
Court and the President were specially armed against Congress,
particularly the House of Representatives, which was viewed as
the greatest, and hence common, threat to their coordinate
status. It is interesting to note that the Constitutional Convention came close to creating an open alliance between the Court

---

[14] Note *ibid.* where, in discussing the "danger from legislative usurpation," Madison
     speaks of "*an* assembly, which *is* inspired, by a supposed influence over the
     people" (p. 322, my emphasis); and No. 51 where Hamilton, or Madison,
     alludes to the Senate as "the weaker branch of the stronger department"
     (p. 338). See also Paul Eidelberg, *The Philosophy of the American Constitution*
     (New York: The Free Press, 1968), *passim.*

and the President in the form of a Council of Revision, combining the executive with members of the judiciary. This Council would have possessed the veto power over acts of Congress, and of the state legislatures as well. The Council had eminent sponsorship. It was part of the Virginia Plan and was vigorously supported by the three leading members of the Convention, James Madison, James Wilson, and Gouverneur Morris. Its main purpose was to strengthen executive resistance to legislative excesses and thereby protect the independence of both non-legislative branches.[15] Put to a vote three times in the Convention, the Council was rejected because it was felt that judicial objectivity in the interpretation of laws might be impaired by having judges participate in the enactment of legislation and that the association of justices with the chief executive in the Council might lead the Supreme Court to share the executive's views excessively.[16]

The strengthening of Presidential and judicial power was designed to help maintain a balance among the three branches of government, and balance was viewed as essential to the preservation of liberty against government. But it appears that the framers also wished to balance the influence of different classes in society through separation of powers so that none would be dominant in the government. There was no special need to guard against the self-interested aims of the propertied classes in the institutional arrangements because, being a minority, the well-to-do could be checked by the majority principle. There was, however, a need to guard against the self-interested claims of the many who were not well-off. The institutional defense against the democratic majority consisted in weakening the impulse of their power by the method used to select the President, senators, and judges, and through the length of the terms given these officials. Only representatives were made directly elective by the people, for brief terms and

---

[15] Farrand, *Records of the Federal Convention*, Vol. I, pp. 21, 94–140; Vol. II, pp. 73–80, 298. The Convention also considered Gouverneur Morris's proposal that the Chief Justice constitute part of a Council of State to assist the chief executive in the conduct of public affairs. (*Ibid.*, Vol. II, pp. 342–344.)

[16] See *Federalist No. 73*, p. 379.

under minor property restrictions (those set by the states for their democratic lower houses). Not only would the President be chosen for a longer term, but his electors would not necessarily be chosen by the people—certainly would not be nominated by them—and would meet in secrecy in the different states to cast their ballots. Senators would be chosen for still longer terms by state legislatures whose upper houses were normally based on a restricted electorate. The judges, who would serve for life, would be selected by the combined action of the President and Senate. Thus the influence of numbers, acting especially through the House of Representatives, was to be balanced by non-democratic influences acting through the other agencies of government. In this sense, the principle of separation of powers was similar in purpose to the classical principle of balance of power, or mixed form of government. But this similarity was limited, for the American scheme was basically republican, and its non-democratic restraints were limited and fragile and, as developments proved, insufficient against the democratic impulse.

Several features of the Constitution make the Supreme Court vulnerable to the actions of the other branches. One concerns the Court's size, which is not fixed in the Constitution at all but is left to ordinary legislation. Another concerns the use of justices for non-judicial purposes. Neither Congress nor the executive branch may under the Constitution have its members serve in the other's ranks, nor may Congressmen hold judicial office; yet nothing prevents Congress and the President, or the latter alone, from making use of judicial officers in executive and other posts. Lastly, the appellate jurisdiction of the Supreme Court (and the entire jurisdiction of lower federal courts) is subject to legislative control. Only the Court's original jurisdiction, which accounts for a negligible proportion of its work, is guaranteed by the Constitution; the other is granted "with such exceptions, and under such regulations, as the Congress [subject to the President's veto] shall make." Inasmuch as exceptions are variations from the norm, it does not appear that Congress could constitutionally deny all, or even a major part, of the Court's appellate jurisdiction. But Congress doubtlessly could take away a sizable share of it.[17]

Where does all this leave the Supreme Court? Did the Constitution make it the equal of the President and Congress? Their inferior? Perhaps their superior? We have Hamilton's oft-quoted words, in *Federalist 78*, that "the judiciary is beyond comparison the weakest of the three departments of power," and the early history of the judiciary seems to support this assessment. In its first three years of life, for example, the Supreme Court had practically no business before it, nor did its case load mount by much during the decade of the 1790s. In this period several justices resigned their positions for other public honors, and several distinguished persons declined appointment to its ranks. John Jay did both, first resigning as Chief Justice, in 1795, upon being elected Governor of New York, and then rejecting President Adams's tender of reappointment in 1800 at the conclusion of his gubernatorial term. The justices at that time—and, indeed, until 1891—had to spend a substantial amount of time holding trial court in the circuits of the county to which they were assigned. In 1801, the outgoing Federalist Congress attempted to end this system by setting up circuit courts of appeal, but the Jeffersonians restored it almost immediately upon taking power. Circuit duty, incidentally, was a major reason in Jay's decision not to return to the Supreme Court, for he had "left the bench perfectly convinced that under a system so defective, [the Supreme Court] would not obtain the energy, weight and dignity which are essential to its affording due support to the national government."[18]

But the early experience of the Supreme Court does not furnish adequate evidence of what the framers intended for it,

---

[17] Constitution, Article III, Sec. 2, para. 2. Most commentaries on this constitutional provision assume that Congress could withdraw all of the Court's appellate jurisdiction, but they ignore the provision's language. See also Henry M. Hart, Jr., "The Power of Congress to Limit the Jurisdiction of Federal Courts," *Harvard Law Review*, **66** (June, 1953), 1362–1402.

[18] Quoted in Albert J. Beveridge, *The Life of John Marshall* (Boston: Houghton Mifflin, 1919), Vol. III, p. 55.

nor does Hamilton's remark concerning the extreme weakness of judicial power despite the frequency with which that remark has been adduced as evidence. Clearly, from the context in which his remark was made, Hamilton was speaking not about the power given to American judges by the Constitution but about judicial power in general. The authority he cited for his statement was Montesquieu's dictum that the power in question was "next to nothing." Hamilton's assessment of the American judiciary, as we shall see, was quite different from that of Montesquieu.

The answer to the question of the Supreme Court's status in relation to the other branches of government depends in great measure upon the answer to another question: To whom does the Constitution give the final authority of interpreting its provisions? Inasmuch as the power to interpret the Constitution includes, necessarily, that of deciding which actions are and are not constitutional, the question is of major significance. The Constitution does not explicitly answer the question we have posed. Three quite different answers were given by those who made up the generation that guided the government during its formative period: Congress, the Supreme Court, and no single branch of government. Let us give some attention to each position before reaching our conclusion.

The doctrine that makes Congress the final arbiter of constitutional questions is one of legislative supremacy. Whatever Congress does is assumed to be constitutional. It must be accepted by the judiciary and, if Congress overrides his veto, by the President. Thus, subject to this qualification, Congress decides whether legislation restricting the President's power to remove executive officers or adding to the Supreme Court's original jurisdiction is constitutional. Congress also decides upon the constitutionality of questions not subject to executive veto, such as whether the President must provide the legislative branch with documents in his possession that it desires. The control over legislative expositions of the Constitution would, under this doctrine, be public opinion and would be expressed through elections and amendments to the Constitution. A number of Republicans of the Jeffersonian period subscribed to this doctrine, but Jefferson himself appears to have done so only well after he left public life, and then only to the extent of conceding that it was a reasonable position to assume.[19]

The key feature of the doctrine of legislative supremacy is the denial of any judicial power to invalidate acts of Congress and the executive. To be sure, the Constitution does not specifically give this power to the courts. It does vest them with judicial power, which requires them to interpret legal and constitutional provisions in the course of deciding cases; it requires them to take an oath to support the Constitution; and it makes laws passed pursuant to the Constitution part of the law of the land. But that is all. On the other hand, the debates in the Constitutional Convention and the ratifying conventions in the states support the existence of judicial power to interpret the Constitution, as do the actions of officials in all three branches from the first years of our constitutional history.[20] No President or federal judge has ever denied the power, and only a few congressmen, mostly in the early years of Jefferson's administration, ever did so. Finally, the doctrine of legislative supremacy, in honoring the representative branch of government, subordinates the President and the judiciary to it in a way quite inimical to the principle of separate-but-equal power.

Opposed to the doctrine of legislative supremacy is the doctrine that makes the Supreme Court the final arbiter of the Constitution. This doctrine does not, to be sure, make the judicial branch the only branch concerned with the constitutionality of government actions. Congressmen and the President, as well as judges, take an oath to support the Constitution, and this oath binds congressmen in exercising their legislative powers, and the President in considering legislation for approval or in exercising his other powers. Neither Congress nor the President, any less than judges, is exempted from the restrictions

---

[19] Letter to W. H. Torrance, June 11, 1815, in Thomas Jefferson, *Writings*, ed. by Andrew A. Lipscomb and Albert E. Bergh (Washington: The Thomas Jefferson Memorial Association, 1903), Vol. XIV, pp. 305–306.

[20] See, for example, Charles A. Beard, *The Supreme Court and the Constitution* (New York: Macmillan, 1912).

of the Constitution. What the doctrine requires is that the interpretations of the Constitution by Congress and the executive
be subject to review by the judicial branch and, once the
judicial branch has made a decision on the meaning of
the Constitution, the other branches must adhere to that
interpretation.

This doctrine is usually called judicial review but it is
more correctly labeled judicial supremacy, for it places the
judiciary over the other branches. The Supreme Court in effect
tells Congress and the President how they are to perform the
duties the Constitution gives them, and settles any disputes
between them. The doctrine, to be sure, has had its powerful
advocates—particularly Hamilton, in his masterful argument in
Federalist 78, and Chief Justice Marshall, in his renowned
opinion in *Marbury* v. *Madison* (1803). The judicial duty, in their
view, is simply to prefer the Constitution to legislative enactments opposed to it. But what if courts should substitute their
own desires for those of lawmakers or the chief executive? What
if they should err in significant matters or act from obvious bias?
Perhaps the most trenchant answer to the doctrine of judicial
supremacy was that given by Abraham Lincoln, in his First
Inaugural Address: "If the policy of the government upon vital
questions affecting the whole people, is to be irrevocably fixed
by decisions of the Supreme Court, the instant they are made,
in ordinary litigation between parties in personal actions, the
people will have ceased to be their own rulers, having to that
extent practically resigned their government into the hands
of that eminent tribunal."[21] Nearly the same comment
may be made of litigation in which the government itself is
involved.

The third answer to the question of who shall finally
interpret the Constitution is: no single branch. It is easier to
describe than to name the doctrine at hand, although coordinate
review might be an acceptable appellation. The doctrine emphasizes the equality of the three branches of government in inter-

[21] Abraham Lincoln, *Complete Works*, ed. by John G. Nicolay and John Hay (New
     York: Lamb Publ. Co., 1894), Vol. VI, p. 180.

preting the Constitution. The President, judges, and members of Congress, according to the doctrine, are bound to support the Constitution as they understand it, and not as it is understood by others, when they perform the duties assigned to them. Thus the interpretations by one branch cannot control those of any other branch. President Jackson's purpose in vetoing the act rechartering the Bank of the United States, in 1832, is often used to illustrate this departmental equality. Congress, in passing the legislation, had decided the question of its constitutionality for itself, then and on two previous occasions. Moreover, the Supreme Court had decided similarly, in the case of *McCulloch* v. *Maryland* (1819). Nevertheless, Jackson did not consider himself to be bound by these opinions and he vetoed the act. The doctrine of coordinate review will result in occasional conflict among the branches, but the framers saw conflict as an essential means of keeping the branches in their proper places. Conflicting interpretations of the Constitution would be settled, in the long run, by the people themselves, and, as Lincoln noted, the agitation by the Democrats against the Supreme Court's *McCulloch decision* "reduced the decision to a nullity."[22]

What we have called the doctrine of coordinate review has much to commend it. It appears to respect, as the other doctrines we have examined do not, the principle of independent and equal branches of government. It can be reconciled, it seems, with the clear evidence that some kind of review of the constitutionality of legislation, involving the judiciary, was intended and required by the Constitution. Finally, the belief that each branch interprets the Constitution for itself has had eminent sponsorship. Thomas Jefferson was its foremost exponent, Martin Van Buren fully shared Jefferson's view, and several other Presidents, including Madison and Jackson, have been represented as sharing it, although their full beliefs are not entirely clear.[23]

[22] Rejoinder at Quincy, *ibid.*, Vol. III, p. 180.
[23] The views of early Presidents on the subject of judicial review are contained in William A. Kolstad, *The Presidents and Judicial Review* (Doctoral dissertation,

The doctrine of coordinate review is nonetheless vitally flawed. Its chief defect, and the one most relevant to our study, is that it is not really a doctrine of coordinate review at all; rather it sets the President over both the judiciary and Congress. If the President disagrees with a constitutional decision of the Supreme Court he may, under the doctrine, disregard it in exercising his own constitutional powers. Consider what this means in practice. The President may properly decline to execute a law he believes to be unconstitutional even though the Supreme Court has found it constitutional. He may also continue to execute a law or perform acts that he considers authorized by the Constitution even though the Supreme Court has found them in violation of the Constitution. Or, if he considers the Court to be mistaken in its interpretation, he may properly refuse to come to the Court's support when one of its decisions is defied by a state. Indeed, he may similarly ignore those Court commands directed at him which he considers to be unconstitutional. And if the President is entitled to refuse to execute a law that the Supreme Court has upheld, he need not execute it in the first place. The doctrine of coordinate review gives Congress precious little in permitting it to decide for itself what legislation it can constitutionally enact, if the President may frustrate its execution; and it gives the judicial branch scarcely more if he can, by failure to put laws into operation, prevent the courts from deciding cases or ignoring the decisions they do make. In summary, the doctrine is one of executive supremacy, of the President acting outside of law.

Political Science Department, University of Texas, 1964). See also William M. Meigs, *The Relation of the Judiciary to the Constitution* (New York: Neale Publ. Co., 1919), pp. 208–240.

The question of Jefferson's consistency in espousing coordinate review is discussed by Samuel Krislov (who, as does the writer, believes that Jefferson adhered to this doctrine throughout his life) in "Jefferson and Judicial Review: Refereeing Cahn, Commager, and Mendelson," *Journal of Public Law*, **9**, No. 2 (1960), pp. 374–381, and "The Alleged Inconsistency: A Revised Version," *ibid.*, **10**, No. 1 (1961), 117–124; and by Wallace Mendelson (who believes that Jefferson shifted from judicial review [supremacy] to coordinate review about 1801, after he became President), in "Jefferson on Judicial Review—A Reply to Professor Krislov," *ibid.*, **10**, No. 1 (1961), 113–117.

Therefore, the answer to the question we posed—To whom does the Constitution give the final authority to interpret its provisions?—must be: the Supreme Court. There is no practical alternative, if the constitutional plan is to be followed. The power to determine the constitutionality of the political branches' acts finally must rest with the Supreme Court, and those political branches must accept that determination as a rule governing their conduct. The alternatives to this conclusion lead to legislative or executive supremacy. Moreover, executive supremacy results in executive review of the judiciary's constitutional interpretations and its judgments in particular cases as well. But, it may be asked, does not the final determination of constitutional issues by the Supreme Court make the Court, in Jefferson's term, a despot over the President and Congress? Our answer to this question is: No, as long as the extent of this power is properly understood.

In the first instance, the Supreme Court's power to make final constitutional determinations is limited by the doctrines of legislative deference and political questions. These doctrines are nothing else but the doctrines of legislative supremacy and coordinate review expressed in a manner compatible with that of judicial review. Legislative deference means that the judicial branch will defer to the decisions of the legislative branch and will not declare them outside the Constitution unless they are distinctly so. Hamilton apparently had this in mind when he stated, in *Federalist 78*, that it would be the duty of the courts "to declare all acts contrary to the *manifest* tenor of the Constitution void."[24] So too Marshall when, in *Marbury* v. *Madison*, he spoke of acts which are "*entirely* void" and "*expressly* forbidden" under the Constitution.[25] Legislative deference simply acknowledges the respect that courts owe to the people's branch of government. The doctrine of political questions postulates that the Constitution has placed the determination of certain questions exclusively in the hands of the President or Congress, or the two branches together. What they have decided on these

---

[24] *The Federalist*, p. 397. Emphasis supplied.
[25] 1 Cranch 137 (1803), at 178. Emphasis supplied.

questions the judiciary cannot review. Marshall recognized this doctrine in *Marbury* v. *Madison*, where he acknowledged that the Court could not "inquire how the executive, or executive officers, perform duties in which they have a discretion." "Questions in their nature political, or which are, by the Constitution and laws, submitted to the executive," he stated, were outside its jurisdiction.[26] In fact, when he was a member of Congress, in 1799, Marshall spoke of questions arising under a treaty as "questions of political law, proper to be decided . . . by the executive, and not by the courts," for the President was, under the Constitution, "the *sole* organ of the nation in its external relations, and its *sole* representative with foreign nations."[27] As the doctrine of legislative deference pays its respect to the lawmaking role of the representative branch, so that of political questions pays its respect to the independent and equal power of each branch to decide fully those constitutional questions confided to it alone.

It is the judicial branch, ultimately the Supreme Court, which decides whether proper deference has been paid to an act of Congress or whether an action of the President is outside judicial cognizance. The doctrines of legislative deference and political questions are, in short, judicially enforced. What assurance is there that the judiciary will adhere to them? What can the President and Congress, or the states for that matter, do if the judiciary does not? In *Marbury* v. *Madison*, where the two doctrines were in essence acknowledged, the Supreme Court, in the eyes of many persons, proceeded to act contrary to them. The Court assumed the power to rule on the legality of an action that Jefferson and his supporters insisted belonged to the executive alone. It also declared a provision of law unconstitutional in spite of the fact that it had been approved by a Congress containing distinguished members of the Constitutional Convention and had never had its validity doubted until the Court's decision.

---

[26] *Ibid.*, 170.
[27] Cited in James B. Thayer, *John Marshall*, reprinted in *James Bradley Thayer, Oliver Wendell Holmes, and Felix Frankfurter on John Marshall*, ed. by Philip B. Kurland (Chicago: University of Chicago Press, Phoenix Books, 1967), pp. 38, 39.

If the Supreme Court fails, in the eyes of the President or Congress, to observe the limitations we have discussed, they need not accept its determination of the Constitution as final. There is a further limitation on the Court's power in this regard. In deciding a constitutional question, the Supreme Court not only interprets the Constitution but makes a judgment concerning the rights of specific parties to a case. To take an example: The Court in *Dred Scott* v. *Sandford*, decided in 1857, adjudged, among other matters, that Scott, a slave, did not gain his freedom by having been carried from a slave state into free territory of the United States, and it based its judgment on the constitutional argument that Congress could not exclude slavery from the territory of the country. Now the final judgments of the Supreme Court, that is, that part of a decision which affects the rights of parties to cases, would seem to be binding upon the President and Congress and everyone else. To deny their binding character would be to deny the essential element of the judicial process. So too are the constitutional interpretations of the Court with respect to the Congressional or executive action at issue: an invalidated action—for example, a law or executive order—cannot be treated as still valid, nor a validated one as without constitutional force. This power, as we have tried to show, rightfully belongs to the judicial branch of government.

But this is as far as the Supreme Court can control the other branches of government, or, for that matter, itself. Beyond this, no one is obliged to be bound by judicial interpretations of the Constitution when these interpretations, to quote Lincoln on the *Dred Scott decision*, lack "claims to the public confidence."[28] Congress may enact new legislation on the subject that incurred the Court's veto; the President may issue new orders and continue in force ones other than the one struck down; and the Court may likewise depart from its own rule in deciding a similar constitutional question in the future. In his first public discussion of the *Dred Scott case*, which occurred in 1857 shortly after the decision was rendered, Lincoln clearly set down the standards

---

[8] Speech at Springfield, June 26, 1857, in Lincoln, *Complete Works*, Vol. II, p. 321.

a constitutional decision of the Court must meet in order to claim the confidence of the public. It must, he said, be unanimous, untainted with apparent partisan bias, in accord with legal public expectations and the practice of the other governmental branches; or, if lacking some of these features, affirmed and reaffirmed by the Supreme Court over a period of years.[29] The *Dred Scott decision* failed these tests, as Lincoln demonstrated in this speech and in his subsequent debates with Stephen A. Douglas, and so he did not accept it then or when he became President. Likewise, no other constitutional decision need compel obedience beyond its immediate situation when it fails to establish its credibility.

What happens when the President or Congress believes that a constitutional interpretation of the Supreme Court is wrong? How is such a dispute resolved? The dispute may arise because the Court upholds the constitutionality of a power which the other branch or branches do not want exercised, or because it rejects the exercise of a power which the others want to exercise. If the interpretation upholds the exercise of power, the answer is easy. Those who contest the interpretation need only prevent that power from being used. This is what President Jackson did in vetoing the Bank bill, and what the Democrats thereafter did in keeping any bank bills from being enacted by Congress. If the Court's interpretation denies the possession of power, on the other hand, the President or Congress may attempt to achieve the same end by means which will satisfy the Court's decision, or they may seek a reconsideration by the Court. They are justified in treating the decision as binding only on the parties concerned and not as a binding interpretation of the Constitution. It is difficult to say how many times they may carry the same constitutional issue to the Supreme Court before it must be considered as fully settled, since that depends on how well a reaffirming Court satisfies the standards we have cited from Lincoln. Perhaps a single reaffirmation would often be enough. The Supreme Court (nearly always) has the final say, but the other branches can influence its

[29] *Ibid.*

pronouncements. The most obvious method is the use of the appointment power. Lincoln appears to have had this means in mind when he spoke of getting the Court to reverse its *Dred Scott decision*. As we shall see, he was not the only President to rely on appointments to bring the Supreme Court into line with the other branches of government.

So much for the obligatory character of judicial interpretations of the Constitution. Let us take up again the character of judicial judgments, which, we have already said, seem to bind all those to whom directed. Inasmuch as they rarely demand anything of Congress, let us ask: Must the President always obey such judgments? Must he enforce those issued against others, such as a state government, and resisted by them? If he considers a judgment, whether directed at the executive branch or others, to be clearly invalid, must he still obey it? What if obedience to a judgment of the Court should place him in perilous conflict with Congress? What if obedience would, in his opinion, endanger the Union itself? Must he still obey? These questions, and the answers some Presidents have given to them, take us to the margins of the Constitution, or perhaps to its core. Fortunately, they have not arisen often. They cannot be easily or, in some instances, definitively answered, but the questions themselves suggest that there may be limits to the Supreme Court's power to control the action of the President in specific cases.

We may summarize as follows. The Constitution did not make the Supreme Court—the judicial branch, in general—supreme over the other branches of the government. It was given possession of neither the purse nor the sword, as Hamilton noted in *Federalist 78*. These powers were confided in Congress and the President. And yet the judiciary was not, in important respects, made markedly inferior to the other branches. As Hamilton also noted, federal judicial power was strengthened by the permanent tenure of those who wielded it and by their power to declare laws void. So strengthened and exercised, the judicial power was to make the courts "bulwarks of a limited Constitution" against an encroaching Congress acting either on its own behalf or upon that of a popular majority stirred by momentary passion. In addition, the courts would, in Hamilton's view, protect the private rights of citizens against unjust and partial—but not unconstitutional—laws by mitigating their severity and restricting their operation. Through such action they would restrain the attempts of legislative bodies to enact legislation of that tenor in the first place. George Washington certainly had an elevated view of the judicial branch's place in the political system, for he called it, at the time he chose its first members, "the keystone of our political fabric" and "the pillar upon which our national government must rest."[30] He matched his words in the quality of his appointments. Five of the original six justices (the number then) had held high office in either the Confederation or their states, and the sixth, James Wilson, was a major architect of the Constitution. All told, three of the justices had participated in the Constitutional Convention and four had participated in their state ratifying conventions. And it is clear that, Jay's prediction notwithstanding, the subjection of the justices to circuit-riding did not prevent the Supreme Court from acquiring energy, weight, and dignity, or from continuing to attract outstanding persons to its ranks.

It seems inevitable that the Supreme Court and the Presidency should come into conflict in the operation of the American political system, for Presidents, as well as Congresses, were bound to challenge the assertions of authority made by the Court under its constitutional mandate. It seems inevitable, too, that relations between the Court and the Presidency should be marked by broad and sympathetic cooperation, in view of the closeness of their functions and outlooks and the constitutional design to draw them together as a check upon the power of Congress.

[30] Cited in Charles Warren, *The Supreme Court in United States History* (Boston: Little, Brown, 1926), Vol. I, pp. 36, 46.

2

Conflict

Perhaps every President has been displeased by some action taken by the Supreme Court. Even so, most have kept their grievances well hidden, and only four have ever carried their displeasure to the point of conflict with the judicial branch. These were, however, all major Presidents: Thomas Jefferson, Andrew Jackson, Abraham Lincoln, and Franklin Roosevelt. Roosevelt was the only one of them who publicly attacked the Court, which he did several times—most severely when he accused it, in a national radio address in March, 1937, of "improperly set[ting] itself up as a third house of the Congress— a super-legislature," of "reading into the Constitution words and implications which are not there, and which were never intended to be there."[1] The conflict in which Lincoln was engaged did

[1] *New York Times,* March 10, 1937, p. 15. One other President, Theodore Roosevelt, also criticized the Supreme Court in his public statements, and other

not actually involve the Supreme Court at all, but rather Chief Justice Roger B. Taney, acting by himself, and with state judges and other federal judges; but its significance merits our consideration. Jefferson's conflict was, for the most part, conducted indirectly and against Supreme Court justices who were acting in a circuit-court capacity as well as against the Court itself. And Jackson seemed as much a bystander as a protagonist in his involvement with the Court.

The encounters between these four Presidents and the judicial branch are interesting in themselves, for in them famous and forceful men came into conflict over important issues. But the encounters also raise basic questions concerning the roles of the President and the judiciary. Therefore, in this chapter we will examine the difficulties each of these Presidents experienced with the judicial branch. We will then consider the constitutional and, broadly speaking, political questions underlying these conflicts.

Jefferson

One is tempted to say that Thomas Jefferson did not so much dislike what the Supreme Court did as he disliked judges as a class, and Chief Justice John Marshall in particular. "I believe that Mr. Jefferson used to boast that he was no lawyer," counsel for a party in litigation was to tell the Supreme Court long after the President's death; "we know that he had no very favorable opinion of lawyers, or of judges. . . ."[2] Jefferson never said anything derogatory about Marshall in public but he frequently condemned the Chief Justice in his private correspondence: for his "twistifications of the law" in three of his major opinions; for "traveling out of his case to prescribe what the law would be in a moot case not before the Court" in

parts of the judiciary as well, but his displeasure did not rise to the level of conflict, probably because the occasion did not happen to occur, Roosevelt was also, of course, a major President.

[2] Counsel for Mississippi, in *Mississippi* v. *Johnson*, 4 Wall. 475 (1866), at 494–495. Jefferson was himself a lawyer and practiced the profession actively for about twelve years.

another; as being a "crafty chief judge" in connection with still another.[3] For his part, the Chief Justice entertained no high regard for Jefferson. At the very threshold of his career on the Court he spurned the plea of his fellow Federalist Alexander Hamilton, who asked him to help influence their party's members in the House of Representatives to support Jefferson over Burr for President when the 1800 election was given to that body for decision. He felt, he said, "almost insuperable objections" to his [Jefferson's] political character, which seemed "totally to unfit him for the chief magistracy," and he never thereafter uttered a kind word about Jefferson in his correspondence or, so far as we know, in private conversation.[4]

But it would be a mistake to put too much weight on personal feelings in explaining relations between Jefferson and the judicial branch. Other considerations were of much greater importance. As we have seen, Jefferson's view of separation of powers did not accord any special status to judicial constructions of the Constitution. "Nothing in the Constitution," he wrote in 1804, in a typical statement, "has given them [the Supreme Court] a right to decide for the executive, more than to the executive to decide for them."[5] This view, we have argued, implied not only executive independence of the judiciary but the supremacy of the executive over both of the other branches of government. Marshall and his colleagues, on the other hand, believed in the binding quality of judicial decisions. As he said in the *Marbury case*, "It is emphatically the

---

[3] The cases are, respectively, *Marbury* v. *Madison* (1803), the *Burr Trials* (1807), at which Marshall presided with a federal district judge in performance of his circuit duty, *Fletcher* v. *Peck* (1810), *McCulloch* v. *Maryland* (1819), and *Cohens* v. *Virginia* (1821). The quoted remarks can be found, respectively, in Charles Warren, *The Supreme Court in United States History* (Boston: Little, Brown, 1926), Vol. I, p. 401; Letter to Justice William, Johnson June 12, 1823, in Thomas Jefferson, *Writings*, ed. by Andrew A. Lipscomb and Albert E. Bergh (Washington: The Thomas Jefferson Memorial Assn., 1903), Vol. XV, p. 447; and Letter to Thomas Ritchie, December 25, 1820, *ibid.*, p. 298.

[4] Albert J. Beveridge, *The Life of John Marshall* (Boston: Houghton Mifflin, 1919), Vol. II, p. 537; Vol. IV, pp. 579–580.

[5] Letter to Mrs. John Adams, September 11, 1804, in Jefferson, *Writings*, Vol. XI, p. 50.

province and duty of the judicial department to say what the law is."[6] The President and the judiciary thus needed only to differ in their views of the Constitution for disagreement to break out between them. And differences were bound to occur given the strong states-rights and republican views held by Jefferson and the solidly Federalist sentiments of nearly all the judges.

Jefferson did in fact disagree with most of the major actions of the judicial branch during his Presidency and long after. Indeed, he came into office breathing out opposition to the convictions resulting from the Sedition Act trials conducted under the Adams administration. (The Act had expired with that administration.) Although the Supreme Court as a body never passed upon the Sedition Act, its members had partici- pated in trials under it in their circuit-judge capacities and had there upheld its constitutionality. Jefferson considered the Act unconstitutional and for that reason when he became President felt justified in pardoning those he found in prison and in discharging those under prosecution.[7] Likewise, the new President entered office opposed to the Circuit Court Act, which had been passed in the closing days of the previous administration and was determined to bring about its repeal. Under that Act, Supreme Court justices were to be reduced in number to five with the next vacancy (one was expected shortly), and their circuit-riding was to be taken over by permanent circuit court judges. Congress quickly responded to Jefferson's wishes in regard to the Circuit Court Act and then moved immediately to other legislation that, by delaying the convening of the Supreme Court for fourteen months, was designed to forestall challenges to the repeal. After considering whether they should accept their reassignment to circuit duty— Marshall was opposed—the justices complied with the new law.

[6] *Marbury* v. *Madison*, 1 Cranch 137 (1803), at 177.
[7] See Beveridge, *Life of Marshall*, Vol. III, Appendix A, pp. 605–606; also, Letters to Mrs. John Adams, July 27, 1804, and September 11, 1804, in Jefferson, *Writings*, Vol. XI, pp. 43–44, 50–51; and Letter to George Hay, June 2, 1807, *ibid.*, p. 214.

The Act delaying the convening of the Supreme Court also delayed the Court's consideration of the explosive case of *Marbury* v. *Madison*. William Marbury had asked the Court in December, 1801, to compel Secretary of State James Madison—really Jefferson—to complete his appointment to a justiceship in the District of Columbia by delivering the commission which Madison's predecessor in office, John Marshall, had neglected to deliver before the Jefferson administration took power. The Supreme Court ordered Madison to show at the Court's next session why he should not be so compelled, and Madison ignored the order. Then Congress enacted its legislation delaying the next session of the Court until February, 1803. In the meantime, threats of defiance were being uttered against what was expected to be a decision in Marbury's favor.

The Sedition Act pardons, the Circuit Court Repeal Act, and the impending *Marbury decision* combined to create great tension between the executive and judicial branches and to set the new Administration upon a campaign to bring the judiciary under control. Thus was launched the move to oust the judges, especially those of the Supreme Court, from their positions. "We *want your offices*," Jefferson's leader in the Senate told a Federalist senator at the pitch of the campaign, "for the purpose of giving them to men who will fill them better."[8] The way of getting them, it was decided, was through impeachment, and the Republicans argued that impeachments were not criminal proceedings but simply a means for removing public officials whose actions were out of line with the popular will.

The first person to feel the impeachment lash was John Pickering, a federal district judge in New Hampshire. Pickering was impeached on February 4, 1803, on Jefferson's instigation in what appears to have been a test case. The Constitution provides that judges shall hold their offices during good behavior (Article III, Sec. 1) and at the same time provides that all civil officers of the United States, including, it has been assumed, judges, shall be impeachable for high crimes and misdemeanors (Article II, Sec. 4). The New Hampshire judge

[8] Cited in Beveridge, *Life of Marshall*, Vol. III, p. 157. Emphasis in original.

had committed no offense, but suffered from insanity, and it was clear that his trial was intended as a preliminary to similar actions against justices of the Supreme Court. The Court was then moving to its decision in the *Marbury case*, and the expected crisis with the executive. In its decision, announced on February 24, however, the Court, speaking through Marshall, declared that its original jurisdiction did not extend to the case before it, and, consequently, that the provision of law under which Marbury had brought the case to it was unconstitutional. Before reaching this conclusion, the Court did lecture Jefferson on his duty to have Marbury's commission delivered to him and declared that executive officials could, in properly brought cases, be controlled by judicial decisions; but it did not order the executive branch to do anything.

Thus, by design or otherwise, Marshall did not in the *Marbury decision* give the Jeffersonians the excuse they needed to launch an assault on the Supreme Court. But one of the Court's members, Samuel Chase, did so a few months later when, in March, 1803, he made some injudicious remarks in addressing a grand jury while on circuit duty in Maryland. Chase had earlier exposed himself to censure by canvassing on Adams's behalf in that state during the Presidential election of 1800. Now he criticized the repeal of the Circuit Court Act and the recent revisions made in the Maryland Constitution and gave vent to his forebodings on the political state of things. "Ought this seditious and official attack on the principles of our Constitution, and on the proceedings of a state, to go unpunished?" Jefferson asked a Maryland congressman (who was to get Chase's seat should it be vacated), and the impeachment machinery was set in motion against the justice.[9] On the day the Senate voted Pickering's conviction on impeachment charges, indeed, within the hour, charges were made against Chase for his allegedly unfair conduct in the trials of Republicans under the Sedition Act, and for less specific offenses. But Chase was to prove only the first justice on Jefferson's impeachment agenda.

[9] Letter to Joseph H. Nicholson, May 13, 1803, in Jefferson, *Writings*, Vol. X, p. 390.

As the President is reported to have put it, "Now we have caught the whale, let us have an eye to the shoal."[10]

Much to Jefferson's chagrin, the Senate in March, 1805, acquitted Justice Chase of the impeachment charges that had been lodged against him, and so ended the President's first great conflict with the Court. Jefferson had failed in his effort to bring the judiciary under the control of the other branches of government. "For the first time since Jefferson's election," as Marshall's biographer has expressed it, "the national judiciary was, for a period, rendered independent. For the first time in five years, the Federalist members of the nation's highest tribunal could go about their duties without fear that upon them would fall the avenging blade of impeachment which had for half a decade hung over them."[11]

Jefferson collided again with the Supreme Court, or rather with Chief Justice Marshall, in the episode of Aaron Burr's alleged plot against the United States. In a message to Congress, Jefferson, in late 1806, accused Burr of planning to attack Mexico and detach the states lying beyond the Alleghanies from the Union. He proclaimed Burr's guilt to be "placed beyond question."[12] Having thus indicted Burr, Jefferson became, behind the scenes, the chief prosecutor against him and his confederates. But at each turn he was countered by Marshall. First, the Chief Justice authored the opinion of the Supreme Court that ordered two of Burr's confederates released from custody (*Ex parte Bollmann and Swartwout*, February, 1807). There was not sufficient evidence, Marshall said, to hold them for trial on the charge of treason, as Marshall defined that crime. Next Marshall, sitting as a circuit judge in Virginia, admitted Burr to bail pending the consideration of his case by a grand jury. In the trial itself, Marshall excluded most of the government's testimony as not bearing upon the charge of treason against Burr, and the jury brought in the unusual verdict that Burr was not guilty "by any evidence submitted to

[10] Cited by Warren, *Supreme Court in U.S. History*, Vol. I, p. 293.
[11] Beveridge, *Life of Marshall*, Vol. III, p. 220.
[12] Burr denied any hostile design against the Union, or against Mexico except in the event of war between it and the United States.

us." The failure to convict Burr of treason forced the government to drop similar charges against the others, and the subsequent trial of Burr for the lesser charge of planning an attack upon Mexico also resulted in a verdict of not guilty.

Tension between the executive and the judiciary grew as the Burr proceedings moved from one stage to the next. To prevent the Supreme Court from considering the cases of Bollmann and Swartwout, Jefferson's spokesman in the Senate sponsored a bill to suspend the writ of habeas corpus, and the legislation was approved by that chamber but was defeated in the House. When Marshall admitted Burr to bail, Jefferson deplored the "fact . . . that the Federalists make Burr's cause their own, and exert their whole influence to shield him."[13] Before Burr was yet indicted, in May, 1807, Jefferson was convinced that Marshall meant to do all he could for Burr, a partiality which showed "the original error of establishing a judiciary independent of the nation."[14] And when Marshall the next month, still before the trial began, granted a defense motion to subpoena Jefferson to appear before the Court with certain documents, Jefferson indignantly denied that the judiciary "could bandy [the President] from pillar to post, keep him constantly trudging from north to south and east to west, and withdraw him entirely from his constitutional duties."[15] Another subpoena was issued against Jefferson in early September, just before the second trial of Burr, and once more he struck out against Marshall's action, referring to it as a "preposterous" proceeding.[16]

It appears that Jefferson planned to have Marshall impeached if Burr slipped from the government's grasp. He even insisted upon the misdemeanor trial of Burr, despite its remote chance of conviction, because he thought Burr's acquittal would "heap coals of fire on the head of the Judge."[17] Marshall's biographer is convinced, moreover, that the President would

---

[13] Letter to James Bowdoin, April 2, 1807, in Jefferson, *Writings*, Vol. XI, p. 186.
[14] See, for example, Letters to Col. G. Morgan, March 26, 1807, and William Giles, April 20, 1807, *ibid.*, pp. 186, 188–191.
[15] Letter to George Hay, June 20, 1807, *ibid.*, p. 241.
[16] Letter to Hay, September 7, 1807, *ibid.*, p. 365.   [17] *Ibid.*, p. 366.

have succeeded in having the Chief Justice removed from office by the Senate if critical foreign problems had not distracted his and the country's attention.[18] But one wonders how much hope Jefferson could have placed in a power which only a few months earlier he had called "a farce which will not be tried again."[19] The President in fact turned his fertile mind to other ways of getting rid of obnoxious judges, including constitutional amendments which would permit executive removal and limit judicial terms to four or six years. But for all his schemes and fulminations, Jefferson never succeeded in limiting the independence of the Supreme Court, by amendment or otherwise.[20] The Republican threat against the judiciary had reached its high-water mark in the Chase impeachment and, although it rose again at the time of the Burr trials, it would be a long time before the judiciary was once more seriously menaced.

If Jefferson was not able to bring the judiciary under the control of the executive and Congress, he could still keep it from controlling his own actions. In his view of the Constitution, it will be recalled, each branch of government had the right to decide for itself the constitutionality of those questions presented to it for action. More specifically, Jefferson held that the courts could not make the executive subject to their commands, and

---

[18] Beveridge, *Life of Marshall*, Vol. III, pp. 530–532. See also Henry Adams, *History of the United States of America during the Second Administration of Thomas Jefferson, 1805–1809* (New York: Charles Scribner's Sons, 1890), Vol. I, pp. 470–471.

[19] Letter to Giles, in Jefferson, *Writings*, p. 191.

[20] In later years Jefferson returned to the impeachment power as a method of removing judges for political reasons. Before Marshall, the Court frequently gave its regular opinions *seriatim*, each justice stating his views of a case; and it was Marshall who led the Court in abandoning this practice in favor of having one justice (often himself) present the opinion of the Court. In fact, concurring or dissenting opinions of any kind were discouraged, and the justices seldom carried their differences in a case into print. Jefferson complained, correctly, that the use of court opinions resulted in "smothering evidence" and wanted the *seriatim* practice resumed in full vigor, so that Congress might denounce those justices with whose views it disagreed and, if they failed to mend their ways, impeach them. To effect this return, he wrote Justice William Johnson and received a promise of support, and urged Madison to write his appointees to the Court. See Donald G. Morgan, *Justice William Johnson: The First Dissenter* (Columbia: University of South Carolina Press, 1954), pp. 170–184. But nothing came of the plan.

that the Constitution had given the executive, more than the other branches, the means to protect itself from outside interference.[21] The Supreme Court never gave Jefferson a chance to act on his view of its authority to control executive action. Although it handed down several decisions which Jefferson considered to be constitutionally improper, none of them required his obedience or execution. The closest the Court came to ordering the President to act against his constitutional judgment was in the *Marbury case*, and there it stopped just short of ordering him (technically, Madison) to deliver up Marbury's commission. For the rest of his life Jefferson disputed Marshall's claim in *Marbury* that the judiciary could control the President's exercise of his constitutional duties, and he made it clear that he believed himself free to disregard any attempts to do so.[22]

On two occasions Supreme Court justices, presiding over circuit courts, ordered executive obedience to what Jefferson considered to be invalid decrees, and it is instructive to observe Jefferson's reactions. The first occasion was that of the Burr proceedings in 1807. As discussed above, the circuit court in Richmond twice subpoenaed Jefferson to produce certain documents requested by the defense, personally or by transmission, and each time he denied the Court's power over him. But both times he uttered his defiance in private communications to the government attorney in the case, and both times he gave the Court what it demanded.[23] The second occasion of lower court action against Jefferson occurred in 1808, in a proceeding conducted under the Embargo Act. Jefferson had, through his Secretary of the Treasury, instructed customs collectors to prevent the coastal movement of vessels carrying certain cargoes, and the validity of the instructions had been

[21] Letter to Hay, June 20, 1807, in Jefferson, *Writings*, p. 241.

[22] See, for example, his letter to Hay, June 2, 1807, *ibid.*, pp. 214–216.

[23] It seems to be commonly believed that Jefferson refused to comply with Marshall's subpoenas, and even Henry Adams states flatly that he defied them. (*Second Administration of Jefferson*, Vol. III, p. 460.) Those holding to the belief have probably taken Jefferson's words for his deeds or thought that the subpoenas required his personal attendance in court.

challenged in the federal circuit court held in Charleston, South Carolina (*Ex parte Gilchrist*). It was Jefferson's own appointee to the Supreme Court, Justice William Johnson, who there ruled that the Embargo Act vested in the collectors the discretion to detain vessels and ordered the ship in question to be allowed to sail. Supported by an opinion from his Attorney General, the President informed the customs collectors in the various ports that they should follow his instructions, and not Johnson's decision, in performing their duties under the Embargo Act, but he did not interfere with the execution of that decision (if, in fact, he learned of it in time to do anything). Jefferson's refusal to be bound by the circuit court's interpretation of the Embargo Act was in accord with his view that judicial interpretations cannot bind the other branches of government. It appears, however, that he had second thoughts about the constitutional, or political, correctness of his interpretation of the Act, for he decided to have Congress grant him the power that he had claimed to possess.

Jefferson never exposed himself publicly in hostile action taken against the judicial branch. In signaling the repeal of the Circuit Court Act (by which the Federalists had reduced the Supreme Court's size and created a circuit court system), Jefferson said no more (in his First Message to the legislative branch) than that "the judiciary system of the United States, and especially that portion of it recently erected, will of course present itself to the contemplation of Congress."[24] In signaling the impeachment of Pickering, he simply transmitted letters and affidavits concerning the judge's behavior to the House of Representatives, "to whom the Constitution has confided a power of instituting proceedings of redress if they shall be of opinion that the case calls for them."[25] And in goading his

---

[24] First Annual Message, December 8, 1801, in Jefferson, *Writings*, Vol. III, p. 337. See the discussion in Beveridge, *Life of Marshall*, Vol. III, pp. 50–100. A contemporary newspaper, cited by Warren, *Supreme Court in U.S. History*, Vol. I, p. 230, reported that "the President is said to have taken a vastly active part in his project for repealing the judiciary—indeed it is regarded as his measure and deemed to be the offspring of his resentment."

[25] Adams, *First Administration of Jefferson, 1801–1805*, Vol. II, p. 143.

Republican spokesman in the House to institute impeachment charges against Chase, the President drew back from personal involvement: "For myself, it is better that I should not interfere."[26] The judiciary's authority to subpoena Jefferson was privately challenged by the President and, by his provision of subpoenaed documents, publicly acknowledged. Jefferson even retreated from his initial refusal to permit Justice Johnson's embargo ruling to control his actions in other situations. He turned to Congress to get the authority the Justice said was required in order to control sailings.

Only once did Jefferson come close to entering into public conflict with the judiciary. This occurred at the time he pardoned the Sedition Act offenders. In his First Message to Congress, Jefferson justified the pardons as follows: "I do declare that I hold that Act to be in palpable and unqualified contradiction to the Constitution. Considering it then as a nullity, I have relieved from oppression under it those of my fellow-citizens who were within the reach of the functions confided to me."[27] But none of the President's fellow-citizens ever saw this justification, for at the last moment he deleted it from the message as submitted. All they saw was the exertion of an undoubted constitutional power for the purpose of relieving a handful of persons from the force of a law no longer on the statute books. Therefore, the public was unaware of the great power that Jefferson claimed with respect to the courts, and to Congress as well. If a President may pardon persons charged with or convicted of crimes under laws he considers invalid, he need not enforce such laws in the first place; and if he may put aside criminal laws he believes to be invalid, he must have the power to put aside all laws which trespass upon his constitutional scruples. Jefferson did not draw these conclusions from his position in the Sedition Act cases, but Martin Van Buren, a constitutional follower of his, did. In a book written after his own term in the Presidency, Van Buren, in justifying Jefferson's pardons in those cases, argued that a President need not execute

---

[26] Adams, *First Administration of Jefferson, 1801–1805*, Vol. II, p. 150.
[27] Beveridge, *Life of Marshall*, Vol. III, Appendix A, p. 606.

at all a law he believes is unconstitutional; if he did he would violate his oath to support the Constitution and would make himself liable to impeachment.[28] This may strike us as a startling assertion, but it accords perfectly with Jefferson's views.

The fact is that Jefferson never openly acted or spoke against the judicial branch, or any decisions rendered by it, or openly expressed his view of the role of the judiciary in the system of separation of powers. His criticisms and other comments were confined to his private correspondence and, we may assume, to non-public discussions. Indeed, we may carry our point regarding Jefferson's reticence a step further. Jefferson never publicly condemned any of the major enterprises of the Federalists, even though they stood in taunting disavowal of the revolution in government that he believed his election in 1800 symbolized. The principle of the Alien and Sedition Acts lived unrepudiated, and those other creations of a centralist monocracy—the Judiciary Act of 1789, the Bank of the United States, a standing army and navy—continued not only unrepudiated but in full vigor during Jefferson's eight years in office. Thus, if Jefferson's war against Marshall and his Federalist colleagues on the bench, and what they represented in terms of constitutional policy, was not won, a major reason was that the Commander in Chief was only half earnest about fighting it, and not at all willing to expose himself on the battlefield.

And so Marshall won almost entirely on the great issue of the nature of the federal union. It was to be one of broad national power, with the states occupying subordinate positions and with manufacturing and commerce finding a climate hospitable to their development. It is ironic that Marshall defeated Jefferson on his own terms, by winning to the Court's side the President's final arbiter on political issues: the people themselves.

[28] Martin Van Buren, *Inquiry into the Origin and Course of Political Parties in the United States* (New York: Hurd and Houghton, 1867), pp. 342–343.

Jackson

Andrew Jackson had only a single encounter with the Supreme Court, but it was a famous one. It resulted not from a decision directed at him or the national government generally, but at the state of Georgia—and it involved Jackson because his help was needed if the decision was to be enforced. The case of *Worcester* v. *Georgia* (1832) concerned white missionaries who had been convicted of operating among the state's Cherokee Indians in violation of a state law requiring them to swear an oath of allegiance to Georgia and to procure a license from the Governor. At issue in the case was the fate of the Cherokee nation, not that of the missionaries, for Georgia was bent upon dealing with its Indians as she wished—and she meant to take their lands, destroy their autonomy, subject them to her will, and, if she could, drive them into the raw territories beyond the Mississippi River. This was not the first time that the Indians and their supporters had taken their plight to the Court, but it was the first opportunity the Court had to declare the oppressive Georgia legislation void. Georgia had, the Supreme Court said, acted contrary to the Constitution and to laws and treaties of the United States, and it ordered the missionaries released. Georgia defied the Supreme Court's judgment, and it is at this point that Jackson is supposed to have remarked, "Well, John Marshall has made his decision, now let him enforce it."

Although it is not likely that the statement was ever made, it does express the President's view of the controversy between Georgia and her Indians. In the first place, Jackson believed that Georgia possessed jurisdiction over the Cherokees, and his own policy was to effect their removal to new lands. Furthermore, he could not have wished to be caught in the missionary controversy when there were other, and to him more important, problems besetting him. The President was at the time locked in struggle with Congress over the rechartering of the Bank of the United States and was, in addition, anxiously watching the storm of nullification gathering in South Carolina. Thus he must have viewed the Court's decision in *Worcester* v. *Georgia* as incorrect and untimely, and the record is clear that he never sought to enforce it against the contumacious state.

The question in the *Cherokee case* is not whether Jackson enforced the Supreme Court's decision, but whether he defied the Court in not enforcing it. It might be argued that the judicial proceeding never reached the stage where Jackson's enforcement was required. The Court did not directly seek Presidential enforcement of its judgment, nor did it act to enforce the judgment itself by instituting a contempt action against the Georgia authorities, an action which would have given it grounds for invoking the President's aid. The Court adjourned in March, 1832, right after announcing its missionary decision, and by the time it reconvened the following January, the Jackson Administration was, according to press reports, seeking a solution to the impasse between it and Georgia. The crisis was finally surmounted a couple of months later when the missionaries, upon their agreement to leave the state, were pardoned by the Governor.[29]

Jackson never claimed the right to disregard those judicial decisions with which he disagreed. In his Bank veto, which has been often interpreted as justifying disobedience, the President asserted no more than that "the authority of the Supreme Court must not . . . be permitted to control the Congress or the Executive when acting in their *legislative* capacities, but to have only such influence as the force of their reasoning may deserve."[30] What Jackson was referring to was his exercise of the legislative power of the veto. Jackson's second Vice President and political heir, Martin Van Buren, was probably speaking Jackson's mind in the *Worcester case* when he wrote as follows on this subject years later: "If resistance is offered to the execution of a [court] judgment or decree . . . too great to be overcome by the civil power, it is the duty of the President, upon the request of the officers of the court, to order out the military power to sustain

---

[29] See Warren, *Supreme Court in U.S. History*, Vol. I, pp. 755–779. Warren points out (*ibid.*, p. 764) that there was then no provision in federal law allowing a habeas corpus to be instituted in order to procure the freedom of the missionaries.

[30] *Register of Debates in Congress*, 22nd Congress, 1st Session, 1832, Vol. VIII, Part 3, Appendix, p. 76. Emphasis supplied.

that of the judiciary. It would be no answer on his part to such a call to say that the right which the decree or judgment seeks to enforce arises under a law which he deems unconstitutional. That is, under the circumstances, a matter that he has no right to inquire into."[31] Inasmuch as the Supreme Court never requested Jackson's assistance in the missionary case, it follows, according to Van Buren, that the President never failed in his duty to the Court.

And yet Jackson showed no disposition to enforce the Supreme Court's missionary decision. As he wrote to a correspondent at the time of the action, "the decision of the Supreme Court has fell [*sic*] still born, and they [the Cherokees] find that it cannot coerce Georgia to yield to its mandate."[32] Jackson's attitude was not, however, one of defiance toward the Court, despite his refusal to heed the plea of the American Board of Foreign Missions that he enforce the Court's decree.[33] In the quoted letter, he proceeded to say that "if orders were issued tomorrow, one regiment of militia could not be got to march to save them [the Cherokees] from destruction . . . if a colision [*sic*] was to take place between them and the Georgians, the arm of the government is not sufficiently strong to preserve them from destruction."[34] The President did, of course, have the national army at his disposal, but he faced another problem, greater than that posed by Georgia's resistance to the Supreme Court: South Carolina's resistance to all national authority. A few months after the missionary decision, a special state convention in South Carolina adopted a Nullification Ordinance proclaiming, under the threat of secession, the right of that, or any, state to void acts of Congress, and specifically voiding the

---

[31] Van Buren, *Inquiry into Political Parties*, pp. 337–338.
[32] Letter to John Coffee, April 7, 1832, in Andrew Jackson, *Correspondence*, ed. by John S. Bassett (Washington: Carnegie Institution, 1929), Vol. IV, p. 430.
[33] Marion L. Starkey, *The Cherokee Nation* (New York: Knopf, 1946), p. 203.
[34] *Ibid.* John Quincy Adams, then a member of Congress, was less charitable concerning Jackson's reason for not acting, noting in his diary that "the executive of the Union is leagued with the state authority, and the two houses of Congress are about as equally as possible divided in the case." *Memoirs*, ed. by Charles F. Adams (Philadelphia: J. B. Lippincott, 1876), Vol. VIII, p. 492.

Tariff Acts of 1828 and 1832. Come what may to the missionaries and the Cherokees, Jackson could not have wanted to take
any action which might have driven Georgia into the hands of
the Nullificationists.

Lincoln

The Supreme Court never gave Abraham Lincoln cause to
complain about its decisions during his Presidency, for the few
it rendered on his wartime policies supported them. The Court
did make Lincoln, or his Attorney General at least, anxious
about how it might rule on the President's suspension of the
privilege of the writ of habeas corpus if that question should
come before it. The Constitution does not specify who may
suspend the privilege of the writ but merely the conditions
under which it may be suspended (when the public safety may
require it in cases of rebellion or invasion). The part of the
document in which the habeas corpus provision is located
(Article I, Sec. 9) is, however, mainly devoted to limitations on
Congress. Lincoln first authorized his military commanders to
suspend the writ along the line between Philadelphia and
Washington in April, 1861; and then, in August and September, 1862, extended its suspension to all rebels, persons
engaging in disloyal practices, and those who interfered with
military enlistments and conscription. Finally, in March, 1863,
Congress either empowered or supported Presidential suspensions of habeas corpus (the law can be read both ways) anywhere in the country. On the basis of the Court's "antecedents
and present proclivities," as well as comments by some of its
members, Attorney General Edward Bates feared, in 1863, that
the Supreme Court would invalidate arrests made under habeas
corpus suspensions and that such a ruling would "do more to
paralyze the executive . . . than the worst defeat our armies
have yet sustained"; and Bates's successor, Joseph Speed, expressed a similar fear two years later.[35]

[35] Cited in James G. Randall, *Constitutional Problems under Lincoln*; rev. ed. (Urbana:
University of Illinois Press, 1951), p. 132.

Although the Supreme Court never passed upon Lincoln's suspension of the habeas corpus privilege, a number of state and inferior federal courts did, often adversely to the government's position. Chief Justice Roger B. Taney also passed upon the issue in the case of *In re Merryman* (1861), but it is not clear whether he did so in his capacity as a Supreme Court justice or as a judge of the circuit court.[36] In either event, Taney's status as head of the Supreme Court gave special weight to his now-famous decision in the *Merryman case*, as did the fact that his was probably the first judicial opinion on the President's authority to make arbitrary arrests. The facts of the case are as follows. In May, 1861, John Merryman, a citizen of Maryland and a Southern sympathizer, was arrested by military authority and incarcerated in Fort McHenry, near Baltimore. Merryman immediately requested Taney, whose circuit included Maryland, to issue a writ of habeas corpus to General George Cadwalader, the commander of the fort, to require the general to produce Merryman before the justice and to show the legal basis of his detention. The proceedings were conducted at the federal circuit court in Baltimore. General Cadwalader did not appear before Taney in response to the habeas corpus writ but sent an aide instead; nor did he produce Merryman. He informed the Chief Justice that Merryman had engaged in treasonous actions and that he (Cadwalader) was "duly authorized by the President of the United States, in such cases, to suspend the writ of habeas corpus for the public safety."[37] Thus disobeyed, Taney issued a writ of contempt against Cadwalader, but the marshal who was sent to serve it reported that he was not permitted to enter the gate of Fort McHenry. Taney, after referring to the marshal's power to summon a *posse comitatus* to help him seize the unyielding general and bring him before the court, excused him from such futile action. The Chief Justice then declared his belief that only Congress,

---

[36] Randall, *ibid.*, p. 131, asserts that Taney heard the case in his circuit judge capacity, while Clinton Rossiter, *The Supreme Court and the Commander in Chief* (Ithaca: Cornell University Press, 1951), p. 20, states that he was acting as Chief Justice of the United States.

[37] *Ex parte Merryman*, 17 Fed. Cas. 144 (No. 9487) (1861), at 145.

and not the President, was authorized by the Constitution to suspend the habeas corpus privilege, and hence that Merryman's detention was illegal. Taney put this opinion in writing a couple of days later and had a copy of it, with the proceedings in the case, transmitted to the President in order that he might "determine what measures he will take to cause the civil process of the United States to be respected and enforced."[38]

Lincoln was convinced that Taney was wrong and that he could, under the conditions stipulated in the Constitution, suspend the privilege of the writ of habeas corpus. As he said in his message to Congress shortly after the *Merryman decision*, the Constitution being silent as to who may suspend the writ in a dangerous emergency, "it cannot be believed the framers of the instrument intended that in every case the danger should run its course until Congress could be called together, the very assembling of which might be prevented, as was intended in this [that is, the *Merryman*] case, by the rebellion."[39] Thus he continued to exercise the disputed power on his own authority until Congress acted two years later.

On a number of occasions subsequent to the *Merryman decision*, courts issued habeas corpus writs to challenge the military arrest of rebels and army deserters, the enlistment of minors into military service, and the military conscription of persons claiming exemption from service; and sometimes they sought to punish by contempt those officers who disobeyed their commands. It seems clear that Lincoln saw no reason for his officers to comply with such writs issued by state courts. As he told his Cabinet, apparently with considerable vexation, in September, 1863, "No honest man did or could believe that the state judges have any such power."[40] This position suggests that

[38] *Ibid.*, p. 153.
[39] Message to Congress in Special Session, July 4, 1861, in Abraham Lincoln, *Complete Works*, ed. by John G. Nicolay and John Hay (New York: Lamb Publ. Co., 1894), Vol. VI, p. 310. Although he did not, he stated, believe he had violated any law in suspending habeas corpus in the *Merryman case*, Lincoln raised a broader point in defense of his action: "Are all the laws but one [the privilege of the writ of habeas corpus] to go unexecuted, and the government itself go to pieces lest that one be violated?" (*Ibid.*, p. 309.)
[40] Edward Bates, *Diary, 1859–1866*, ed. by Howard K. Beale (Washington: Government Printing Office, 1933), p. 306.

federal judges, in his opinion, did have the power to issue writs against officers of the federal government. A War Department report issued two months after the Cabinet meeting indicated that military officers had been following Lincoln's distinction in treating habeas corpus writs from the two sets of judiciaries: "The practice in regard to those issued by United States courts has been to obey the writs and abide the judgment of the court. In the cases of like writs issued by state courts, the practice has been . . . [that of] requiring the officer on whom the writ was served to make return denying the jurisdiction of the state courts, and declining to produce the person held."[41]

But military officers, under Presidential instructions, also disregarded the processes of federal courts. The *Merryman case* is to the point. General Cadwalader, under instructions from his military superior, refused Chief Justice Taney's command to produce Merryman in court, and when Taney sent a copy of his opinion to Lincoln, "no attention," we are told by Lincoln's private secretaries, "was paid to the transmitted papers,"[42] although Merryman was shortly afterwards turned over to civil authority and charged with a criminal offense. On at least a few other occasions, too, the writs of federal judges were resisted.[43] Indeed, resistance to all judicial authority was sanctioned by a War Department order approved by the Cabinet and issued in September, 1863, instructing military officers to cite Presidential authority as their reason for holding persons demanded by any courts issuing habeas corpus writs, and to resist any attempts by courts to arrest them for disobedience.[44]

We do not know the constitutional ground upon which

[41] "Report of the Provost Marshall General," dated November 17, 1863, in *Message of the President of the United States, and Accompanying Documents, to the Two Houses of Congress*, House of Representatives, Executive Document No. 1, 38th Congress, 1st Session, p. 112.

[42] John G. Nicolay and John Hay, *Abraham Lincoln: A History* (New York: Century, 1914), Vol. II, p. 176.

[43] See the discussion in Glendon Schubert, *The Presidency in the Courts* (Minneapolis: University of Minnesota Press, 1957), pp. 185–187, 323–324.

[44] *The War of the Rebellion: A Compilation of the Official Records of the Union and Confederate Armies* (Washington: Government Printing Office, 1897), Series III, Vol. III, p. 818.

Lincoln based his disobedience to federal judicial authority. We do know the ground on which his Attorney General justified Lincoln's disobedience, for it was expressed in a formal opinion to the President in July, 1861, with the Merryman incident, among others, in mind. "If it be true," the Attorney General said, "that the President and the judiciary are coordinate departments of government, and the one not subordinate to the other, I do not understand how it can be legally possible for a judge to issue a command to the President . . . to submit implicitly to his judgment and in case of disobedience treat him as a criminal, in contempt of a superior authority, and punish him as for a misdemeanor by fine and imprisonment." Or, more broadly stated: "No court or judge can take cognizance of the political acts of the President or undertake to revise and reverse his political decisions."[45] We should note that Attorney General Bates considered acts performed by the President's subordinates as done by the President's own hand.

The Attorney General's position is not free of difficulty. For example, he also averred in his opinion that judicial determinations were binding upon the parties involved in litigation. Perhaps Bates meant that the President was exempted from obeying only those judicial decisions that would subordinate him to the courts; but do not all judicial decisions so subordinate him? And does it do any good to say, by implication, that the President's non-political decisions can be controlled by the courts, if the President is thought to be "eminently and exclusively political in all his principal decisions"?[46] Furthermore, inasmuch as Congress is also an independent and co-equal governmental branch, it too must be free to disregard those judicial actions that would subordinate the legislature or control its political decisions. Finally, if the President—and Congress—may decide which judicial decisions they should and should not submit to, are they not made judges not only of their own powers under the Constitution but, in the most important respects, of those of the federal judiciary as well?

[45] *Ibid.*, Series II, Vol. II, p. 26.
[46] *Ibid.*

Whether Lincoln agreed with Attorney General Bates on the subject of executive obedience to judicial commands is hard to say. In view of his belief that judicial decisions bound the parties concerned, expressed not only in his First Inaugural Address but in his 1858 debates with Stephen A. Douglas, it is hard to see how Lincoln could agree with Bates. Yet Bates himself, as we observed, subscribed to Lincoln's belief in the binding quality of decisions. It may be that Lincoln based his resistance to the federal courts on the higher ground that the President's ordinary duty to obey judicial commands may be superseded, in extraordinary circumstances, by his higher duty to "preserve, protect, and defend the Constitution." Such a position would be consistent with the one he took in defending his suspension of the habeas corpus privilege, for he there argued that one part of the Constitution might be violated in order to save the government as a whole.

Franklin Roosevelt

The conflict between Franklin Roosevelt and the Supreme Court has become known as "the Court-packing fight." When Roosevelt launched it, however, he was careful not to give it the appearance of being a controversy at all. The President said, in a message to Congress in early February, 1937, that he was concerned about the judicial backlog of cases and with the efficiency of the federal courts in general. He wanted to provide assistance to those courts that had aged and infirm members, and so, he stated, he was proposing certain administrative and procedural changes in the court system. The changes included improved retirement benefits and Presidential authority to appoint additional judges to courts whose members had reached the age of seventy. For the Supreme Court, a maximum size of fifteen justices was proposed.

Roosevelt was not primarily concerned with the federal courts in general, but with the Supreme Court; and his interest, contrary to outward appearances, was not in helping the Court but in packing it with half a dozen of his own appointees. The

Supreme Court at that time had six members beyond the age of seventy, four of whom had been united in their opposition to the New Deal, and a fifth of whom had often sided with them. Roosevelt evidently was unwilling to put his real reasons before the public in making his proposal because of the stigma that would be attached to Court-packing: He himself had called it a "distasteful idea" a year earlier in discussing with his Cabinet the problem of the Court's obstruction.[47] In thus masquerading his designs, Roosevelt did not avoid the opprobrium of Court-packing but merely added that of duplicity. On March 9, a month after he unveiled his plan, Roosevelt put the issue somewhat more squarely when, in criticizing the failure of the "third member" of the "three-horse team" to pull in "unison" with the others, he spoke as follows in a national radio address: "By bringing into the judicial system a steady and continuing stream of new and younger blood, I hope, first, to make the administration of all federal justices speedier and therefore less costly; secondly, to bring to the decision of social and economic problems younger men who have had personal experience and contact with modern facts and circumstances under which average men have to live and work."[48]

The President was still caught up in his disguise, and not so cleverly as to be immune to exposure. Expose him Chief Justice Charles Evans Hughes did, in a letter to the Senate Judiciary Committee, the body considering Roosevelt's plan. Hughes easily demolished the tableau of backlogged and overworked justices by pointing out that the Supreme Court was (as it had not been when its members were younger) well abreast of its work, and he observed that the addition of justices to its number would, by adding voices to its deliberations, increase— not lighten—the Court's burden. Roosevelt's March address also heaped a gratuitous insult upon Justice Louis D. Brandeis, who was both well over eighty and proud of his liberalism. It was Brandeis who suggested to the chairman of the Judiciary

[47] Harold L. Ickes, *Secret Diary* (New York: Simon and Schuster, 1953), Vol. I p. 495.
[48] *New York Times*, March 10, 1937, p. 15.

Committee, a foe of the Court plan, that Hughes be asked for a letter commenting upon the Court's ability to perform its labors.[49]

In baiting the trap which Chief Justice Hughes sprang on him, Roosevelt acted with surprising ineptness, but then his behavior throughout the Court controversy was uncharacteristic. Usually careful to submit his projects to discussion, the President evolved his plan in an atmosphere of conspiracy into which only Attorney General Homer Cummings and perhaps three Justice Department aides were fully admitted.[50] The President's principal advisers were, at the insistence of Cummings, excluded from any part in the preparation of the plan. Usually astute in assuring political support for his projects, Roosevelt failed even to let his Cabinet and congressional leaders know anything about the Court plan until it was on its way to the legislative branch. Almost always clear-sighted about his political situation, Roosevelt seemed blind to the extent of opposition to Court-packing. He remained confident of victory even after the Court undercut his position by upholding national and state social-welfare legislation. The need to infuse new blood into the Court now seemed unnecessary, especially so when Justice Willis Van Devanter announced, on May 18, that he would retire from the Court at the end of the term, in June. As late as July 20, just two days before the Senate killed his bill by recommitting it (its Judiciary Committee had recommended against passage), Roosevelt told one of his Cabinet that he thought he had the votes to get his plan enacted.[51] Finally, Roosevelt, the pragmatist, refused to consider any compromises until it was too late. His Senate opponents promised to support a constitutional amendment giving the

---

[49] Joseph Alsop and Turner Catledge, *The 168 Days* (Garden City, N.Y.: Doubleday, Doran, 1938), p. 126. Brandeis permitted Senator Burton K. Wheeler, the Committee's chairman, to inform the Chief Justice that he was making his call from Brandeis's residence.

[50] William E. Leuchtenburg, "The Origins of Franklin D. Roosevelt's 'Court-Packing' Plan," in Philip B. Kurland, ed., *The Supreme Court Review, 1966* (Chicago: University of Chicago Press, 1966), p. 392. See this study generally on the development of Roosevelt's Court proposal (pp. 347–400).

[51] Ickes, *Secret Diary*, Vol. II, p. 166.

federal government the power the Court had denied it if he would give up his plan, but he refused. If he had acted in time he might have obtained legislation adding two new justices. Senator Wheeler, the leader of the opposition to the Court plan, offered him this as well as assurance of procuring Justice Sutherland's resignation (Van Devanter had at this time already announced his), but again Roosevelt refused to compromise. In fact, Roosevelt was obsessed with the fear that his Senate leader might agree to a compromise on the number of justices to be added. As a result, Roosevelt got nothing—except legislation improving the retirement system for federal judges.

Roosevelt was both encouraged and goaded into taking on the Supreme Court. The encouragement came from the great victories in the 1936 elections, which not only won him all but two states, but gave him an overwhelmingly Democratic Congress. The goading, of course, came from the Court. In nine cases decided between 1934 and 1936, it had invalidated national laws, in whole or partly, in thirteen decisions, and state and local legislation in thirty-six decisions. These actions constituted about one-fifth of the total number of national invalidations during the country's history until then, and about one-twelfth of the state and local invalidations; and nearly all of them involved legislation dealing with social welfare or the regulation of business. In addition, the Court had rendered the exercise of executive and regulatory functions difficult by still other decisions, and in the two years prior to his Court-packing attempt lower federal judges had issued about 1,600 injunctions against government officials engaged in the administration of national laws.

The Court has sometimes been portrayed as eagerly seeking opportunities to strike at the New Deal, but this accusation overstates the situation. Generally, it acted with caution, turning away cases where it could, and accepting the government's narrow definition of the issues in others. The government itself caused the constitutionality of the National Industrial Recovery Act to be decided upon (*Schecter Poultry Corporation* v. *United States*, 1935). The Act was due to expire shortly and the government could have delayed action on the case until it became moot for that reason. It is likewise an exaggeration to say that the Roosevelt administration suffered its constitutional defeats at the hands of the Court's four conservatives (Butler, McReynolds, Sutherland, and Van Devanter) aided by one or both of its moderates (Hughes and Roberts), while it was defended against judicial extremism by its three liberals (Brandeis, Cardozo, and Stone). Actually, the Court was unanimous in over half its invalidations of national laws or, in one case, nearly so. This fact should temper the common view that a liberal President and a liberal Court minority were engaged in a fight against a conservative majority of justices. In addition, only a few of the Court's legislative invalidations, perhaps no more than three, struck at important parts of the multifaceted New Deal, although it should be added that the Court was sharply divided in these instances.

One of the Supreme Court's invalidations (*United States* v. *Butler*, 1936) struck at a critically important part of the New Deal: its regulation of farm production. Other important parts had not yet undergone their ordeal in the Court, and Roosevelt was understandably anxious about legislation that regulated labor–management relations, public utilities, and stocks and bonds; established a system of social security and unemployment insurance; provided for a national public-works program; and created the Tennessee Valley Authority. These and other programs were considered to be in serious danger. Worse still, the Court's interpretations of key constitutional provisions left some doubt as to whether it would accept any new departures in social welfare and economic regulation. In short, the very existence of the New Deal, and its state counterparts, was made doubtful by the Hughes Court. Thus challenged, Roosevelt felt impelled to act.

Roosevelt had been moving toward a showdown with the Supreme Court for two years. In January, 1935, the Court was considering several cases challenging the government's power to repudiate its gold-support of the dollar. At this time, the

President toyed with the notion of creating turmoil in the financial market so that, if the decisions went against the government, the people would, in his words, say, "For God's sake, Mr. President, do something"—and, he added, "if I do, everybody in the country will heave a sigh of relief and thank me."[52] Roosevelt apparently planned to defy the Court in the event of unfavorable decisions, and had a radio message prepared for the purpose,[53] but the decisions, announced in February, did not upset the government's policy.[54] (Roosevelt again privately threatened defiance in 1942 when the Supreme Court undertook to determine whether he could establish a special military commission to try the cases of eight saboteurs who had attempted to penetrate the country's shoreline defense by landing from a German submarine. "I want one thing clearly understood, Francis," Roosevelt told Attorney General Biddle on that occasion, "I won't give them up . . . I won't hand them over to any United States marshal armed with a writ of habeas corpus. Understand?"[55] Once more the Court's decision did not require him to act on his threat.)

The *Gold-clause cases* only partially eased the tension between Roosevelt and the Supreme Court, and this only for a few months. The Court dealt the New Deal several new blows in May, 1935,[56] and additional ones in the first months of 1936.[57]

---

[52] Arthur M. Schlesinger, Jr., *The Age of Roosevelt: The Politics of Upheaval* (Boston: Houghton Mifflin, 1960), Vol. III, pp. 257–258.   [53] *Ibid.*, p. 258.

[54] The decisions were *Norman* v. *Baltimore and Ohio Railroad Company, Nortz* v. *United States*, and *Perry* v. *United States*, in the last of which the Court held the legislation repudiating gold-clause contracts in government bonds to be unconstitutional, an empty gesture inasmuch as it rejected the claim based on the illegality of the repudiation.

[55] Francis Biddle, *In Brief Authority* (Garden City, N.Y.: Doubleday, 1962), p. 331. The case was *In re Quirin.*

[56] The National Recovery Act was voided in *Schechter Corporation* v. *United States*, the farm-bankruptcy law in *Louisville Joint Stock Land Bank* v. *United States*, and the railroad workers' retirement law in *Railroad Retirement Board* v. *Alton Railroad Company*; and the President was told he could not remove members of regulatory agencies at his pleasure in *Humphrey's Executor* v. *United States.*

[57] These cases were *Butler* v. *United States*, voiding the Agricultural Adjustment Act; *Rickert Rice Mills* v. *Fontenot*, voiding amendments to that Act; *Carter* v. *Carter Coal Company*, invalidating legislation designed to fix prices and control working conditions in the coal industry; and *Ashton* v. *Cameron County District*, invalidating a municipal bankruptcy law.

Roosevelt was incensed. He privately declared that it was not possible to "draw an act that would pass the scrutiny of the Supreme Court in its present outlook on New Deal legislation," and he seemed to be hoping that the Court would make a clean sweep of the New Deal so that the issue would be indelibly marked between him and it.[58] Indeed, the President seemed convinced that the Court, following the course it had set, would do just that. It was in this atmosphere that Roosevelt began to devise ways of protecting his New Deal. He swore, when the agricultural production law was invalidated in January, 1936, that he would bring the Court "into line" if he had to pack it or deny it appellate jurisdiction,[59] and he also considered constitutional amendments that might get him around the seeming impasse.[60] Finally, toward the end of 1936, the President, fresh from his victory at the polls, decided upon Court-packing.

To be fully understood, the controversy between the Supreme Court and President Franklin Roosevelt must be seen as transcending the particular cases involved and even the issue of the powers of government. It concerned the character of American society, no less than did the great struggle between the Supreme Court and President Jefferson. In the more recent, as well as the older, controversy, Congress was not so much a contestant as an arbiter. In both controversies, too, each side was convinced of the correctness of its constitutional position. In the New Deal controversy, the constitutional issues were mainly concerned with the scope of the power to regulate commerce, the taxing and spending powers, the power of the President to receive Congressional delegations of legislative power and to control executive personnel, and the reserved powers of the states. Behind the exercise of these powers lay the questions of the government's power broadly to regulate economic activity, to provide economic security for the people,

---

[58] Ickes, *Secret Diary*, Vol. I, pp. 530–532.

[59] Alsop and Catledge, *The 168 Days*, p. 17. See also Ickes, *Secret Diary*, Vol. I, p. 372.

[60] Carl B. Swisher, *American Constitutional Development*; 2nd ed. (Boston: Houghton Mifflin Company, 1954), pp. 940–942, discusses different alternatives which the President took under review.

and to reduce economic and other class differences: in brief, to benefit the many at the general expense of the well-to-do. The President had public opinion behind him on the issue of the regulatory powers of the government; the Court had not been able to convince the people of the correctness of its constitutional position. Where the Marshall Court by-and-large established its position over that of its formidable adversary, the Hughes Court failed.

UNDERLYING ISSUES

With one exception, the issues underlying the conflicts we have considered have been given little treatment. This is surprising, for they are basic to the relationship between the Supreme Court and the Presidency. They concern: the propriety of Court-packing (the issue that has received attention); the binding character of judicial interpretations of the Constitution; the obligation of the President to enforce judicial judgments against others; and the President's obligation to obey such judgments directed at him or his subordinates.

Packing the Court

Court-packing has to do with the appointment of justices to the Supreme Court so as to influence the Court's decisions. But not all attempts to influence decisions of the Court through the appointment process qualify as Court-packing. Nearly all Presidents have chosen their justices with at least some attention to views on important matters that might come before the Court, and yet for this they cannot be accused of having tried to pack the Court. As the term has been generally used in American politics, Court-packing is accomplished through means that are considered to be unconstitutional or otherwise improper. It is perfectly proper for a President to concern himself with a man's views on constitutional or other legal questions. The stigma of Court-packing would be attached to an appointment in which a justice committed himself to act in a certain way on the Court. There is no evidence that such a pledge has ever been sought by a President, although it was one ground upon which President Grant's appointment of Joseph P. Bradley in 1870 was denounced as Court-packing. (Bradley was supposed to have agreed to uphold the constitutionality of legal-tender legislation.)[61] Grant did, however, have private information as to how the Court was going to rule on the legal-tender question, and made use of it to get the ruling reversed through his nominations of Bradley and William Strong to the Court. This action might properly be called Court-packing.[62]

The charge of Court-packing has been most often made in connection with efforts to increase the size of the Supreme Court. The most spectacular instance of attempted Court-packing in the Court's history was, of course, Franklin Roosevelt's proposal that Congress permit him to add up to six members to the Court. Roosevelt's proposal was not unconstitutional in the strict sense: the Constitution gives Congress the power to determine the size of the Court, and Congress has in fact varied the number of justices six times. But the purpose for which Roosevelt sought his increase was extreme. Never in the past had Congress increased the size of the Supreme Court because it, or the President, wished to affect the Court's decisions—and, for that matter, there is no convincing evidence that it enacted either of its two decreases for that purpose. Furthermore, the Court had been fixed at nine members since 1869, long enough for most people to consider its size almost as set by the Constitution itself.

Before Roosevelt made his attempt, every increase in the size of the Supreme Court had been related to the circuit duties of the justices, although patronage considerations had some influence on the timing. As the country grew, new circuits were needed for the conduct of judicial business, and additional justices were required for these additional circuit courts. The

[61] Charles Fairman, "Mr. Justice Bradley's Appointment to the Supreme Court and the Legal Tender Cases," *Harvard Law Review*, **54** (May, 1941), 1142.
[62] See pp. 54–55, including n. 47.

Supreme Court was established in 1789 with six members, added a seventh in 1807, two more in 1837, went to ten members in 1863, and found its present level six years later. It was feasible to set the number of justices and circuits at nine in 1869, and not to increase them thereafter because Congress in that year lightened the circuit duties of justices, and eliminated them entirely in 1891.[63]

The constitutional irregularity of Roosevelt's plan helps explain the great resistance it encountered. Perhaps the opposition of the organized bar was to be expected, and yet it is striking that only one of six lawyers polled by the American Bar Association favored the plan.[64] The Senate that killed the plan was four-fifths Democratic. Even the American public, which had given the President and his policies such emphatic support the previous November, backed away from the idea of tampering with the Supreme Court. The closest Roosevelt came to gaining a popular endorsement, according to a survey of public opinion, was in March, just after he had carried his case to the public in two nationwide radio addresses and before Chief Justice Hughes wrote his explosive letter; even then 51 per cent of those with an opinion were against the Court plan. From there popular opposition steadily rose, and by June it stood at 59 per cent.[65] Even Felix Frankfurter, who in 1937, while on the Harvard Law faculty, was a frequent adviser to the President, refrained from openly endorsing Court-packing. Although Frankfurter furnished considerable behind-the-scenes assistance to the President, he maintained a public pose of neutrality

---

[63] In 1801 Congress reduced the size of the Supreme Court from six to five members because it at the same time abolished circuit-riding; perhaps, too, it wished to frustrate the incoming President Jefferson. In 1866 it reduced the Court from ten to seven members to frustrate Andrew Johnson. The Jeffersonians undid the Federalist shackle a year after it was attached, before any vacancy occurred and the Radical Republicans in 1869, with Johnson gone, restored the Court to its pre-1863 size of nine members.

[64] Cited in Carl A. Auerbac, *et al.*, *The Legal Process: An Introduction to Decision-making* (San Francisco: Chandler Publ. Co., 1961), p. 679. The number of lawyers taking part in the poll was 19,136.

[65] For these and other Gallup Poll figures on the Court question, see Walter F. Murphy, *Congress and the Court* (Chicago: University of Chicago Press, Phoenix Books, 1965), p. 61 n.

on the question, told his closest friends that he had no role in the affair, and was prepared, if asked, to be similarly deceptive with the Senate Judiciary Committee at the time of his nomination to the Court in 1939.[66] Although espoused by a most popular President at the peak of his public acclaim, Court-packing was not a popular cause.

If Roosevelt's Court plan was an extreme way of dealing with the Supreme Court, the circumstances in which the President acted, we must remind ourselves, were also rather extreme. There was the gravity of the Depression, the damage the Court had already inflicted on the New Deal, and the judicial danger that seemed to lie ahead. One might criticize Roosevelt for not trying to steer the Court by the normal method of waiting for vacancies to appear among the elderly justices, but he had already waited four years. No other President except Monroe had gone so long without the opportunity to name a justice,[67] and Roosevelt was understandably impatient. "You know," he told his Secretary of Labor in discussing what the Court might do to the National Recovery Act, "I have been in office for two years and haven't had an appointment for the Supreme Court. . . . What that Court needs is some Roosevelt appointments. Then we might get a good

---

[66] Frankfurter's part in the Court-packing episode is told, mostly through documentary evidence, in *Roosevelt and Frankfurter: Their Correspondence, 1928–1945*, annot. by Max Freedman (Boston: Little, Brown, 1967), pp. 376–406; and the statement he prepared for use before the Senate Judiciary Committee is printed *ibid.*, p. 15. The justice explained his public deception on the ground that Roosevelt telephoned him after the Court plan was announced and "exacted" a "most solemn oath of silence and public neutrality" from him because he wanted someday to put the law professor on the Supreme Court and didn't want him entangled in the Court controversy (*ibid.*, p. 372). The published correspondence between the two men gives no support to this explanation and, indeed, evidence against it. See, for example, Frankfurter's letter of March 30, 1937, in which he states that he will not give Roosevelt's enemies "a new line of attack against your proposals" by getting publicly into the controversy ("There are various ways of fighting a fight!"), and Roosevelt's reply of April 5: "You are dead right in keeping—*for the moment*—wholly out of the hearings. As you know, we are carrying out the dignified process of keeping still and watching each new witness damn the proposal and offer a new remedy." (*Ibid.*, pp. 392, 396; emphasis supplied.)

[67] Woodrow Wilson made no appointments in his second term in office, but he did make three in his first term.

decision out of them."[68] He was not sanguine about his chances of getting appointments, once remarking that he expected his great nemesis, McReynolds, still to be on the Court at the age of 105.[69] Since the Court first reached its size of nine members (in 1837), Presidential appointments had averaged two or three per term; Roosevelt was led to wonder, not without some cause, whether he would get any in two terms.[70]

Accepting the Court's Interpretations of the Constitution

As we observed in the last chapter, the Supreme Court's interpretations of the Constitution are not necessarily binding upon the President, nor upon anyone else. It is the Constitution that the President swears to support, and not what the Court says about the Constitution. Judges do, of course, have a special duty to say what the Constitution, and law in general, mean, for those who apply law to particular cases must also explain it; and so great deference is owed to the pronouncements of the judiciary. But judges are neither infallible nor the constitutional superiors of Presidents and congressmen. Nor do they, in consequence, have the power to fix the meaning of the Constitution the moment they speak upon it.

All four of the Presidents we have considered adhered to the position we have set forth. Despite judicial views to the contrary, Jefferson held that the Sedition Act had been unconstitutional, that the President had control over appointments until the commissions to them had been delivered, and that he had the authority under the Embargo Act to instruct

---

[68] Quoted in Frances Perkins, *The Roosevelt I Knew* (New York: Viking Press, 1946), p. 249.

[69] Ickes, *Secret Diary*, Vol. I, p. 705.

[70] In such circumstances, suspicions and misunderstandings were almost bound to arise between the President and the Court. On Roosevelt's side, for example, there was the belief that the justices had failed to appear for the delivery of the State of the Union Message in January, 1937, because they had been alerted by someone that the President planned to criticize the Court in it (Ickes, *Secret Diary*, Vol. II, p. 32); and that the Court had deliberately snubbed him in October, 1936, by not paying its usual courtesy visit to the White House at the start of its term (Merlo J. Pusey, *Charles Evans Hughes* [New York: Columbia University Press, 1963], Vol. II, pp. 749–750).

port collectors on the detention of vessels. (In the last case, Jefferson was asserting his right to interpret legislative, not constitutional, provisions for himself.) Jackson put aside the opinions of both the Supreme Court and Congress in deciding that the Bank of the United States was unconstitutional and, mainly for that reason, vetoed legislation to recharter it. Likewise Lincoln continued his suspensions of the habeas corpus privilege despite the views of Chief Justice Taney and some other judges. And Franklin Roosevelt made it clear that he did not accept the interpretation given by the Supreme Court to the commerce clause and other provisions of the Constitution and, in his attempt at Court-packing, sought to bring the Court back to a proper constitutional perspective.

There is, as we have demonstrated, nothing constitutionally improper in a President's asserting his right to interpret the Constitution for himself and in refusing to accept an interpretation placed upon it by judges when he is convinced that they are wrong. To hold differently would, as Jefferson and Lincoln and others have pointed out, place the chief executive and everyone else under a judicial despotism. It is indeed those who, especially in recent years, have pronounced everyone, including the President, to be under judicial rule who have taken a position which is constitutionally untenable. That they have included justices of the Supreme Court does not mitigate the error.[71]

Enforcing Judicial Judgments

It appears that the only President who refused to enforce a judicial decree (if indeed he did so refuse) was Andrew Jackson. We do not know whether Jackson believed that the President was bound by the Constitution to enforce judicial judgments against others. We do know that Martin Van Buren, writing long after the decision in *Worcester* v. *Georgia*, believed that Jackson was so bound. Although Van Buren expressed his belief with that case apparently very much in mind, we cannot

[71] See, for example, *Cooper* v. *Aaron*, 358 U.S. 1 (1958), at 18.

say for sure that Jackson shared his view in 1832, when the case was decided. Even if Jackson considered himself bound to enforce judicial judgments directed at others, we still cannot say that he failed in his duty in this case. In the first place, the Supreme Court had asked nothing of the President. (Van Buren, it will be recalled, stated that the President's assistance must be requested by the judiciary in order for his constitutional obligation to be operative.) In the second place, we must keep in mind that the President is obligated to do more than enforce judicial mandates; he is also charged, in his oath, to "preserve, protect, and defend the Constitution." What if the Constitution were imperiled by Presidential enforcement of a decision? Must he enforce the decision and endanger, perhaps undo, the Constitution? The nullification crisis did endanger the Union; and the use of force against Georgia on the Cherokee question might have given South Carolina an ally— perhaps other states sensitive about their rights would have gone over, too. And if Georgia could not be subdued by federal force, as Jackson feared it could not, would not the South Carolinians have been encouraged to pursue their collision course with the national government? Under the circumstances, Jackson, if no other motive had stayed his hand, was justified in seeking a political, and not a military, means of resolving the missionary controversy.

Finally, we may ask whether the President is at all required by the Constitution to enforce judicial decrees. Nothing in the Constitution says that he must, and President Jackson certainly gave no sign that he was consciously violating it by not coming to the Supreme Court's assistance in the *Worcester case*. It might be argued that his duty to take care that the laws be faithfully executed includes judicial decrees, at least those decrees based upon an interpretation of laws.[72] On the other hand, Hamilton, in *Federalist 78*, seemed to put the judiciary at the mercy of the

---

[72] On this question, see the opposing positions taken by Alfred J. Schweppe, "Enforcement of Federal Court Decrees: A 'Recurrence to Fundamental Principles,'" *American Bar Association Journal*, **44** (February, 1958), 113–116, 187–190, 192; and Daniel H. Pollitt, "The Executive Enforcement of Judicial Decrees," *ibid.*, **45** (June, 1959), 600–603, 606.

President's favorable disposition in his remark that it "must ultimately depend upon the aid of the executive arm even for the efficacy of its judgments."[73] And it is worth noting that the legislation providing for executive enforcement of judicial decisions, enacted in 1792, authorizes the President to use military force only where rebellion or other disturbance makes it impracticable to enforce the laws by ordinary judicial proceedings.[74]

Thus, however we regard Jackson's behavior in the case of *Worcester* v. *Georgia*, the question of whether he was constitutionally obliged to come to the assistance of the Supreme Court cannot be given an easy answer.

Obeying Judicial Commands

The most difficult question arising from judicial–executive conflict concerns the President's obligation to comply with judgments and other processes of the judiciary. Two of the four Presidents we have considered threatened to disregard judicial actions aimed at them. In each instance, the threat was privately made, and in neither was it carried out. Jefferson said long after the fact in *Marbury* that no court could make him deliver an appointment, and Roosevelt said before the favorable decisions in the *Gold-clause* and *Nazi Saboteur cases* that he would not obey the Supreme Court if the decisions went against him. Jefferson also said, in the Burr proceedings, that the President could refuse to obey a court subpoena. He claimed to have ignored a second subpoena issued against him in those proceedings, although it appears that he did not actually do so.

Andrew Johnson is the only President who ever openly threatened to disobey an order of the judicial branch. Speaking through his Attorney General, in oral argument in the case of *Mississippi* v. *Johnson* (1867), the President indicated that he would not comply with a decision enjoining him from enforcing two Reconstruction Acts just passed by Congress. But the

---

[73] *The Federalist*, p. 396.
[74] *United States Code*, Title 10, Ch. 15, Sec. 332.

circumstances of Johnson's threat were most extenuating and the threat itself most respectful, for the President faced impeachment by a hostile Congress if he failed to execute the Acts (they had been passed over his vetoes). The Attorney General intimated that the President would accept the judicial consequences of any disobedience, but the Court was unwilling to make Johnson choose between legislative impeachment and judicial imprisonment (or, perhaps, as it suggested, executive defiance of the Court's process), and it dismissed the litigation.[75]

Only two Presidents, Jefferson and Van Buren, appear to have claimed the constitutional right to disobey judicial decisions that they considered to be unwarranted by the Constitution. Lincoln's Attorney General made a similar claim on Lincoln's behalf, but we do not know whether Lincoln shared his view. Whatever the case, Jefferson and Lincoln nullified judicial actions, Jefferson in his Sedition Act pardons[76] and Lincoln in ignoring judicial writs directed against arbitrary arrests.

Must the President, under the Constitution, obey all judicial actions directed at the executive branch or see that they are obeyed by his subordinates? May he, for example, undo judicial decisions through the use of his power of pardon? The Constitution gives the Supreme Court and such other courts as may be established the power of deciding cases and controversies which come within the federal judicial power. This power is basic to law courts. For a party to a case to disregard or subvert the judicial settlement of it would be to act against the Constitution. Courts must apply law in deciding cases, and thus are required to interpret the law, including the law of the Constitution. Their interpretations of law must be accepted in the particular cases involved (but not necessarily, as we have seen, as binding future actions). The President, who is charged with the faithful execution of laws, must accept the

[75] *Mississippi* v. *Johnson*, at 485–487, 500–501.
[76] "But the executive determined that the Sedition Act was a nullity under the Constitution, and exercised his regular power of prohibiting the execution of the sentence." Letter to George Hay, June 2, 1807, in Jefferson, *Writings*, p. 214.

law as it is judicially defined and applied in particular cases. Thus, it would seem, the decisions of the judicial branch must be obeyed by the President as well as by others.

Yet a reservation or two must be made concerning the President's obligation to allow his actions to be controlled judicially. Judges need not comply with decisions of the President or Congress regarding the scope of judicial power when they consider the decisions to be palpably wrong. Might it be argued that the President and Congress, in a system of coordinate branches, possess a similar power with respect to judicial decisions? But our main reservation concerns the President's obligation not only to obey judicial decisions but also to "preserve, protect, and defend the Constitution" as a whole. The Constitution would not have been imperiled if the Supreme Court had ordered Thomas Jefferson to deliver Marbury's commission of office to him. And it is unlikely that it would have been imperiled if the Court had told Franklin Roosevelt that he could not try the Nazi saboteurs by special military commission. But the Constitution was placed in peril by judicial attempts to interfere with the military detention of persons thought by the executive to be dangerous to national safety during the most serious crisis through which this nation yet has passed. Fully conscious of the dangers involved in an affirmative answer, we still must ask: Are there not circumstances in which a President may be justified in refusing to comply with the commands of the judiciary—even of the Supreme Court itself?

3

Out-of-Court Relations

The Constitution does not attempt to define the extent to which officials in the three branches of government may cooperate with each other or influence each other's actions. There has always been considerable political interaction between members of Congress and the executive branch, of course, but not between congressmen and executive officers on the one hand, and judges on the other. This is to be expected. The executive and legislative branches are constitutionally linked in a number of ways, but the judiciary is linked to the other two branches only in appointments and in the rarely used impeachment power. The framers did consider other points of contact. As we noted in an earlier chapter, there was strong support in the Constitutional Convention to have Supreme Court justices participate with the chief executive in a Council of Revision to approve legislative enactments. The framers also contemplated a proposal to join the Chief Justice with the heads of executive departments in a Council of State to advise the President in the conduct of public affairs. Yet another proposal would have required the Supreme Court to furnish the other branches, upon request, with advisory opinions on legal and other matters.

The framers rejected all of these moves to insinuate the Supreme Court into the affairs of the Presidency and Congress. But they did not specifically prohibit the Court or its members individually from advising the other branches, and they turned down a proposal which would have disqualified justices from simultaneously holding any other office. Instead, the Constitution stipulates only that members of Congress may not at the same time hold office in either the executive or the judicial branch. As we shall show, Supreme Court justices have entered into various extra-curiam relationships with their colleagues in other parts of the government. They have done so more often, it appears, than have lower-court judges, and much more often with the Presidency than with Congress.

NATURE OF THE RELATIONS

The out-of-Court activities of Supreme Court justices with the Presidency and Congress have taken three forms. First, justices have engaged in activities related to their judicial responsibilities. These have consisted of the performance of quasi-judicial tasks, usually at the designation of the President; advising the chief executive on judicial appointments; and advising both the chief executive and Congress on legislation affecting the judiciary. Second, they have accepted temporary service in some executive capacity, nearly always at the behest of the President. And third, they have acted as political advisers to Presidents. Inasmuch as these three kinds of extra-curiam activity differ so sharply, they will be treated separately in the following pages.

Judicial-related Activities

The Supreme Court decided, just after it was formed, that it would not advise the other branches of government on the

legality of actions under their consideration. The issue came
before the Court in 1793 when President Washington, through
Secretary of State Jefferson, asked the Court if it would be
willing to pass judgment upon a number of perplexing questions
concerning this country's relations with Great Britain and
France. The Court informed the President that both the principle of separation of powers and its own role as a court of last
resort precluded its helping him.[1] The Court appears to have
deviated from this rule only once, in 1822, when it complied
with President Monroe's request for an opinion on Congress's
power to provide for internal improvements, such as the building of roads and canals.[2] Perhaps the only deviation from the
rule by an individual justice occurred in 1796, when Chief
Justice Oliver Ellsworth, acting for himself, advised President
Washington that the House of Representatives could not constitutionally demand papers connected with the negotiation
of the Jay Treaty.[3] Of course, Presidents may have requested
and received constitutional advice from individual justices informally on other occasions, and justices have sometimes been
willing to proffer it. During the Civil War, for example, Chief
Justice Roger B. Taney gave the Secretary of the Treasury the
unasked-for opinion that the government had no authority to
levy an income tax on judicial salaries, and Justice David Davis
acted similarly in giving President Lincoln his opinion that
the trial of civilians by military courts where the civil courts
were open was outside the Constitution.[4] But the Supreme
Court's refusal to advise Washington on the legal aspects of
the country's international relations pretty much settled the

---

[1] Charles Warren, *The Supreme Court in United States History* (Boston: Little, Brown,
    1926), Vol. I, pp. 108–111.   [2] *Ibid.*, pp. 595–597.
[3] George Washington, *Writings*, ed. by Worthington C. Ford (New York:
    G. P. Putnam's Sons, 1892), Vol. XIII, p. 177. In 1792, a year before the
    Court took its position on advisory opinions, Chief Justice John Jay advised
    Alexander Hamilton with respect to the constitutionality of proclamations
    dealing with the Whiskey Rebellion and American neutrality in the
    belligerency between Great Britain and France. (Warren, *Supreme Court in
    U.S. History*, Vol. I, p. 109 n.)
[4] Samuel Tyler, *Memoir of Roger Brooke Taney* (Baltimore: John Murphy, 1872),
    pp. 432–435; Willard L. King, *Lincoln's Manager: David Davis* (Cambridge:
    Harvard University Press, 1960), p. 254.

question of whether that tribunal would serve as a Presidential advisory council on constitutional issues. It meant that the President would have to get his legal uncertainties resolved elsewhere or through regular judicial proceedings.

Supreme Court justices have, however, considered themselves free to perform quasi-judicial duties for the other branches. They have done so in about a dozen instances, mostly at the request of the President, in a few instances at the joint request of Congress and the President, and, concerning the special commission established to resolve the disputed Presidential election of 1876, once at the behest of Congress alone.[5] In these assignments the justices have been called upon to render judgments after considering evidence and arguments; the proceedings have usually been adversary in character; and the judges have generally acted as members of a collegial body. Such assignments thus do not in themselves seem inappropriate for members of the judicial branch. The assignments include Justice Samuel Nelson's service, by President Grant's appointment, as an arbitrator in a dispute between the United States and Great Britain that arose from the Alabama incident during the Civil War; the work of Chief Justice Melvin W. Fuller and Justice David J. Brewer, by Cleveland's selection, as arbitrators in a dispute between Great Britain and Venezuela concerning Venezuela's boundary with British Guiana (now Guyana); and Fuller's designation by Theodore Roosevelt as an arbitrator in a dispute between Great Britain and France concerning the use of the French flag by a North African sultanate. American interests, when involved at all, were aligned on only one side of these disputes, and judicial litigation was highly unlikely. And yet a Supreme Court justice could find his participation in quasi-judicial proceedings embarrassing, as Justice Owen J. Roberts did in his service in 1932 on a mixed-claims commission. Appointed by President Hoover as an umpire in proceedings to determine the German government's liability for fires and

---

[5] For a critical discussion of the non-judicial employment of federal justices and judges, see "Independence of Judges: Should They Be Used for Non-Judicial Work?" *American Bar Association Journal*, 33 (August, 1947), 792–796.

explosions that occurred in New York harbor during the First World War, Roberts was accused of bias by the German commissioner, who walked out of the meeting.

Supreme Court justices have been appointed to quasi-judicial assignments less for their possession of needed knowledge or skills than for their prestige. Judicial participation in such assignments has offered assurances of impartiality and has helped to obtain an acceptance of the decisions reached. The need to draw upon the Court's prestige seems to have been the primary reason for President Franklin Roosevelt's selection of Justice Roberts to head the commission of inquiry appointed to investigate the Pearl Harbor disaster immediately following the Japanese attack. We might cite as other examples President Kennedy's proposal to management and labor in the railroad industry in July, 1963, that Justice Arthur J. Goldberg arbitrate a bitter dispute between them, or President Johnson's designation of Chief Justice Earl Warren to head the commission to investigate the assassination of President Kennedy.

The justices' second service related to their judicial responsibilities has concerned the operations of the judicial branch itself. Presidents have freely consulted with justices on judicial appointments, as has Congress on legislation affecting the judiciary; and justices have felt fairly free to offer their advice to both on these subjects. It is likely that many, if not most, Presidents have consulted, or have been consulted by, Supreme Court justices in the filling of vacancies on the Court, and consultations on lower-court appointments have not been infrequent, either. Probably no other justice matched Chief Justice William Howard Taft's interest in staffing the bench. He frequently prodded the administrations of Harding, Coolidge, and Hoover in his effort to have more attention paid to quality and less to patronage in the appointment of federal judges. In this crusade Taft was only partly successful, for his advice was not usually sought after, and he had to contend with political pressures from the Senate; but he at least was able to keep a number of the worst judicial candidates from receiving the Presidential favor.[6] His greatest service was in successfully opposing, as "totally unfit," a circuit court judge who, with strong backing, aspired to the Supreme Court and who ended his career convicted of accepting large sums in bribes from litigants.[7]

Taft was also active in legislative matters concerning the judiciary. His efforts with the executive and legislative branches produced two acts instituting major reforms in the judicial system, and he was responsible, too, for the legislation that finally gave the Supreme Court its own quarters.[8] Taft's involvement in legislative business was somewhat unusual in its intensity, but Supreme Court members have had some part in most of the serious legislative proposals affecting the judiciary. As early as 1793, the protests of the justices effected a change in a law under which courts passed upon the invalid pension claims of war veterans (their decisions were subject to revision by the Secretary of War and by Congress). They also enlisted the support of Presidents Washington and Adams against circuit-riding and, under Adams, obtained short-lived legislative relief from the practice. Taft's colleagues on the Supreme Court had, before he joined them, drafted other legislation concerning the judiciary, and those who followed him to the bench have likewise taken an interest in such legislation.

Executive Service

Four Supreme Court justices have been employed in executive capacities, but none of them participated in judicial deliberations while engaged in extra-curiam service. Most of the service was performed by the first three Chief Justices: John Jay (on two occasions), Oliver Ellsworth, and John

---

[6] Alpheus T. Mason, *William Howard Taft: Chief Justice* (New York: Simon and Schuster, 1964), pp. 157–191, contains ample evidence of Taft's appointment efforts, although it exaggerates their significance (one chapter, for example, being called "[Taft's] Packing the Court").

[7] See David J. Danelski, *A Supreme Court Justice Is Appointed* (New York: Random House, 1964), pp. 59–60, 73–75, 195–197.

[8] Mason, *Taft*, pp. 88–137; Walter F. Murphy, "Chief Justice Taft and the Lower Court Bureaucracy," *Journal of Politics*, 24 (August, 1962), 453–476.

Marshall. It must be kept in mind that neither the Constitution nor considerations of judicial ethics at the time precluded the non-judicial employment of judges. The sharp line of separation between the judicial and the other branches—especially the executive branch—had not yet been drawn, and, moreover, judges were eligible to hold other public offices in a number of states. Thus George Washington felt free to employ Jay as Minister Plenipotentiary to Great Britain in 1794 to negotiate the famous treaty of settlement that bear's Jay's name. Thus, too, John Adams had no qualms in appointing Ellsworth in a similar capacity to France in 1799 to seek to avert open war between that country and the United States. The other two early instances of double office-holding by justices are not only extenuating for the reasons we have given but trivial. Jay had been Secretary of Foreign Affairs under the Confederation government, and he agreed to hold the reins of that office for several months after his appointment in September, 1789, as Chief Justice under the new government until Thomas Jefferson, newly returned from France, was able to assume the post. And Marshall continued as Secretary of State for the few weeks that remained of the Adams administration after his appointment to the Court in January, 1801.

The next and only other Supreme Court justice to serve in an executive (as distinguished from a quasi-judicial) assignment was Robert H. Jackson. President Truman designated Jackson in 1945 to negotiate the executive agreement providing for the trial of the vanquished German war leaders and to serve as chief American prosecutor at the Nuremberg proceedings. The tradition of judicial abstention from service in the executive branch which had grown between the employment of Jay, Ellsworth, and Marshall, and that of Jackson caused Truman's action to be roundly criticized, with the consequence that the tradition appears to be once more firmly established.

In only one instance did the executive employment of Supreme Court justices seem motivated by a desire to make use of the prestige of the Court. Jay and Marshall merely lent themselves to administrative convenience in briefly holding on

to their secretaryships. President Washington sent Chief Justice
Jay to Great Britain because of the latter's vast diplomatic
experience under the Confederation, not because of his prestige
as Chief Justice. Ellsworth had been a leader in the Federalist
party before his appointment to the Court, and his designation
as special minister seemed designed to draw the party's support
behind President Adams's overtures to revolutionary France.
But Jackson's service was dictated neither by a towering reputation nor by special proficiency. (His experience in trial courts
had been concluded many years earlier.) What Jackson brought
to Nuremberg was the eminence of the Supreme Court, a
needed commodity in proceedings whose legal foundations
were none too firm.

Political Advising

Political advising by Supreme Court justices has consisted
of private counseling, the preparation of speeches and other
written materials, and the like. The President has been the
beneficiary of such activity. However, unlike the justices'
performance of executive duties, their political advising has
been screened from public view, and conducted without leave-
taking from the Court.

The purpose of political advice, whether given by justices
or others, is to assist a President in the performance of his
duties. Thus Presidents have not drawn advisers from the
Supreme Court in order to exploit the Court's reputation but
primarily to avail themselves of valued and trusted assistance,
although a secondary motivation might sometimes have been
to obtain a justice who would be favorably disposed toward
Presidential policies in litigation before the Court. Those justices
who can give Presidents the needed assistance must be political or personal friends; but friendships have rarely, if ever,
developed between Presidents and sitting justices, and rarely
have Presidents happened to be friends of justices appointed by
someone else. Informal judicial–executive collaboration, then,
has nearly always occurred between Presidents and friends

appointed by them. And, since Presidents have personally known most of their appointees to the Court, the number of their potential advisers has been large.

We are interested in political advising by Supreme Court justices which has been at least of some significance, not that which has been episodic and trivial. We are also interested in political advising which Presidents have sought or to which they have at least been receptive, not that which has been unwanted and, so far as we can tell, nearly always disregarded. Most instances of judicial advice-giving have been minor or unsolicited, and have sometimes been exaggerated. For example, Justice David Davis frequently gave President Lincoln his advice, but, by the justice's own account, Lincoln never asked him for it on any subject. "When I have given any, I have thrust it upon him," said Davis, without, it may be added, important effect.[9] Stephen J. Field undertook to instruct President Cleveland on the making of executive appointments in California, but he was ignored.[10] Hugo L. Black wanted President Franklin Roosevelt to know, as America was preparing itself for the Second World War, that the government should manufacture its own military aircraft, to which advice we do not, perhaps fortunately, know Roosevelt's reaction.[11] William H. Moody gave judicial assistance at the President's request, and yet we could not, in a serious sense, call Moody an adviser to Theodore Roosevelt on the basis of his known activities: attendance at a dinner to discuss a social problem and suggestions for a speech.[12] To speak of justices as Presidential advisers in political matters requires more substantial activity than what we have described.

The confidential character of political advising makes it difficult to say how many justices have engaged in more than a

[9] King, *Lincoln's Manager*, p. 206.
[10] Carl B. Swisher, *Stephen J. Field: Craftsman of the Law* (Washington: Brookings Institution, 1930), pp. 316–317.
[11] Harold L. Ickes, *Secret Diary* (New York: Simon and Schuster, 1954), Vol. III, pp. 177–178.
[12] Theodore Roosevelt, *Letters*, ed. by Elting E. Morison (Cambridge: Harvard University Press, 1952), Vol. V, p. 801; Vol. VI, p. 1336. Moody also served on a commission to study certain needs of the Navy (*ibid.*, Vol. VI, p. 1487).

minimal amount of it. On the basis of published material, at most nine justices would qualify. They are, in order of appointment: John Jay, Roger B. Taney, Louis D. Brandeis, William Howard Taft, Felix Frankfurter, William O. Douglas, James F. Byrnes, Fred M. Vinson, and Abe Fortas. All of the justices except Jay and Taney have served on the Court in this century; the last two seem to have been most involved in advising. Their assistance was rendered primarily to the Presidents who appointed them, and all except Taft were appointed by Democrats. It will be recalled that Democratic Presidents, much more than Republican, have selected their justices from their political entourage and with an eye to political views. An ex-President, Taft had trouble keeping his mind off executive matters. All seven of the Democratic-appointed justices enjoyed an advisory relationship with their appointers before going on the Court.

Jay appears to have been a fairly active adviser to Washington and to Washington's Secretary of the Treasury, Alexander Hamilton, although written evidence is lacking on much that apparently took place between them. We do know that Jay frequently visited Washington and Hamilton, and we do have a record of several advisory transactions. For example, Jay is known to have counseled the President on the propriety of seeking Senate advice concerning the places to which diplomatic officers should be posted; on the proposal of an Anglo–American alliance put forward by a special British agent; and on several of Washington's public messages. He advised Hamilton on how to deal with the Whiskey Rebellion and on various aspects of foreign relations. As Jay's biographer has expressed his subject's role, "Jay continued to advise Washington and Hamilton during his entire tenure of the chief justiceship," but "at the same time he insisted upon a strict separation of the three great departments of government."[13] The conduct of Jay must be placed in the context of the 1790s. The creation of a Council of Revision had been vigorously backed in the Consti-

---

[13] Frank Monaghan, *John Jay: Defender of Liberty* (Indianapolis: Bobbs-Merrill, 1935), p. 347. See also pp. 344–346.

tutional Convention, and the Cabinet-like Council of State also had its influential advocates there. Thus there was, as we have already noted, a widespread belief in the propriety of the President's drawing upon the Court's members for assistance. It was in this spirit that Washington and Hamilton turned to Jay for political advice, and that Jay satisfied them. The President even addressed formal notices to the Chief Justice as well as to the heads of the executive departments in requesting suggestions for proposals to be submitted to Congress. But as the Cabinet emerged in Washington's administration as the proper body for advising the President, judges came rather quickly to be pretty much regarded as having their rightful place outside the executive advisory system.

There is some question as to whether Taney, Brandeis, and Taft were sufficiently involved in the political affairs of the executive branch to merit inclusion with the other five justices we have named. Taney's assistance to his appointer, Andrew Jackson, consisted in preparing a veto message that Jackson did not use; contributing to Jackson's last annual message to Congress; and taking a major hand in writing the President's Farewell Address. Perhaps Taney would have done more for Jackson if he had not assumed his office only about a year before Jackson vacated his. The Chief Justice did respond to a request in early 1837 for fiscal and economic advice from Jackson's successor, Martin Van Buren (Taney and Van Buren had served together in Jackson's administration), but no traces of Presidential advising by Taney appear after that.[14] Brandeis's main biographer, who had long conversations with him late in the justice's life, calls him "Wilson's Adviser" in one of the chapters of his biography.[15] The only evidence he gives of Brandeis's activities on Wilson's behalf, however, are a talk between the two men in late 1917 concerning the appointment of a wartime agency head; and a memorandum the justice wrote the following year, at the request of an aide to Wilson, on

---

[14] Taney's advisory relations with the two Presidents is recounted in Carl B. Swisher, *Roger B. Taney* (New York: Macmillan, 1935), pp. 496–502.

[15] Alpheus T. Mason, *Brandeis: A Free Man's Life* (New York: Viking Press, 1946), p. 526.

the work of such agencies. Both Brandeis and Wilson obviously considered their discussion of a political matter to be highly irregular. The justice declared that he could visit the White House on such a matter only at the President's request, and Wilson responded that he could not invite the justice there for that purpose; thus, Wilson visited Brandeis at the latter's residence. There is no record of other visits, and, furthermore, Wilson stated his agreement with the position of Chief Justice Edward D. White that a Supreme Court justice (specifically, Brandeis) should not perform executive jobs.[16] Whatever other help Brandeis gave Wilson seems to have been transmitted nearly entirely through subordinate executive officials. Writing nearly three decades later, Wilson's Secretary of the Navy reported that "not once but a number of times in discussing humanitarian or progressive policies, he [Wilson] would say to me: 'I wish you would go see our friend Brandeis, acquaint him with the problem and get his reaction.'"[17] Such indirect help did not, from the available records, amount to much; nor could it have continued very long, for, by late 1918, a little more than two years after he mounted the bench, Brandeis was saying uncomplimentary things about the President in his correspondence.[18]

William Howard Taft was certainly active in the affairs of the other governmental branches. Most of his activity, however, concerned the judiciary and has already been noted; and most of the rest is of dubious relevance from the standpoint of Presidential advising. Several times during the Harding administration, and a few times in the Coolidge and Hoover administrations, Taft supported persons for appointment to non-judicial offices, but in only one minor instance is there evidence that his support had any weight. The former President

[16] *Ibid.*, pp. 519–526. See also Walter F. Murphy, *Elements of Judicial Strategy* (Chicago: University of Chicago Press, 1964), pp. 148–149.

[17] Josephus Daniels, *The Wilson Era: Years of Peace, 1910–1917* (Chapel Hill: University of North Carolina Press, 1944), p. 548.

[18] Mason, *Brandeis*, p. 528. Although I have relied on them for most of my facts, my evaluation of Brandeis's relations with Wilson after his appointment to the Supreme Court differs radically from those offered by Mason in this work and by Murphy in *Elements of Judicial Strategy*.

also intruded into other executive business on a few occasions. For example, he commented on a message Harding had prepared for delivery to Congress; and he recommended that Coolidge veto some acts making charges on the Treasury and take care to safeguard government oil interests. His influence in such matters does not appear to have been much greater than it was in political appointments. What Taft said (with some understatement) of his role in judicial appointments is an accurate description of the part he played as a Presidential political adviser: "I can only make my recommendations known by affirmative and unsolicited action." We can add that his political recommendations went generally unheeded.[19] The three Presidents whose terms of office coincided with Taft's were rarely interested in his political advice, and even then, it appears, only in matters of minor importance. Hence our skepticism as to whether the Chief Justice should be considered a Presidential adviser on political subjects.

Franklin Roosevelt seems to have maintained the most extensive political contacts with members of the Supreme Court. (He also filled the largest number of vacancies, nine, including his designation of Justice Harlan F. Stone as Chief Justice.) Also, he knew most of those he appointed. Roosevelt's personal secretary reported that "four Supreme Court justices were frequent off-the-record White House callers": Felix Frankfurter, William O. Douglas, Robert H. Jackson, and Frank Murphy; and that "their counsel was often of great help to the President."[20] Another source refers to "numerous stories of visits by Douglas and Frankfurter to the White House for the purpose of advising the President";[21] still another source indicates that Hugo L. Black, who was less well known to Roosevelt at the time of his appointment, also gave some advice to him.[22] And James F. Byrnes has given his own account of the

[19] My facts are from Murphy, *Elements of Judicial Strategy*, pp. 149, 152–154; and Mason, *Taft*, pp. 138–152, with the citation at p. 162.

[20] Grace Tully, *F.D.R.: My Boss* (New York: Charles Scribner's Sons, 1949), p. 290.

[21] Alpheus T. Mason, *Harlan Fiske Stone: Pillar of the Law* (New York: Viking Press, 1956), p. 707.

[22] Ickes, *Secret Diary*, Vol. III, p. 514.

service he provided the President in the months following the Japanese attack on Pearl Harbor.[23]

Frankfurter and Byrnes appear to have been the two most active justices in Roosevelt's advisory circle. The relations between the other New Deal justices and the President were apparently more social than political, and their political contacts, the quoted statements to the contrary, do not seem to have been extensive. Frankfurter kept up a heavy correspondence (mostly from his direction) with the President. He had an important part in developing lend-lease legislation and in preparing a number of Presidential speeches, including the one accepting the Democratic nomination for the Presidency in 1940. When the United States entered the Second World War, the justice authored a detailed and influential memorandum on how manpower and resources should be mobilized in the struggle. In addition, he recommended to Roosevelt a number of appointments, including that of Henry L. Stimson as Secretary of War, and that of Chief Justice Stone to study and make recommendations concerning the wartime scarcity of rubber. Stimson's appointment was made, but Stone, unaware of Frankfurter's role, summarily rejected his on the suspicion that the President was trying to exploit his judicial position. When Frankfurter described himself in November, 1940, as having been an "outside insider" in the Roosevelt administration for seven years, he made no distinction between the five years of that administration in which he was a free spirit at the Harvard Law School and the two years in which he was supposedly enclosed in the cloister of the Supreme Court.[24]

Byrnes's collaboration with the President was, by contrast, more modest. He had been the Democratic floor leader at the time of his appointment to the Court in 1941, and Roosevelt asked his help with some emergency legislation immediately after Pearl Harbor. For a month or so, Byrnes was consulted by the Attorney General on all emergency war legislation and

[23] James F. Byrnes, *All in One Lifetime* (New York: Harper, 1958).
[24] See *Roosevelt and Frankfurter: Their Correspondence, 1928–1945*, annot. by Max Freedman (Boston: Little, Brown, 1967), pp. 524–525, 531–533, 538, 546, 549, 582, 628–632, 662. The quoted words were taken from p. 549.

executive orders and given the additional assignment of helping to expedite the passage of such legislation by Congress. The President's need for Byrnes's assistance then decreased until October, 1942, when he wanted someone to be Director of Economic Stabilization, a new position which, incidentally, appears to have been developed from one of Frankfurter's recommendations. Byrnes, told that he would be a kind of "assistant President" handling home-front problems, resigned from the Court in order to take the job.[25]

The assistance that Franklin Roosevelt's justices willingly gave him was helpful and, we may assume, gratifying to him. He had privately remarked during his great controversy with the Supreme Court in 1937 that he needed to increase the Court's size to fifteen members to be assured of a Court which would cooperate with him. "He needed six new justices who would be friendly and approachable, men with whom he could confer, as man to man, on his great plans for social and economic reform and experiment."[26] This kind of Court Roosevelt finally got through the normal process of appointment, but he got it only after 1937 when it was no longer a critical matter to him. When he needed the Court's cooperation, he could not get it. As the story has been told, Roosevelt, as a "first step" to getting along with the Hughes Court, suggested a "sort of consultative relationship" with the Chief Justice at the start of the New Deal. "He had intimated that he would like to talk over with the Chief Justice all his important plans concerning the general welfare, to get the Court's slant on them before acting. But," the story continues, "instead of accepting the overture in a friendly spirit, the Chief Justice had been Olympianly chilly. He had given the President to understand that the strictest separation between the Court and the White House was not only advisable but necessary."[27]

Our knowledge of what Chief Justice Vinson and Justice Fortas did for Presidents Truman and Lyndon Johnson,

---

[25] Byrnes, *All in One Lifetime*, pp. 147–155.
[26] Joseph Alsop and Turner Catledge, *The 168 Days* (Garden City, N.Y.: Doubleday, Doran, 1938), p. 155.
[27] *Ibid.*, p. 16.

respectively, suffers from the recency of their judicial service. The records of their relationships with the White House have not yet been opened, and so what we know of their activities comes from incomplete reports. These reports contain enough, however, to allow the judgment that both justices were extensively involved as political advisers to the Presidency. The obituary on Vinson published in the *New York Times* stated that "the Chief Justice's friendship with President Truman was one of the most important facts of their lives. . . . Throughout the Truman administration Mr. Vinson was regarded as one of the real inner circle at the White House, one of the 'top ten.'"[28] Vinson is referred to in a Presidential biography as one of Truman's "intimates . . . who came and went unannounced."[29] We know further that Truman nearly sent Vinson to Moscow in 1948 as his special negotiator with Stalin, that Vinson regularly accompanied or visited Truman on his rest trips to Key West, Florida, and that the two men regularly discussed Presidential matters on the telephone.[30] It seems safe to say that none of Vinson's predecessors equaled his activity as a Presidential adviser.

Only Abe Fortas, it appears, can rival Fred M. Vinson in this respect. Fortas was a close political confidant to President Lyndon Johnson when Johnson was first a senator and then the Vice President, and their relationship did not change much after Johnson became President, nor, it seems, after Fortas went on the Supreme Court in 1965. According to a well-informed source, President Johnson never considered that Fortas's new position might make improper his continued calls upon Fortas for help, which he sought on such varied subjects as executive appointments, steel-price increases, strikes in the railroad industry, race riots, and foreign policy.[31] According to

---

[28] *New York Times*, September 9, 1953, p. 26, cited by Murphy, *Elements of Judicial Strategy*, pp. 232–233, n. 94.

[29] Alfred Steinberg, *The Man from Missouri: The Life and Times of Harry S. Truman* (New York: G. P. Putnam's Sons, 1962), p. 350.

[30] *New York Times*, September 9, 1953, p. 26.

[31] Fred P. Graham, "The Many-Sided Justice Fortas," *New York Times Magazine*, June 4, 1967, p. 94.

one supporter of the justice, he "was a close and confidential adviser on everything from race riots to Vietnam."[32] At the time of his nomination to the chief justiceship, in July 1968, one news report stated that "few important Presidential problems are settled without an opinion from Mr. Justice Fortas."[33] Another said, "He has been witness to nearly every great decision that Johnson has made," and that "no one outside knows accurately how many times Fortas has come through the back door of the White House, but any figure would probably be too low."[34] In his appearance before the Senate Judiciary Committee on his nomination, the justice minimized his services for President Johnson, and maintained that he had participated very seldom at White House conferences and then only on the two subjects of Vietnam and race riots.[35] But it is clear from other parts of his testimony, not to mention the cited reports of his activities, that the justice had other advisory contacts with the President and perhaps with other executive officials.[36] It is possible that Justice Fortas's avowal of his activities as a Presidential adviser is not inconsistent with other evidence, but was rather less than ingenuous. He did not, after all, deny having advised the President over the telephone or at places other than the White House or, for that matter, in private sessions, as contrasted to conferences, at the White House itself. What does not seem possible is to take his avowal at its intended value, although it may be that some of the accounts of his extra-

---

[32] Fred Rodell, "The Complexities of Mr. Justice Fortas," *ibid.*, July 28, 1968, p. 65.

[33] *Newsweek*, July 8, 1968, p. 18.

[34] *Time*, July 5, 1968, pp. 16, 17.

[35] Senate Committee on the Judiciary, *Nominations of Abe Fortas and Homer Thornberry, Hearings, July 11–12, 16–20, 22–23, 1968*, 90th Congress, 2nd Session, 1968 (Washington: Government Printing Office, 1968), pp. 103–107.

[36] See, for example, Fortas's testimony that "officials of the government" had sometimes asked his opinion about "various persons" being considered for appointment (*ibid.*, p. 103). When asked whether he made a telephone call to a businessman friend conveying the President's displeasure with a statement that person had made concerning Vietnam war costs, the justice made the broad reply that he would not "go into any conversations . . . that I have had with the President." (*Ibid.*, p. 167.)

curiam political activities on President Johnson's behalf are exaggerated.[37]

PROPRIETY OF THE RELATIONS

Presidents have sought, or accepted, the cooperation of the Supreme Court in extra-curiam matters for quite different reasons depending upon the nature of the cooperation. There have been three main, though not necessarily exclusive, reasons: to draw upon the Court's reputation, to utilize abilities possessed by its members, and to grant the Court a voice in questions concerning it. Consultations between Presidents or their subordinates and members of the Supreme Court on judicial appointments, especially on those to the Court itself and above all to the chief justiceship, seem to have been intended to satisfy the last reason, as have consultations on legislative questions affecting the Court and other parts of the judiciary; but Presidents have also, of course, made use of the special knowledge of the justices. Presidents (and Congress) have appeared mainly interested in exploiting the Court's reputation in appointing justices to quasi-judicial duties. Presidents have made use of the abilities rather than the prestige of some justices in the political advice they have obtained from them. The reasons for using justices on a few occasions in executive capacities have been mixed.

Should justices of the Supreme Court (any judges, for that matter) engage in non-judicial activities? There are two circumstances under which such activities are clearly inappropriate. One is where they would seriously interfere with a justice's judicial responsibilities. Probably most justices who have performed services for the other branches have not had their judicial work significantly impaired. Only three justices

---

[37] Nor could Justice Fortas properly maintain that he never discussed anything with President Johnson which might possibly come before the Supreme Court, for both the Vietnam War and race riots have produced judicial litigation. And it is hard to credit his claim that his only function at White House discussions was to summarize the arguments made by others (*ibid.*, pp. 104–106).

have been drawn away from the Court for extended periods by outside work. Chief Justices Jay and Ellsworth went abroad on their diplomatic missions at a time when the Court's business was light, but Justice Robert Jackson's year-long absence as prosecutor of the Nazi war leaders was quite different. Chief Justice Stone used the occasion of refusing a request made by President Truman (that Stone head a committee on traffic safety) to inform the President of "the extra work imposed on all the justices, and especially the Chief Justice, because of Justice Jackson's absence."[38] Of course, even fairly minor outside engagements may require a justice's colleagues to assume some of his load, and it was apparently to avoid this burden that Justice Brandeis declined President Wilson's request in 1916 that he serve on a commission to settle a border dispute with Mexico. After discussing the matter with Chief Justice Edward White, Brandeis told the President: "I find the state of the business of the Supreme Court at the present time to be such that it is my duty not to undertake this important additional task."[39]

The second circumstance under which it is inappropriate for justices to engage in outside activities is the more important: where the integrity of the judicial branch might be impaired. Judicial integrity depends greatly upon the reputation that judges have for impartiality and independence, as well as upon the possession of the qualities themselves. The Supreme Court's reputation can only suffer when its members accept controversial executive business, as Jay and Ellsworth did in their diplomatic ventures. Nor is the Court adequately shielded when the controversial business is given a quasi-judicial form, as in the inquiry which Warren headed into the assassination of President Kennedy. Such assignments are bound to generate partisan attack: Observe Presidential aspirant Jefferson's sneering reference to the Court's "would-be ambassadors" in 1794, at the time of Jay's mission to England, and another President-aspirant's charge in 1968 that President Lyndon Johnson's employment of Warren "could in no way be squared with the

[38] Cited by Mason, *Stone*, p. 719.　　　　[39] Mason, *Brandeis*, p. 512.

intention of the framers of the Constitution."[40] Thus such activities should be avoided. That the Court encounters controversy in its regular adjudication is no reason why it should add
to the burden through the involvement of its members in extra-
constitutional activities of the kind we have described. And
there is a strong reason why they should not do so. Chief Justice
Stone's statement is worth quoting. It was Stone's reply to
President Franklin Roosevelt's attempt to get him to investigate the wartime rubber shortage, a problem which had deep
political overtones. Stone wrote the President: "When [a
judge's] action is judicial he may always rely upon the support
of the defined record upon which his action is based and of the
opinion in which he and his associates united as stating the
ground of decision. But when he participates in the action of the
executive or legislative departments of government he is without
those supports. He exposes himself to attack and indeed invites
it, which because of his peculiar situation inevitably impairs
his value as a judge and the appropriate influence of his
office.[41]

When Supreme Court justices serve as political advisers to
occupants of the White House, the Court's reputation for
impartiality and independence need not suffer, at least immediately, because the fact may not become known until well
after the event, if at all, and then not to the public at large. But
impartial and independent justice is nonetheless endangered by
this kind of out-of-Court activity if that activity is carried on to
any appreciable extent; indeed, the greatest threat to judicial
integrity must occur when justices enter upon the part-time
career of White House politician. Although the confidential
advising of Presidents and other government officials was not a
topic of public controversy before Justice Fortas's nomination
to the chief justiceship in 1968, it had been a subject of informal concern within the legal profession since Franklin

---

[40] Letter to James Madison, December 28, 1794, in Thomas Jefferson, *Writings*, ed.
     by Andrew A. Lipscomb and Albert E. Bergh (Washington: The Thomas
     Jefferson Memorial Assn., 1903), Vol. IX, p. 295; Eugene J. McCarthy,
     First Things First (New York: Signet Books, 1968), p. 41.
[41] Mason, *Stone*, p. 711.

Roosevelt's administration. We may excuse Chief Justice Jay for answering George Washington's requests for ideas on legislative proposals and for advice as to whether Great Britain should be permitted to march troops across American territory in the event of war between that country and Spain.[42] These episodes took place at the very threshold of this country's history, when the Court's relationship to the executive branch was still unclear. More recent justices have not had Jay's excuse for rendering assistance to the executive branch, nor Washington's for seeking it in the first place.

We may summarize to this point. Much of the extra-curiam activity in which Supreme Court justices have engaged has not been sufficiently consequential to matter, and much that has been consequential has come to light only after it has taken place. Reports of the most questionable activity, the confidential advising of Presidents, have been the slowest in coming to the surface. On the other hand, the most publicly criticized activity, the quasi-judicial resolution of domestic issues, has been relatively innocent in terms of effects upon judicial impartiality and independence. In any event, all these things would have been better left undone, with justices confining their out-of-Court activity with the Presidency, and Congress, principally to matters pertaining directly to the judicial branch. The most appropriate kind of extra-curiam activity is that in which the justices have the greatest concern and can be of the greatest assistance to the other branches: advising on judicial appointments and legislation affecting the judiciary; but here, too, propriety sets limits to judicial involvement. There appears, moreover, to be no impairment of judicial integrity when justices serve on quasi-judicial commissions dealing with international problems that lie outside of domestic political controversy, if indeed such exist today.

There is one important exception to our argument. Political crises may occur that require all the moral authority the society can muster for their peaceful resolution. In such circumstances,

---

[42] George Washington, *Writings*, ed. by John C. Fitzpatrick (Washington: Government Printing Office, 1939), Vol. XXXI, pp. 354, 102.

the other governmental branches may properly invoke the assistance of the Supreme Court even though the Court runs the risk of sacrificing part of its reputation in order to support the political order as a whole. The one time the Court's assistance has clearly been invoked in such a cause was in the disputed Presidential election of 1876, and then it was Congress, not the President, that did the invoking. Whether the Republican Rutherford B. Hayes or the Democrat Samuel J. Tilden won that election depended on how disputed election returns from the states of Florida, Louisiana, South Carolina, and Oregon were counted, and commission was established by law to examine the returns and to recommend action to the legislative branch. The ten Congressional members of the commission, five drawn from each chamber, consisted of an equal number of Republicans and Democrats, and the statute, in effect, named two Republican and two Democratic members of the Court and provided that these four justices would select the commission chairman from among their judicial colleagues. Thus constituted, and with a Republican named as its fifth justice, the commission resolved the crisis, but not without leaving the Supreme Court marked by scars: on every important vote within the commission, the judicial members joined with their party colleagues in Congress in voting along strict partisan lines. A Democratic congressman justified such irregular employment of Supreme Court justices on this ground: "It is not well to drag the Supreme Court of this country into the slough of politics. But in times of high political excitement like the present, when the members of that body are the only ones whose decisions and determinations of the Presidential question the parties of the country will respect, they can for a moment, with propriety, lend their saving influence and services to avert evils incomprehensible from our land."[43] Nothing need be added to this argument.

[43] *Congressional Record, Appendix*, 44th Congress, 2nd Session, 1877, p. 26.

CONCLUSION

In 1800 Senator Charles Pinckney, a framer of the Constitution, sought to control the extra-curiam activities of Supreme Court justices by a constitutional amendment and then by legislation that would have prohibited any federal judge from holding another public office. "If the President can hold out to the judges the temptation of being envoys, or giving them other offices," said Pinckney, with the Jay and Ellsworth experiences in mind, "it might have a tendency to influence them in opinion."[44] We shall consider the possible influence of Presidential association upon the judicial actions of justices in a later chapter. It is enough at this point to observe that Pinckney's idea never got far, although Justices Robert Jackson and Roberts (after his retirement from the Court) gave it their support based upon personal experience.[45]

The prohibition of double office-holding would not affect the most serious breach in the line between the executive and judicial branches: the informal, confidential advisory relationship. This relationship does not appear to be amenable to legislative cure but depends primarily upon the exercise of restraint by both Presidents and justices. It is, of course, limited in duration by the fixed Presidential tenure in office, since Presidents almost always confine their informal relations to men they have appointed to the Court. But the judicial role itself appears significantly to affect relations between Presidents and their former political advisers. If nothing else happens, an adviser-turned-justice finds himself drawn from the main current of politics by the burden of judicial work and finds, too, that he must act with greater circumspection. Even the level

[44] *History of Congress*, Senate, March 5, 1800, pp. 98–99.
[45] John J. McCloy, "Owen J. Roberts' Extra Curiam Activities," *University of Pennsylvania Law Review*, **104** (December, 1955), 350; "The Association and the Supreme Court," *American Bar Association Journal*, **32** (December, 1946), 862–863. Jackson was willing to exempt foreign policy assignments and such essentially judicial tasks as membership in international arbitration tribunals from the prohibition, although he felt that even here justices should be rarely used.

of Fred M. Vinson's activity on behalf of President Truman dropped substantially after he left the Cabinet for the Court, although he was, as we estimated, one of the two most active justice–advisers.[46] But President and advising justice also adapt their relationship to the judicial proprieties. An example is the way Justice Frankfurter performed his services for Franklin Roosevelt after his appointment to the Court. As one of Roosevelt's former aides described the change: "We were always careful—as was the President—never to discuss anything with him that might later embarrass him in his judicial capacity."[47]

It would not be surprising if justices became somewhat inhibited in their advice-giving under these circumstances. In this connection, we might cite President Jackson's comment that suggestions he received from Chief Justice Taney for his last annual message to Congress, furnished just after Taney went on the Court, lacked some of his old message-writer's accustomed energy.[48] Nor would it be surprising if Presidents discovered that the usefulness of their political friends as advisers had diminished as a result of strains produced by the new relationship. Thus, even before a President's departure from office resolves it, the pressures of the judicial role tend to ameliorate the problem of political relations between a President and his judicial appointees. In nearly all instances where they have occurred, they have diminished in intensity, if indeed they have not atrophied, with the passage of time. But still the problem exists, and Presidents will still be tempted to go to the Supreme Court when they want to borrow the talents of its members or exploit their reputation. And justices will still find it difficult to resist a Presidential invitation offered out of obligation or friendship.

[46] "I valued his judgment and advice very highly, and until he was appointed to the Supreme Court he was in on nearly every conference on every subject." Harry S. Truman, *Memoirs: Year of Decisions* (Garden City, N.Y.: Doubleday, 1955), Vol. I, pp. 327–328.

[47] Samuel Rosenman, *Working with Roosevelt* (New York: Harper, 1952), p. 208.

[48] Swisher, *Taney*, p. 334.

4

Appointments

Since it is, next to the Presidency, the most eminent public office in the United States, the position of Supreme Court justice has been highly coveted. Thus, many hopes and ambitions, and not a few pressures, are attached to appointments to the Court. In making his appointments, a President must submit his candidates not only to the Senate for approval, but in an important sense to the bar and to a considerable part of the public as well. There are no constitutional or statutory qualifications for the office of justice, but there are professional and other norms that set the boundaries within which a President is expected to make his choices. Every President has been aware that the men he puts on the Court will, through their decisions, help shape public policy and perhaps basic relations between the Supreme Court and the Presidency itself. In view of these considerations, it is understandable that President John F. Kennedy found his first appointment to the Supreme Court "one of the hardest decisions he had to make."[1]

The opportunity for a President to appoint a Supreme Court justice does not occur often. Through mid-1970, ninety-eight persons have served in regular appointments to the Court, and the thirty-three Presidents who appointed them have averaged one appointment every twenty-two months.[2] Like many averages, this one may be misleading. First, the appointment rate has been somewhat higher since 1861 than it was to that date, and since 1937 it has averaged one every seventeen months. In the second place, the use of averages obscures the great variations among Presidents in placing persons on the Court. Three Presidents—Taylor, William Henry Harrison, and Andrew Johnson—made no appointments, Franklin D. Roosevelt made eight appointments, and Taft made five. Nine justices served under Washington's regular appointments, although only three replaced sitting members.[3]

There is, as one would expect, a connection between the number of justices a President can appoint and the length of time he serves in office. Of the eleven Presidents who appointed four or more justices, seven served more than six years; and of the eighteen Presidents who appointed two or fewer justices, only two served more than six years. Clearly, Presidents who serve only a term, or a little more than a term, in office have scant chance of remaking the Court. Thus, they have little

---

[1] Arthur M. Schlesinger, Jr., *A Thousand Days: John F. Kennedy in the White House* (Boston: Houghton Mifflin, 1965), p. 698.

[2] Grover Cleveland is counted once as President, and Charles Evans Hughes, who served twice on the Court under different Presidential appointments, is counted twice. The promotions to Chief Justice from within the Court, of William Cushing (who declined the honor), Edward D. White, and Harlan F. Stone, are not counted as separate appointments, and John Rutledge was eliminated because he relinquished his first appointment without actually having participated in the Court's deliberations and was rejected by the Senate in a second, interim appointment after having served a brief time. Edwin M. Stanton died before he could sit with the Court, and is not counted.

[3] Rutledge's successor in 1791 is not counted as having replaced a sitting member of the Court, and Rutledge is not counted as having replaced a sitting member when he was reappointed to the Court in 1795, for the reasons given in footnote 1.

chance of reshaping judicial doctrine or, in other words, of having the Court associated in the public mind with their administration of the country's affairs. Taft is a notable exception for, despite his single term of office, he placed five justices on the Court in addition to promoting one of the sitting justices to the chief justiceship. Two full terms in office do not necessarily assure a President of numerous vacancies on the Court: Madison and Monroe both served eight years but Madison appointed only two justices, and Monroe but one. Nor does making numerous appointments assure a reshaping of judicial doctrine. Few persons would consider Earl Warren or William J. Brennan to be in the constitutional or political mold of Dwight Eisenhower, the President who put them on the Court; and Charles E. Whittaker, another of Eisenhower's five appointments, stayed on the Court less than five years, too short a time to have much impact upon public law. One may speak of a Taft or Roosevelt or Truman Court, but hardly of an Eisenhower Court.

When the vacancy to be filled on the Supreme Court is the chief justiceship, the President has a special opportunity to leave his mark upon that institution. The Chief Justice is the Court's leader. He presides over its public sessions and its closed deliberations; he assigns the preparation of opinions when he does not dissent, and often reserves the most important opinions for himself; and he does much else that a non-elected ruler of an otherwise democratically organized group can be expected to do. Most Presidents have wanted to select their own Chief Justice rather than promote someone from within the Court, and twelve of the fourteen Chief Justices in the Court's history were appointed in this way. Most of our recent Presidents—Hoover, Franklin D. Roosevelt, Truman, Eisenhower, and Nixon—have appointed one, and Nixon's appointment would have been Lyndon Johnson's if the nomination of Abe Fortas by Johnson had not been successfully filibustered in the Senate.

SELECTING CANDIDATES

Advising the President

Presidents have had ample advice in their search for men to place on the Supreme Court. According to one informed estimate, the number of candidates advanced for the some eighty positions filled between 1789 and 1932 "lies in the thousands and not in the hundreds."[4] If we assume that about four thousand candidates were proposed, an average of fifty persons were advanced for each opening on the Court. No one knows how many communications were addressed to the President or other high executive officials on behalf of these candidates, but the number must be staggering. A study of a single judicial appointment, that of Pierce Butler, in 1922, uncovered the names of about fifty persons who supported the successful candidate just in the forty-four days from the opening on the Court to President Harding's action to fill it.[5] But most letters have at best a limited effect. Most appear to be written by the uninfluential on behalf of the undistinguished and gain nothing—if we overlook the appointment of the little-known Edward T. Sanford, which was achieved with the aid of three to four hundred letters written in great part by "the most nondescript group of unimportant little people ever organized."[6] But even communications on behalf of significant persons have the narrow purpose of supporting persons already under serious Presidential consideration.

The fact is that Presidents do not select candidates for the Supreme Court on the basis of popularity contests, whether conducted by writing letters or other means. Presidents have been concerned with public opinion in making their choices,

[4] Daniel S. McHargue, *Appointments to the Supreme Court of the United States: The Factors that Have Affected Appointments, 1789–1932* (Doctoral dissertation, Political Science Department, University of California at Los Angeles, 1949), p. 549.

[5] David J. Danelski, *A Supreme Court Justice Is Appointed* (New York: Random House, 1964), pp. 156–158. Danelski does not present figures on the support given other candidates for the position.

[6] McHargue, *Appointments to the Supreme Court*, p. 457.

but their principal advisers have not come from the public at large but that narrow segment that has a strong interest in the operation of the judiciary. Most important as Presidential advisers, probably, have been those governmental officials whose constitutional or statutory responsibilities have given them a legitimate ground for giving advice: the Attorney General, United States senators, and the justices themselves.

The President's main helper in selecting justices has been, understandably, the Attorney General. He is the chief legal adviser to the President and a member of his Cabinet; he and his department maintain close relations with the courts and with leading members of the legal profession; and he is often a person with considerable political experience. These factors combine to assure the President that his Attorney General is not only the appropriate official upon whom to lean, but a useful one as well. He can expect the Attorney General to be acquainted with many of the candidates who come up for consideration, to exercise good judgment about them, and to obtain reliable information about them when it is needed.

Not all Presidents have made use of their attorneys-general in making appointments. In fact, this officer has not always been regarded as having a special responsibility in the appointment process, and it was not until 1840 that he assumed responsibility from the Secretary of State for the administrative handling of judicial appointments. (It was Secretary of State Madison who refused to deliver Marbury's appointment to him in the famous proceeding of the Jefferson administration.) Until the Civil War the President consulted more generally with different members of his Cabinet in making Supreme Court appointments than he has appeared to do since then, and much more with the Secretary of State than with the Attorney General. Although a number of attorneys-general have been nominated to the Court, none was before the Buchanan administration. Since the Civil War, most attorneys-general have probably done leg-work for their Presidents and transmitted information culled from various persons. Yet in only a small number of instances have they substantially shaped their superior's decision.

United States senators rank after attorneys-general as a source of Presidential help in the selection of justices. The constitutional ground for this activity is the Senate's duty to give its advice and consent to nominations of the President. It is not clear whether the framers intended the Senate to act as an advisory council that sits with the President to consider nominations, as the word "advice" suggests, or whether they intended it simply to approve, or reject, his nominations, as Hamilton assumed in *The Federalist*.[7] The Senate has never acted as an advisory council in the appointment process, although President Washington made a single and frustrating effort to seek its collegial advice, as well as its consent, in the making of a treaty. In the appointment of Supreme Court justices, all senatorial advising of the President has been done informally through the activity of single senators or small groups of senators. Moreover, those senators whom Presidents consult, or seriously listen to, have nearly always been members of the chief executive's political party: senatorial advising is conducted not only informally, but along partisan lines.

We do not know just how extensive or important the participation of senators has been in the selection of justices. Perhaps senators have been involved in most selections, but usually their advice has been offered, not sought; and it has not figured significantly in the specific decisions of Presidents. Individual senators, according to an informed estimate, were influential in the selection of only a handful of justices down to 1932.[8] This

---

[7] Alexander Hamilton, John Jay, and James Madison, *The Federalist*, ed. by Max Beloff (Oxford: Basil Blackford, 1948), No. 76. The Constitution's language is: The President, "by and with the advice and consent of the Senate, shall appoint ambassadors, other public ministers and consuls, judges of the Supreme Court, and all other officers of the United States, whose appointments are not herein otherwise provided for."

[8] McHargue, *Appointments to the Supreme Court*, p. 544. The instances cited are Senator Sumner's activity with President Lincoln on behalf of Salmon P. Chase, Senator Hoar's activity with President Benjamin Harrison on behalf of Howell Jackson, Senator Lodge's activity with Theodore Roosevelt on behalf of William Moody, Senator Warren's activity with President Taft

estimate seems unduly low, and it does not include appointments since the Presidency of Franklin Roosevelt nor those in which groups of senators have been influential. President Jefferson, for example, leaned heavily on the senators from the geographic areas from which he chose two of his three justices. Senatorial advice has figured significantly in perhaps fifteen selections of candidates for the Supreme Court. (We should note here that, for reasons we shall shortly suggest, the influence of the Senate was considerably greater in the nineteenth century than it has been in the twentieth.)

The third more-or-less regular and influential source of advice to Presidents in selecting members of the Supreme Court has been the justices themselves. Once again, precise measurement is not possible, but fairly important judicial participation has been evident in at least a dozen Supreme Court appointments. Sometimes the advice is sought by the President, as when President Kennedy, through his Attorney General, asked for the Court's views on a successor to Justice Whittaker in 1962; but more often the advice is volunteered by the justices. Those who give the advice are usually of the President's political party, even if they have not been appointed by him, and they generally urge the merits of a favored candidate rather than seek only to present the qualifications of several persons or discuss the qualities needed upon the Court. But the justices have also indulged in negative advice. Joseph P. Bradley prepared a report on his possible successors in which he averred that no one from his native New Jersey was qualified to sit on the bench; and Hugo L. Black and another justice variously identified as William O. Douglas and Frank Murphy let President Truman know in 1946 that they would resign from the Court if their colleague Robert H. Jackson was designated as successor to Chief Justice Stone.[9]

Beyond these three sets of officials—attorneys-general,

on behalf of Willis Van Devanter, and Senator Borah's activity with President Hoover on behalf of Benjamin N. Cardozo.

[9] The threat by Black and Douglas/Murphy is reported by Eugene C. Gerhart, *America's Advocate: Robert H. Jackson* (Indianapolis: Bobbs-Merrill, 1958), pp. 258, 492.

senators, and justices—regular and direct sources of advice to Presidents faced with the task of filling vacancies on the Supreme Court are hard to discern. In the early years of the Court, some persons acquainted with the President proposed themselves as suitable candidates. James Wilson, John Rutledge, and Henry B. Livingston did so, successfully, and there were probably others, but since the 1820s only William Howard Taft appears to have gained entry to the Court in this manner. During most of the Court's history, ambitious men have had either to hope that their merits would draw Presidential attention to them or to engage others to take up their cause with the President. Thus the custom of appointment to the Supreme Court has tended to neutralize those who wish to be appointed by making the office seek them and, at the same time, has increased Presidential discretion in the choice of Supreme Court justices.

The major agent in Supreme Court selection has been the President himself. The Attorney General and his staff have rendered valuable assistance in the filling of Court vacancies, but this has been more by helping the President sift and investigate candidates than by guiding the Presidential choice. Senators have offered Presidents advice in filling most vacancies on the Court, but the frequency of their advice-giving has far outrun its influence. Supreme Court justices have generally hesitated to offer a President advice, and have not been very successful in the advice they have given. Clearly, in that minority of appointments where an Attorney General, a senator, or a justice has played an influential role, it is usually not possible to say that his influence was decisive.

Others have advised Presidents in the choice of justices: members of the House of Representatives, special Presidential advisers, governors, leaders of the bar, labor union officials, magazine editors, law school professors; but none has had a sufficiently important part in the selection process to deserve separate consideration. The bar comes closest. At different times, bar leaders or local bar groups have pressed their candidates for Presidential consideration, and in 1953 a committee of the American Bar Association made the unprecedented offer to help the Attorney General in his search for someone to succeed Chief Justice Vinson. The offer was turned down, and the Association's formal role in the appointment process has been limited to commenting upon the professional qualifications of persons already chosen, if and when asked by the President or Senate to do so.

Most advice directed to the President on Supreme Court appointments is given not to propose candidates but rather to support persons already under scrutiny. Such advice may be important in helping to structure the President's choice: The quality and quantity of support given different candidates attach political weights to the claims based on merit which were made on their behalf by their sponsors. But it is easy to exaggerate the secondary, or structuring, role of advice and pressures. In announcing his nomination of Thurgood Marshall to replace Justice Tom Clark, President Johnson commented that he had received "very little pressure of any kind" in connection with the selection.[10] If so, the President did not solicit advice, and the unsolicited advice directed to him came from persons outside the circle of influence and never reached his ears.

Presidential Control over Selection

The President has much greater control over selecting Supreme Court justices than he has over selecting inferior federal judges, even though the same constitutional provision governs both kinds of appointments. For inferior federal judges, the selection process has in large part passed into the hands of the Attorney General, senators and some other political leaders, and the judiciary itself. "In most cases, the choice of a federal judge is the Attorney General's to make"; the power of nomination "must be shared with individual senators and selected leaders of the President's party"; and "in virtually *all*

---

[10] *New York Times*, June 14, 1967, p. 18.

cases the views of some judges are solicited or offered."[11] Two reasons go far to explain Presidential control over appointments in one instance and not in the other: *knowledge* and *power*. Each deserves some extended remarks.

Knowledge. The President cannot possibly know about the great majority of serious candidates for lower federal judicial posts. These posts are many, are limited to small areas, and do not as a rule attract men who are nationally prominent. Since the President cannot spend much time in finding out about these candidates, he must delegate the task—especially to his Attorney General and the Justice Department, but sometimes also to senators, congressmen, and others. And since the President cannot spend much time evaluating the advice given him, he must for the most part accept the recommendations of these others. But there are only nine positions to be filled on the Supreme Court. They may be filled from anywhere in the country, and normally they are filled by persons who have been nationally prominent. Most Presidents were themselves active in public life before reaching their position and so do not usually have to seek out advice on possibilities for the Court. No one had to tell Harry S. Truman about Fred Vinson, an old friend who, at the time of his selection, was Truman's Secretary of Commerce. No one had to tell John F. Kennedy about Byron F. White, also an old friend, chairman of the National Citizens' Committee for Kennedy's election in 1960, and his Deputy Attorney General. And no one had to tell Lyndon B. Johnson about Thurgood F. Marshall, who had been politically active and nationally prominent since the 1930s and was Johnson's Solicitor General.

Presidents who have had limited or no prior public experience, such as Dwight D. Eisenhower, have needed much more assistance in finding suitable Supreme Court candidates. Eisenhower was somewhat acquainted with (and, at that time, at least, favorably disposed toward) Earl Warren when he selected him for the chief justiceship in 1953, and he was

[11] Joel B. Grossman, *Lawyers and Judges: The ABA and the Politics of Judicial Selection* (New York: John Wiley, 1965), pp. 25, 30, 39. (Italics in the original.)

slightly acquainted with John M. Harlan, whom he appointed in 1954; but he did not have personal knowledge of any of his other three Supreme Court choices. As we have seen, when a President has been deficient in his knowledge of possible candidates, he usually has sought additional information from the Attorney General. As a lawyer himself, and usually prominent in public life, the Attorney General sometimes finds that, in performing the labor of John Alden, he himself wins the Presidential favor instead of watching it bestowed upon some Myles Standish waiting off-stage.

Presidents usually select those they know personally, and of course favorably, for positions on the Supreme Court, and this circumstance explains why they have been able to retain control over their appointments there. In about three-fifths (approximately 82) of the 134 nominations they had made to the Court to mid-1970, Presidents had personally known their candidates.[12] In a number of instances in which they had no personal acquaintance, they had first-hand information about them. Thus, in only a small proportion of appointments were Presidents compelled to rely upon information and advice supplied by others, and even here they frequently made their own inquiries. Rarely has a Supreme Court appointee been so little known to an appointing President as Samuel F. Miller was to Lincoln, who was under the impression that he was putting a congressman and not a private citizen on the Court. Indeed, Presidents have sometimes been personal or political friends of the men they have chosen, and since the 1930s most nominations have been of this sort. Nearly all of the justices chosen by Presidents Franklin Roosevelt, Truman, Kennedy, and Johnson had at least a fairly confidential relationship with them prior to their appointment. In the whole history of the republic, it is doubtful whether any group of officials whose

[12] Included are the four sitting justices nominated for the chief justiceship (William Cushing, Edward D. White, Stone, and Fortas) and the three persons nominated on two occasions by the same President (John Rutledge, Taney, and King). Only one of Paterson's nominations is counted, however, for his initial nomination was withdrawn for a technical reason and the nomination resubmitted a few days later.

appointment has required the concurrent action of the President and Senate, including Cabinet officers, has been as well known to the chief executive who selected it as have the justices of the Supreme Court.

Power. Presidents have for the most part been able to control their Supreme Court appointments, in contrast to district court appointments, largely because of their power in relation to the Senate. Presidential power in appointments varies with the size of the judicial area and the number of positions to be filled. There are about 330 federal district judges, and all of them serve within particular states. Therefore, the senators of a President's party from the states in which appointments are to be made can claim the right to propose or pass upon candidates for these positions. A President will usually acknowledge their claim because he fears that they will call upon the support of their fellow senators if he does not, and most senators will usually respond to such a call because they, too, want to control judicial appointments within their states. This rallying behind a beleagured colleague is called senatorial courtesy. The situation is far different for the Supreme Court. The Court serves the entire country, its members may be selected from anywhere in it, and there are only nine of them; hence, individual senators lack firm ground upon which to claim the right to have their wishes heeded in appointments to that body.[13]

But the President does not fully dominate the Senate in Supreme Court appointments. A general indication of the strength of the Senate in these matters is in the record of Senate rejections of nominations. Through the middle of 1970 the Senate had rejected, directly or by refusing to act, 25 of the 134 nominations made to the Court, or 19 per cent of the total.[14] The rate of rejections has varied. Few appointments were

---

[13] The courts of appeals come between the district courts and the Supreme Court in number of personnel and size of area, and also in the degree of Presidential–Senate influence in the selection of their members.

[14] The rejected nominees, with the year of nomination, are: John Rutledge (1795), Wolcott (1811), Crittenden (1828), Taney (1835), Spencer (1844), Walworth (1844), King (1844, nominated twice), Read (1845), Woodward (1845),

defeated during the era of the Federalist Court, between 1789 and 1829, or during those of the generally Conservative Court of 1897–1937 or the Liberal Court that followed upon it. Six nominations, or 8 per cent of those made, were defeated during the 112 years covered by these periods. Indeed, until Abe Fortas failed to obtain Senate approval in 1968, no Presidential nomination had failed to pass the Senate in thirty-eight years. By contrast, the Jacksonian Court of 1829–1861 and what, for want of a better name, we may call the Republican Court of 1861–1897 had a total of eighteen nominations rejected, nearly a third of all those made during sixty-eight years.[15] When the Senate has been strong enough, and willing, to defeat the nominations of Presidents to the Supreme Court, it has also, we may assume, been in a position to compel chief executives to accommodate their choices of candidates to its dominant temper. As we shall demonstrate shortly, this assumption is supported by evidence.

Why have Presidents been able to retain control of Supreme Court appointments at some times and not at others? When the conditions under which the Senate has acted on nominations are examined, certain factors emerge as having an important bearing on the outcome. They are partisanship, the timing of appointments, and the threat of senatorial courtesy.

When the President and a majority of the Senate have been of the same political party, Presidents have been much more likely to get their nominations approved than when they have been of different political parties. Fortunately for them,

Bradford (1852), Badger (1853), Micou (1853), Black (1861), Stanbery (1866), Hoar (1870), Williams (1873), Caleb Cushing (1874), Matthews (1881), Hornblower (1893), Wheeler Peckham (1894), Parker (1930), Fortas (1968), Haynsworth (1969), and Carswell (1970).

President Lyndon B. Johnson nominated Thornberry to fill Fortas's seat at the same time that he nominated Fortas for the chief justiceship in 1968. Because the Senate did not act on the Fortas nomination, there was, strictly speaking, no vacancy for Thornberry to fill.

[15] A precise breakdown of Senate rejections is as follows: 1789–1829: three (11 per cent) of twenty-eight nominations; 1829–1861: eleven (42 per cent) of twenty-six nominations; 1861–1897: seven (23 per cent) of thirty-one nominations; 1897–1937: one (5 per cent) of twenty-two nominations; and 1937–1970: three (11 per cent) of twenty-seven nominations.

Presidents have had the Senate politically aligned with them in 108 nominations and politically opposed in only 26. When the two have been aligned, Presidents have almost always (that is, in 98 instances) had their nominations accepted; and when they have been opposed the chief executives have infrequently (that is, in 11 instances) had their nominations accepted.[16] Thus, partisanship is related to Presidential control of Supreme Court appointments. The timing of appointments is also connected with the Senate's reaction to them. When they have been made in the first three years of a President's term of office, nominations have been overwhelmingly accepted (in eighty-seven instances out of a hundred). When, on the other hand, they have been made in the last year of a term or in the interregnum between the non-re-election of a President and his successor's assumption of office, they have met with much less success (twenty-two instances out of thirty-four).[17]

The Senate should naturally be less generous with Presidential appointments when it is controlled by the opposition party than when it is politically aligned with the President, or when appointments are made toward the end of a President's term. At the end of his term, he is likely to have diminished influence over both parties in the legislative branch. But it is neither partisanship as such nor the timing of appointments as such that accounts for most Presidential troubles in Court nominations, but rather the two factors in combination. When

[16] I have considered Presidents John Tyler and Andrew Johnson to be Democrats dealing with opposition Whig and Republican Senates, respectively, and the Senate to be opposition-controlled at the time of Taney's first nomination. Tyler was an anti-Jackson Democrat elected Vice President on the Whig ticket with William Henry Harrison in 1840, and he sought the nomination of the Democratic party for President in 1844. Johnson was a pro-Union Democrat elected with Lincoln on the Unionist ticket in 1864, and he was later elected to the Senate as a Democrat. The Senate was under the control of a coalition of Whigs and anti-Jackson Democrats when it rejected Taney's first nomination on March 3, 1835, and, in fact, John Tyler was that very day chosen as its President Pro Tempore.

[17] Prior to the 1936 Presidential election, the interregnum period extended from early November to March 4, and since then from early November to January 20. Where a President has nominated a candidate for the Court between his own re-election and re-assumption of office, the nomination has been counted as though it had occurred during the first three years of a term.

Presidents have given opposition Senates end-of-term nominations, these have usually been defeated. To be sure, partisanship
and the timing of appointments do have some independent
bearing upon Senate treatment of nominations. Thus opposition Senates are more inclined to reject nominations made
during the first three years of a President's term than are
Senates that are politically aligned with the President. Similarly, the Senate is more likely to reject end-of-term nominations
than nominations made during the first three years of a Presidential term, regardless of who controls it.

Observe, however, the combined effect of the two factors.
When opposition Senates have received nominations during the
first three years of a Presidential term (eleven instances), they
have usually approved them (seven instances). When they
have received them in Presidential election years (six instances)
or interregnums (nine instances), on the other hand, they have
usually rejected them (four and seven instances, respectively).[18]
In the last year of a President's term, the opposition party in the
Senate appears to be moved by a strong desire to have Court
vacancies held for the next President in the hope that he will be
of its political persuasion, and the desire increases in intensity
when its candidate has won the Presidential election but has not
yet assumed office.

It follows that Presidents must exercise considerable
caution, if not outright accommodation, if they wish to get their
Supreme Court appointments accepted by opposition Senates in
Presidential election years or interregnums. They must, in fact,
be careful when the opposition is less than a majority but can
influence dissident majority senators. Indeed, the Republican
and Southern Democratic opponents of Lyndon Johnson's

---

[18] Nominations made during the first three years of a Presidential term have been
approved in nine of thirteen instances by opposition Senates and in seventy-
eight of eighty-seven instances by politically aligned Senates. Opposition
Senates have approved end-of-term nominations in four of fifteen instances,
and politically aligned Senates have done so in eighteen of nineteen instances.

Opposition Senates rejected Spencer, Walworth, King, and Bradford
during election years; Crittenden, King, Read, Badger, Micou, Black, and
Matthews during interregnums; and Taney, Stanbery, Haynsworth, and
Carswell at other times.

nominations of his close friends Abe Fortas and Homer
Thornberry in 1968 were sufficiently aroused that, although in a
minority, they prevented Senate action upon the appointments
by conducting a filibuster against them.

Thus, if they wish to avoid trouble with a politically
uncertain Senate in end-of-term appointments to the Court,
Presidents must often allow their discretion to be influenced by
legislative considerations. The two nominations that opposition
Senates have approved in election years suggest that Presidents
have followed this rule. In 1888 the Democratic Cleveland
presented Melville W. Fuller's name to a Senate which contained thirty-seven Democrats and thirty-nine Republicans.
Fuller was an Illinois Democrat who originally lived in Maine,
and Cleveland made a special effort to enlist the support of the
senators, all Republicans, from these two states. And in 1956
Dwight D. Eisenhower chose William J. Brennan, his only
Democrat among five appointments, for the approval of a
Democratic Senate. The two appointments approved by
opposition Senates during Presidential interregnums are also
interesting because in neither instance could partisan profit be
gained from rejection. A Whig Senate accepted the Democratic
Tyler's nomination of Samuel C. Nelson, also a Democrat, in
February, 1845, the alternative to allowing the incoming
Democratic Polk to make the appointment. Similarly, if the
Democratic majority in the Senate had rejected the Republican
Hayes's nomination of William B. Woods, in December, 1880,
it would simply have turned the appointment over to the
Republican Garfield. At that, Hayes exercised considerable
caution in making his interregnum choice: Woods, a Repub-
lican, was a resident of Georgia but was born in the North and,
as the first Southerner to be nominated to the Court since the
Civil War, drew nearly unanimous Southern Democratic
support in the Senate.

The third factor limiting the President's ability to control
his Supreme Court nominations is the threat of senatorial
courtesy. We have noted that senatorial courtesy depends upon
the Senate's willingness to support the claimed right of indi-

vidual senators to propose or pass upon candidates for judicial positions and that senatorial courtesy lacks a firm basis in the filling of Supreme Court vacancies. But it has not been absent there. The conditions for senatorial courtesy exist whenever a particular state is presumed to be favored in the filling of a vacancy on the Court, for then the senator or senators of the President's party from the state, if there are any, can raise their claim. The claim cannot be raised as strongly as in district court appointments, for other senators will not be as eager to support a claim that most of them will never be able to raise on their own behalf; further, nothing requires a President to fill Supreme Court vacancies from any particular state. It appears, however, that Presidents have in fact been more disposed to consult with senators of their party when Court vacancies have been widely assumed to more-or-less belong to the states represented by these senators.

When a President nominates a justice from a state that has received at least the two immediately preceding nominations for the seat in question, we may assume there was, at a minimum, a fairly strong presumption that the nomination might go to that state. When such a presumption exists, the senators of the state can claim the right to be consulted on the nomination if they are of the President's party. Three states have given their senators the opportunity to claim this right: New York, on nine occasions; Pennsylvania, on seven occasions; and Ohio, on one occasion.[19] All told, the threat of senatorial courtesy was present in seventeen nominations to the Court, according to our assumption. In nine the candidate was approved by the Senate. In some of the Senate's actions, the threat of senatorial courtesy

[19] New York's seat was established by the nominations of Livingston and Thompson, and *Spencer*, *Walworth*, Nelson, Hunt, Conkling, Blatchford, *Hornblower*, and *Wheeler H. Peckham* were then nominated to fill it; and, after the chain had been broken, Stone and Robert H. Jackson re-established the seat and Harlan was nominated to it. Pennsylvania's seat was established by the nominations of Baldwin and *King*, and *King*, *Read*, *Woodward*, Grier Stanton, and Strong were nominated to fill it. McLean and Swayne established Ohio's seat and Matthews (second nomination) was designated to fill it. The persons whose names are italicized failed to get approved by the Senate. Only those nominations to fill established seats are included in which one or both of a state's senators were of the President's party.

might not in fact have been a significant reason at all. In five of the eight rejections, for example, the nominations were made to opposition-controlled Senates in the last year of a Presidential term or in the interregnum following a Presidential election, and four of these were supported by the senators of the President's party from the states concerned. Senatorial courtesy was clearly the main factor in the rejections of William B. Hornblower and Wheeler H. Peckham in 1894. President Cleveland had appointed them to fill the New York seat vacated by Samuel Blatchford, but had refused to clear his choices with his fellow Democrat from that state, Senator David B. Hill. Senatorial courtesy also figured in the election-year rejection of Reuben H. Walworth for the New York seat in 1844 and of George W. Woodward for the Pennsylvania seat in 1846.[20]

Thus, the exercise of senatorial courtesy has negated the President's power of appointment to the Supreme Court on at least a few occasions. In addition, the threat of its exercise appears to have limited that power on other occasions when the conditions for it have existed. It may compel a President to appoint somebody practically demanded by the Senate, as in President Grant's "reluctant" nomination of Edwin M. Stanton in 1869 to fill the Pennsylvania seat vacated by Robert C. Grier.[21] Or it may lead a stubborn President to turn away from a state in order to avoid the veto power of its senators. When the Senate rejected President Cleveland's nominations of William B. Hornblower and Wheeler H. Peckham in 1894, Cleveland, rather than submit to Senator Hill of New York, gave that state's seat to Edward D. White of Louisiana. In addition to being safely out of Hill's jurisdiction, White was the Democratic majority leader in the Senate.

As these examples indicate, the threat of senatorial courtesy induces Presidents to be cautious, if not compliant, in selecting Supreme Court justices. It also often softens into Presidential courtesy, in which Presidents assume as a matter of course that

[20] See Henry J. Abraham, *The Judicial Process* (New York: Oxford University Press, 1962), p. 79.
[21] See Charles Warren, *The Supreme Court in United States History* (Boston: Little, Brown, 1926), Vol. II, p. 504.

they should consider the wishes or interests of their party colleagues in the Senate in appointments that belong to those senators' states. President Grant was not intimidated by his friend Senator Roscoe Conkling of New York into consulting Conkling on New York's vacancy on the Court in 1872 (or into accepting Conkling's recommendation of Ward Hunt); nor was President Arthur intimidated into giving the New York seat to Conkling himself a decade later (Conkling declined the completed appointment).

In summary, Presidents have made 26 of their 134 Supreme Court nominations under conditions that have limited their control over them. Fifteen nominations were made toward the end of Presidential terms when the Senate was in the opposition's hands, and seventeen were made when senators were in a position to claim senatorial courtesy, on eleven of which occasions the end-of-term condition was not also present. On fourteen of the twenty-six occasions the Senate did not consent to the nominations. Inasmuch as the Senate has rejected a total of twenty-five nominations, the two conditions we have discussed have accounted for most rejections although they have existed in only a small portion of nominations made. Furthermore, another five nominations were rejected when made toward the end of a Presidential term or when the Senate was opposition-controlled, but when these factors were not combined with each other or with the threat of senatorial courtesy.[22] Other factors than those discussed have, we should add, limited Presidential discretion on still other occasions: there were, after all, six nominations rejected under conditions not covered in our categories.[23] It does seem possible to conclude, nonetheless, that Presidents have, in relation to the Senate, been able to keep control of most of their Supreme Court appointments because the main conditions that inhibit their control have been infrequently present in the history of the Court.

Between 1894 and 1968 the Senate refused only one Supreme Court nomination, that of John J. Parker in 1930.

[22] The nominations were of Taney (1835), Stanbery, Fortas (1968), and Thornberry.
[23] John Rutledge (1795), Wolcott, Hoar, Williams, Caleb Cushing, and Parker.

Two reasons have been frequently given to explain why Presidents have nearly always had their way during this period of time. One is that the Senate either had abdicated, or been forced from, its role of seriously examining nominations to the Court. The other is that the Senate used to judge nominees on the basis of party regularity, but shifted to examining their views on public issues—with the intimation that the first is the more severe standard.[24] The first explanation actually tells us very little and the second is only partly correct, for partisan judgments in the nineteenth century usually embodied judgments about public views. Our inquiry into the Senate's treatment of Supreme Court nominations leads us to suggest that Presidential success between 1894 and 1968 can be ascribed largely to the general absence of those conditions under which the Senate's power in appointments is exerted. During this long time, only Truman and Eisenhower had to face opposition Senates in making appointments, and only Eisenhower did so in an election year. Herbert Hoover had only a fragile Republican majority in the Senate in 1932 when he appointed Benjamin N. Cardozo to the Court, and Cardozo, like Brennan (Eisenhower's election-year choice), was a Democrat.[25] There were no interregnum appointments during these years, and only when John M. Harlan of New York replaced Robert H. Jackson in 1955 could a state expect an appointment to be made from among its citizens.[26] The rejections of Fortas (1968), Haynsworth (1969), and Carswell (1970) shattered this record of success, but in such a way as to be consonant with our thesis: the first rejection occurred in a Presidential election year and the other two rejections were administered by an opposition Senate.

[24] Both explanations are presented, but not necessarily endorsed, by Glendon Schubert in *Constitutional Politics* (New York: Holt, Rinehart and Winston, 1960), pp. 45–46.

[25] The Senate consisted of forty-eight Republicans, forty-seven Democrats, and one Farmer Laborite (Henrik Shipstead), and among Cardozo's strongest supporters was a small group of progressive Republicans.

[26] Even this was not quite within our definition of a situation in which a claim to consultation can be raised. Jackson had not been appointed to replace a New Yorker on the Court but rather to join one, having filled Harlan F. Stone's seat in 1941 when Stone was moved up to the chief justiceship.

Thus, personal knowledge of candidates and power in relation to the Senate have enabled Presidents for the most part to control their appointments to the Supreme Court. When they have not known candidates for Court positions personally, they have usually relied upon the judgments of close advisers who themselves have usually known them. When they have had to face opposition Senates in Presidential election years or in the interregnums, they have usually accommodated their choices to Senate demands or faced the threat of having them rejected. So, too, when appointments have been viewed as belonging to particular states and when the senators of those states have been of the same party as the nominating Presidents. But these adverse conditions have not been dominant in the history of the Supreme Court, and thus Presidents have usually been masters of the appointment process there.

THE PERSONS CHOSEN

We turn now to the ninety-eight persons who have served in regular appointments to the Supreme Court through the middle of 1970. Our interest is in the attributes which Presidents have considered important in appointing justices. Three kinds of attributes are of particular interest: those having to do with the merits of persons chosen for the Court; those that link the justices to significant portions of the American public; and those relating to the candidates' views on constitutional and other public matters. We shall, in the following discussion, refer to these sets of attributes as *professional qualifications, representational qualifications,* and *doctrinal qualifications* for service on the Supreme Court.

Professional Qualifications

Although neither the Constitution nor law requires it, every person appointed to the Supreme Court has been a lawyer. Every justice, moreover, practiced law at some stage of his career and, in fact, made either the practice or the teaching of law a major part of his career. But the category of lawyer covers a multitude of situations and does not tell us how qualified those persons were who reached the Supreme Court. Persons who have served on the Supreme Court have traditionally been of high moral character, eminent in their public or private careers, and, generally, prepared by their careers for the responsibilities of a Supreme Court justice.

The men whom Presidents have appointed to the Supreme Court have as a group been of unblemished probity. It is true that Samuel Chase was impeached for his intemperate treatment of counsel in the Sedition Act trials and his remarks to a grand jury concerning the drift of political affairs, but the impeachment charges, motivated by partisan animosity, were not upheld by the Senate. It is true, too, that the moral character of a few justices was questioned at the time of their appointment. Louis D. Brandeis was opposed for confirmation by leading members of the bar on the ground that he had engaged in improper practices as a private attorney; and Hugo L. Black, at the time his nomination was before it, misled the Senate into believing that stories of his former Ku Klux Klan membership were false. Both men, it should be added, enjoyed distinguished careers on the Supreme Court.

The accusation of impropriety was not seriously directed at sitting justices until William O. Douglas and, especially, Abe Fortas came under criticism in 1969 for certain of their out-of-Court activities. It was revealed in early May of that year that Fortas had in January, 1966, shortly after joining the Court, arranged to receive from a small private foundation an annual stipend of $20,000 for life, with his wife continuing to draw the stipend if she outlived him. The foundation was controlled by a person who was, at the time of the arrangement, in difficulty with the federal government because of stock manipulations and who was subsequently tried and convicted for them. Moves were under way in Congress to impeach Fortas when, on May 14, he resigned his judicial position. Douglas was also associated with a private foundation and had, in fact, been its president for several years, at a salary reported to be nearly $13,000 in 1967, when the Fortas controversy broke out. Douglas's foundation had been investigated for possible federal taxation irregularities (it had engaged Fortas's wife, a lawyer, to help it out) and, amid various charges, including one that Douglas might have given it legal assistance in its tax problems, the justice resigned from it, just one week after Fortas resigned from the Court. These activities and certain non-judicial writings and associations of the justice led to a formal move in 1970 to impeach Douglas.

The great majority of Supreme Court justices had already gained eminence by the time they were selected for the Court—in judicial or other public office, as attorneys, or as legal scholars. Consider, for example, the public careers of most of the forty-one persons appointed in this century. Nine had been members of the federal Cabinet, six had been judges of federal courts of appeals, six state supreme court judges, five United States senators, and two each state governors and United States solicitors-general. One person, William Howard Taft, was a former President; one, Charles Evans Hughes, a former justice of the Supreme Court itself; and one had headed a federal regulatory agency. Most of the remaining eight justices, among whom were four outstanding practicing attorneys and one highly regarded law school professor, had been eminent in private careers.[27] Similarly, most of those appointed to the Court prior to the twentieth century had achieved high public office or fame in the practice of law.[28] If the pre-eminent were not always included with the eminent in Supreme Court appointments, yet one can not but be impressed with the roster of persons who have been put on the Court. To cite names only from this century, there have been, in addition to the afore-mentioned Taft and Hughes, Oliver Wendell Holmes, Louis D. Brandeis, Benjamin N. Cardozo, Felix Frankfurter, Earl

[27] Where a justice achieved success in more than a single career, the more eminent one has been chosen. For instance, William Howard Taft had been Solicitor General of the United States, a federal appellate judge, Governor of the Philippines, and a Cabinet member before he became President.

[28] In *Supreme Court in U.S. History, passim,* Warren makes his own and cites from contemporary evaluations of the eminence of those who received appointments to the Supreme Court.

Warren, and Thurgood Marshall. Not all of these persons were great justices, but all of them brought distinguished reputations to the Court.

Finally, in considering the professional qualifications of persons appointed to the Supreme Court, we must ask how well prepared the justices were by their previous careers for their judicial service. Other things being equal, experience on other federal and on state courts should help a person in the performance of his duties. Such experience would be more likely to help nurture impartiality, reflection, and detachment than would be experience confined to advocacy at the bar or to political and other public activity. Further, when previous judicial service was on an appellate court, the justice would have received at least some experience in handling the kinds of issues that come before the Supreme Court as well as considerable experience in the process of hearing, deciding, and writing cases.[29]

Presidents have frequently disregarded prior judicial experience as an important qualification in a Supreme Court justice or have regarded it as secondary to other considerations. Only fifty-eight of the ninety-eight justices have had such experience, and only forty-one had over five years service on another bench. Thus, about 60 per cent of the justices had either no or limited judicial experience at the time of their appointments, and some of those who had served over five years in other judicial capacities had also held political or other public office. In fact, just half of the members of the Supreme Court had led primarily political careers, as distinguished from careers as judges, practicing lawyers, or law school teachers, before their appointments.[30] Finally, only thirty-nine

---

[29] Justice Felix Frankfurter argued that service on inferior federal courts was of little value for the work of a Supreme Court justice, and that service on state courts was irrelevant. See, for example, "The Supreme Court in the Mirror of Justices," *University of Pennsylvania Law Review*, 105 (April, 1957), 781–796. His argument is not convincing. What Frankfurter did demonstrate is that inferior federal judges and state judges still have a lot to learn after they become Supreme Court justices, and that the largeness of view and cultivated mind so important to work on the Court can be found outside of the judicial system as well as within it.

[30] John R. Schmidhauser, "The Justices of the Supreme Court: A Collective Portrait," *Midwest Journal of Political Science*, 3 (February, 1959), Table II,

justices held judicial posts at the time they were appointed to the supreme bench.

The importance of prior judicial service appears to vary by historical period and by the party of the President. Such service was most evident in appointments during the Federalist period of the Court, from 1789 to 1829, and least evident in the most recent period, since 1937. Republican Presidents have been far more disposed to select state and lower federal court judges for the Supreme Court than have Democratic Presidents, having done so in twenty-three of forty-two appointments since the Civil War; the Democratic record is a scant three appointments out of twenty-three. These figures agree with other evidence (some of which will be discussed elsewhere in this study) that Republican Presidents have usually been more legal, or legalistic, and have certainly been less political than have Democratic Presidents in their dealings with the Supreme Court. Men do not necessarily make better justices because they have served in other judicial capacities, however, for there is more to the work of the Supreme Court than adjudicating disputes and writing opinions. Furthermore, in choosing persons without prior judicial service for the Court, Presidents have not necessarily derogated the value of a judicial temperament, for one need not be a judge to be a judicious man. It would be hard to argue that the Court's most distinguished men were more those justices with previous judicial experience than those without it.[31] Among the distinguished justices who did not reach the Court through the ranks of the judicial system were John Marshall, Joseph Story, Roger B. Taney, Joseph Bradley, Louis D. Brandeis, and, if we exclude his brief service as a police judge twenty-six years

p. 33, reports that forty-nine of the ninety-one justices appointed through 1957 had been "primarily politicians." None of the seven men appointed since then fall into the politician category.

[31] Frankfurter, "Supreme Court in the Mirror of Justices," p. 784, considering those justices appointed to the Supreme Court through 1932, concluded that "of the sixteen justices whom I deem pre-eminent, only six came to the Court with previous judicial experience, however limited." The finding is more impressive inasmuch as a clear majority of all justices have had some prior experience.

before his appointment to the Court, Hugo L. Black.

On the basis of the indirect evidence presented here, we may conclude that Presidents have been concerned with appointing persons of high professional merit to the Supreme Court. This point needs making because it is sometimes said that Presidents have been much more concerned with the political and other qualifications of Supreme Court candidates than with their professional qualifications. The views of Theodore Roosevelt are worth citing in this connection. Roosevelt was intensely interested in what he called the social philosophy of judicial candidates and yet he believed that "a judge's views on progressive social philosophy are entirely second in importance to his possession of a high and fine character."[32] And in his extensive study of Supreme Court appointments, Daniel McHargue found that the qualifications most often stressed in letters recommending candidates for the Court were their ability, character, and judgment.[33]

Representational Qualifications

By "representational qualifications" we refer to those attributes which Presidents seek in their justices that link the appointees to significant portions of the American public. Presidents consider the possession of these attributes important because people wish, in a certain sense, to see their own kind on the Supreme Court. We are not speaking of the representation of constitutional or other public viewpoints but of what we might call symbolic representation. Those attributes which have been especially relevant as representational qualifications are political party affiliation, section of the country, religion, and, now perhaps, ethnicity.

It is probable that most Americans have always felt that Supreme Court justices should be chosen without reference to political party affiliation. The press has generally applauded

---

[32] "Annual Message to Congress," *Congressional Record*, 60th Congress, 2nd Session, Vol. 43, Pt. 1, December 8, 1908, p. 21.

[33] McHargue, *Appointments to the Supreme Court*, p. 562.

Presidents when they have appointed justices from the other major party. Yet eighty-nine of our ninety-eight justices have been of the same party as the men who appointed them, although the two promotions from within the Court to the Chief Justiceship were across party lines. Presidents consider political party an important qualification for the highest judicial office because of pressures from that limited public of leading lawyers and politicians which is intensely interested in Court appointments, and not because of pressure from the public at large. The lawyers and politicians want the appointments for themselves or their fellow partisans. The practice of partisan appointments to the Supreme Court is buttressed by the Senate's treatment of lower court appointments as patronage positions. It is usually likewise supported by the President's desire to put men of generally acceptable views on the Court, an important indication of which is party persuasion. Since the present party divisions were formed over a century ago, neither Republican nor Democratic Presidents have been overly generous in making cross-party appointments to the Court, but the Democrats less so. Republican Presidents have appointed nearly two-thirds of the sixty-five justices who have sat during this period, but they have also made seven of the eight cross-party appointments. The Democrats clearly had looked upon representation almost entirely as a partisan issue.

Presidents have wanted the Supreme Court to have sectional balance, and thus have generally been concerned with the place of residence of the men they have appointed. This concern has existed throughout the Court's history. Thus, we find Washington commenting in his appointment of James Iredell in 1790 that North Carolina had received no federal posts; Lincoln expressing a reluctance to fill the two "Southern vacancies," created at the start of the Civil War, with Northerners; and, in more recent years, Franklin Roosevelt telling Wiley Rutledge that "we had a number of candidates for the Court who were highly qualified, but they didn't have geography—you have that."[34] Speaking more broadly, once

[34] Wesley McCune, *The Nine Young Men* (New York: Harper, 1947), p. 200.

they have obtained representation on the Court the major sections of the country have almost never been without it. New England and the Northeast have had unbroken representation since 1789. The South suffered only in the aftermath of the Civil War, from the death of James M. Wayne of Georgia in 1867 to the designation of John M. Harlan of Kentucky ten years later. The Midwest has been continuously represented since Thomas Todd's appointment in 1807 from the then western state of Kentucky, and the West has, since 1861, been deprived of representation for only the fifteen years between Willis Van Devanter's resignation in 1937 and Earl Warren's appointment in 1953.[35] Added together, the five sections of the United States have, from the time they first obtained representation, been deprived of it during only 3 per cent of their subsequent history.

Presidents have not, by and large, attached the same weight to sectional representation since the end of the nineteenth century that they had attached to it before then. The change in attitude is reflected in a declining disposition since 1897 to fill a vacancy on the Supreme Court, directly or within two or three years, from the section that had held the vacated seat.[36] Three-fourths of all vacancies from 1789 to 1897 were filled by same-section appointments, as we have defined them, but only two-fifths were so filled from 1897 to mid-1970.[37] A decrease in sectional feeling in the United States may underlie this change, although it is hard to believe that sectionalism was as weak in the first part of the twentieth century as it has been in

[35] Maryland has been included as part of the Northeast; Kentucky as part of the Midwest until 1837 and then as part of the South; Texas as part of the South; and Montana and the states below it as part of the West.

[36] Some Presidents have rotated appointments among sections in such a way as to maintain the pre-existing sectional arrangement. Taft did this in appointing Lurton (Tennessee) to the seat vacated by Peckham (New York) in 1909 and then, three years later, Pitney (New Jersey) to the seat vacated by Harlan (Kentucky). Peckham himself had been appointed by Cleveland in 1895 to Jackson's Tennessee seat less than two years after White (Louisiana) had been appointed to Blatchford's New York seat.

[37] The figures on same-section appointments by periods are as follows: 1789–1829, eight of twelve; 1829–1861, eleven of twelve; 1861–1897, fifteen of twenty-one (the Civil War causing some shifts); 1897–1937, eight of twenty; and 1937–1970, eight of twenty-three.

more recent decades; yet the rate of same-section appointments was about as low from 1897 to 1937 as it has been since 1937. The abolition of circuit-riding in 1891 certainly deprived sectionalism of a strong prop in Supreme Court appointments. Until that date the justices of the Court had to perform trial court duties in various parts of the circuits to which they were assigned, and there were as many circuits as there were justices. It thus made sense for Presidents to select their justices from the circuits in which they would ride and whose law and local conditions they would presumably know, and Presidents usually did so.[38] The circuits were fairly well contained within sectional boundaries, so that same-circuit appointments usually meant same-section appointments as well.[39]

Two more observations will conclude our discussion of sectional representation. One is that Republican and Democratic Presidents seem to have their favorite sections, or perhaps are pressured into such favoritism by senators and other leaders of their parties. At any rate, the Midwest, East, and West have received kinder treatment from Republican than from Democratic Presidents since the Civil War, and the reverse has been true of the South.[40] The other observation is that certain states seem to be favored in appointments, and that the six most favored are old ones: New York, with fourteen appointments; Ohio, with nine; Massachusetts, with eight; and Tennessee, Kentucky, and Pennsylvania, with six each.

The decline of sectionalism as a qualification for judicial service has been accompanied by the rise of religion and ethnicity. Except for a few years, there has been a Catholic seat on the Supreme Court since McKenna's appointment in 1898 and a Jewish seat since Brandeis's appointment in 1916, although in

---

[38] See McHargue, *Appointments to the Supreme Court*, pp. 521–528, for appointments made through 1891.

[39] For an effort to relate actual representation on the Court to "deserved representation," see Cortez A. M. Ewing, *The Judges of the Supreme Court: A Study of Their Qualifications* (Minneapolis: University of Minnesota Press, c. 1938), pp. 56, 59.

[40] Democratic appointments since 1861 from New England, the East, the South, the Midwest, and the West were, respectively: three, three, nine, seven, and one; and Republican appointments were: four, thirteen, six, fourteen, and five.

each instance the religious consideration did not control the selection of the justice but rather emerged from the justice's presence on the Court. Thus, Chief Justice Stone counseled against the appointment of Charles Fahy to the Court as James F. Byrnes's replacement in 1943, for, Stone thought, if Fahy, a Catholic, were appointed, the Catholic hierarchy would feel that it was "regularly entitled" to his seat as well as the one already held by the Catholic Frank Murphy.[41] The first clearly ethnic appointment to the Supreme Court was that of Thurgood Marshall, in 1967, and it seems likely that, for some time at least, Negro representation on the Court will be deliberate. Religious and ethnic representation have generally been gained at the expense of sectional representation and, in Goldberg's appointment to succeed Frankfurter, in 1962, it cost Massachusetts the representation it had held continuously since 1881. It is difficult to say which groups will next obtain representation on the Court, although it is not improbable that a woman's seat should be established in the near future.

Our examination of representation on the Supreme Court brings us back to the matter of the President's control over the selection of justices. Representational qualifications restrain his freedom of choice, for they tend to guide that choice within the framework of party, of section, and sometimes of religion and ethnicity. Yet representational considerations help him in choosing justices. First, they tend to simplify that choice by directing it to persons and areas with the desired credentials. If, for example, the Catholic seat or the New England seat is vacant, the search for a justice may be restricted to eminent lawyers of that religion or from that section. In simplifying the President's task, representational qualifications may also free him and his chief advisers from considerable political pressure, for, to continue our example, supporters of non-New Englanders or non-Catholics are less likely to make efforts on behalf of their candidates and can be turned away when they do with the explanation that the vacant seat belongs elsewhere. Secondly, a President seldom has his hands tied by representational quali-

[41] Francis Biddle, *In Brief Authority* (Garden City, N.Y.: Doubleday, 1962), p. 193.

fications. Sectional claims often are ambiguous; population changes justify shifts in sectional balance; and a President may be able to choose between honoring a claim based upon section and honoring one based upon religion or ethnicity. In short, Presidents may use representational considerations to maintain their control over appointments.

Doctrinal Qualifications

The views of a judicial candidate are relevant to his actions as a justice because law is necessarily incomplete. As Lincoln once put the matter: "No foresight can anticipate, nor any document of reasonable length contain, express provisions for all possible questions." From unprovided-for questions, he added, "spring all our constitutional controversies."[42] The necessary incompleteness of law also gives rise to controversies over the meaning of legislative enactments. A person's views are also relevant to his judicial actions, of course, if he subscribes to the theory of jurisprudence that his is the task of adjusting that meaning or otherwise substituting his values for it. Whatever the case, constitutional and other statutory controversies have been present in all periods of American history, at varying levels of intensity, and have almost always made their way to the doors of the Supreme Court. In choosing men for the Court, a President cannot easily ignore the consequences his decisions may have for the way in which these controversies are resolved. As another President, Theodore Roosevelt, once expressed the point in a letter to his friend and fellow Republican, Senator Henry Cabot Lodge: "I should hold myself as guilty of an irreparable wrong to the nation if I should put [on the Court] any man who was not absolutely sane and sound on the great national policies for which we stand in public life."[43]

---

[42] From the First Inaugural Address, printed in Abraham Lincoln, *Complete Works*, ed. by John G. Nicolay and John Hay (New York: Lamb Publ. Co., 1894), Vol. VI, p. 178.

[43] *Selections from the Correspondence of Theodore Roosevelt and Henry Cabot Lodge, 1884–1918* (New York: Charles Scribner's Sons, 1925), Vol. II, p. 519.

Presidents have varied greatly in the extent of their concern with the views of Supreme Court candidates. Sometimes they appear to have disregarded a dissimilarity of views in making appointments or to have deemed the matter of viewpoints to be of less importance than other considerations. One thinks of the Republican Hoover's selection of the liberal Democratic Cardozo for a justiceship in 1932. A number of Presidents appear to have limited their concern to an assurance that their choices were loyal members of their party, or to other general indicators of views; for example, Wilson declared that he chose John H. Clarke for the Court in 1916 because Clarke could be relied upon to give the law a "liberal and enlightened interpretation."[44] But most Presidents have probably wanted further indications of how their candidates would react to important and controversial matters that might come before them as justices. Again we cite Lincoln and Theodore Roosevelt, who were both specific as to what they expected in some of the men they selected for the Supreme Court. One reason why Lincoln appointed Salmon P. Chase as Chief Justice in 1864 was that "we wish for a Chief Justice who will sustain what has been done in regard to emancipation and the legal tenders."[45] And Roosevelt, once again writing to Lodge, said of Horace H. Lurton, one of the persons he was considering for a justiceship in 1906: "He is right on the Negro question; he is right on the power of the federal government; he is right on the insular business; he is right about corporations; and he is right about labor. On every question that would come before the bench he has so far shown himself to be in much closer touch with the policies in which you and I believe than even [Justice Edward D.] White, because he has been right about corporations, where White has been wrong."[46]

It appears that only once has a President chosen a justice in order to influence the outcome of a case before the Court.

[44] Ray Stannard Baker, *Woodrow Wilson: Life and Letters* (Garden City, N.Y.: Doubleday, Doran, 1937), p. 116.
[45] Cited in Warren, *Supreme Court in U.S. History*, Vol. II, p. 401.
[46] *Roosevelt–Lodge Correspondence*, Vol. II, p. 228. But it was left to William Howard Taft to place Lurton on the Court.

In 1870, informed in advance that a divided Supreme Court would invalidate legislation that made paper money legal tender, President Grant nominated William Strong and Joseph Bradley to fill vacancies on the Court on the very day the *Legal-Tender decision* was announced. Grant had reason to be confident that both men believed in the constitutionality of the legislation and, once their nominations had been confirmed, the government asked the Court to reconsider its decision. With the new justices participating, the Court agreed to take up the question again and reversed its initial action.[47]

Those conditions under which Presidents are likely to be most interested in the specific views of their candidates are as follows. Public controversy over important matters, which, as we noted, usually assumes a form in which it may receive judicial treatment, must be at a high level of intensity; the President must have a policy for dealing with these matters; and the Supreme Court's position on the policy must be uncertain, if not hostile. These conditions have been notably present when major Presidents have been in office, that is, at critical times in the country's history. They were clearly present during the Civil War and explain Lincoln's policy of seeking justices who were strongly pro-Union and who could be depended upon to support the extraordinary military and political measures he employed to preserve it. They were clearly present also during Theodore Roosevelt's administration, and Roosevelt responded to them by statements such as the one

[47] Warren, *Supreme Court in U.S. History*, Vol. II, pp. 515–527, argues that Grant did not know in advance what the Court's first legal-tender decision would be and that he had decided upon Strong and Bradley considerably before the announcement of the decision. But Sidney Ratner, in "Was the Supreme Court Packed by President Grant?", *Political Science Quarterly*, 50 (September, 1935), 343–358, seems to have the better case. Chief Justice Chase had told Grant's Secretary of the Treasury two weeks before the decision what the outcome would be, and Ratner believes this information was most likely conveyed to the President. In addition, Ratner is able to produce supporting evidence, not available when Warren wrote, in the form of a statement by Grant several years after the incident that he had desired in his appointments of Strong and Bradley that the constitutionality of legal tender should be sustained by the Supreme Court (*ibid.*, p. 351).

The first legal-tender decision was *Hepburn* v. *Griswold*, 8 Wall. 603 (1869), and the second was *Knox* v. *Lee*, 12 Wall. 457 (1870).

quoted in setting forth what he wanted in his justices. And Franklin Roosevelt's anxiety to put trusted New Dealers on the Supreme Court was incited by the Court's treatment of his New Deal programs. When he was filling his first Court vacancy, Roosevelt remarked to Harold Ickes, his Secretary of the Interior, that he could not afford to give the appointment to Senator Joseph Robinson, who expected it. Although Robinson, as Senate majority leader, had loyally supported Roosevelt's programs, and had even stood to the end by the President's attempt to gain control of the Court by increasing its membership, Roosevelt did not consider him sufficiently devoted to the New Deal.[48] In fact, Roosevelt drew all of his early appointments from among those who appeared to be ideological New Dealers and who had, in addition, favored his Court proposal.

When the Supreme Court has posed no threat to their programs, Presidents have tended to relax their guard in selecting justices. Thus, Franklin Roosevelt was willing to have his sixth justice, James F. Byrnes, be less than pure in his New Deal principles and an opponent of the Court-increase plan, too. But Byrnes had been generally loyal to the Administration as a senator, and, by the time of his appointment in 1941, the Court was safe for the New Deal. The only appointment Roosevelt did not take much interest in was his last (in 1943) — that of Wiley B. Rutledge, the only one of his justices whom Roosevelt did not know, even though he had appointed him to the federal court of appeals. After listening to his Attorney General describe the candidate as a "liberal who would stand up for human rights" but not one who would be "extreme or Messianic," Roosevelt asked where Rutledge came from and then, satisfied as to geography, he said simply, "He'll do."[49]

---

[48] Harold L. Ickes, *Secret Diary* (New York: Simon and Schuster, 1954), Vol. II, p. 143; see also p. 153. Roosevelt told Ickes he could appoint Robinson if he had three or four appointments to make and, according to Ickes, told Robinson he would need at least four vacancies.

[49] Biddle, *In Brief Authority*, pp. 193–194. Even so, Roosevelt decided to talk to Rutledge before submitting his nomination to the Senate (*ibid.*, p. 194).

Similarly, Presidents have been less concerned with the views of their candidates on public questions during periods of relative political calm. And occasionally a President has seemed more concerned with political tactics than with political views in naming a person to the Court, as when Andrew Jackson appointed John McLean in 1829 in order to get his Secretary of the Treasury, who was a critic of his United States Bank policy, out of the Cabinet.

Thus, the environment in which Presidents have made their appointments has influenced the extent and specificity of their interest in the views of their candidates. When the need to control the Court or to satisfy the Senate or other groups has not narrowed their range of choice, Presidents have in selecting justices put more emphasis upon the two other considerations we have discussed. Theodore Roosevelt, for example, decided that he should not "pay heed to where a man comes from"[50] after he was made to realize the great importance of the Court's decisions during his administration, and Franklin Roosevelt made a man's residence a prime consideration only after the Court had been secured. As they have paid less attention to the matter of viewpoints in comparatively unstrained circumstances, Presidents have correspondingly paid more attention to the professional qualifications of their candidates. We can put the matter differently: In relatively calm periods, Presidents have tended to regard the Supreme Court in its legal role, as an institution which applies the law to specific cases involving particular parties. Such an institution is, consequently, best served by persons of judicial temperament who are deeply knowledgeable about the law and, preferably, have judicial experience. In times of stress, however, they have tended to regard the Court in its political role, as an institution which exercises discretion in construing law. Such an institution is best served by persons of statesman-like temperament who have a deep political understanding, and experience in the other branches of government. Needless to add, the statesmen who are sought are those sharing the President's views on the

[50] *Roosevelt–Lodge Correspondence*, p. 228.

Constitution and statutes. Yet rarely, if ever, have Presidents emphasized one role of the Court to the exclusion of the other. Usually they have been able to keep in view the representational role of the Court as well, but representational criteria are not as fixed as are professional and political criteria, and they have been, at least in this century, subordinated to them, especially to a concern with views on public questions.

How have Presidents assured themselves that persons with acceptable views would receive appointments? One way has been to appoint justices of the same party, or of the same wing of a divided party. Most Presidents appear to have assumed that party has some relation to beliefs, for, as we noted in the previous chapter, all but eight of the ninety-eight justices appointed through mid-1970 were of the same party as the appointing President.[51] But, knowing that party attachment does not always reveal the whole of a person's politics, few Presidents have ceased their inquiry with this external evidence. There is no record of a President asking a person, before tendering an appointment, how he would decide on particular matters, for, as Lincoln stated it, "if we should, and he should answer us, we should despise him for it."[52] But a few Presidents have come dangerously close. In what appears to be the most recent instance, Dwight D. Eisenhower, by his own account, talked to Earl Warren about his "basic philosophy" a few months before the death of Chief Justice Fred Vinson, with the idea, which he conveyed to Warren, of giving the California Governor a Supreme Court appointment should a vacancy occur. Eisenhower was "quite pleased that [Warren's] views seemed to reflect high ideals and a great deal of common sense," but he took the added precaution of sending his Attorney General, Herbert J. Brownell, to California to speak further with Warren when the Vinson vacancy occurred. With Brownell's "helpful

[51] The cross-party appointments were of Stephen J. Field, Howell E. Jackson, Horace H. Lurton, Joseph R. Lamar, Pierce Butler, Benjamin N. Cardozo Harold H. Burton, and William J. Brennan. In addition, two justices, Edward D. White and Harlan F. Stone, were elevated to chief justiceships by Presidents of the other party.

[52] Quoted by Warren, *Supreme Court in U.S. History*, Vol. II, p. 401.

report" before him, Eisenhower made his selection.[53]

A more dignified and, as Eisenhower discovered, dependable way of gauging how a person will act in a judicial capacity is to examine his record on public issues. Most justices have had substantial careers in government service, and of the thirteen who lacked such careers, some, notably Louis D. Brandeis and Felix Frankfurter, were active governmental advisers.[54] Better yet, Presidents might select persons whom they, or their trusted advisers, know personally and, of course, favorably, for in such appointments a President may be most sure of his men. Most appointments, as we showed in the previous chapter, have been of this character. The importance of the personal factor can be inferred from President Kennedy's selection of Byron R. White in 1962. Kennedy had considered several other persons for the seat opened by Justice Charles E. Whittaker's resignation in that year, among whom the leading candidates were Paul Freund of the Harvard Law School, Walter B. Shaeffer of the Illinois Supreme Court, Roger J. Traynor of the California Supreme Court, and William Hastie of the federal court of appeals. As Robert Kennedy explained the elimination process, "You wanted someone who agreed generally with your views of the country," and only White and Arthur J. Goldberg seemed to meet that requirement.[55] Goldberg was President Kennedy's Secretary of Labor (and was wanted then in the Cabinet), and White was an old friend of the President's and Robert Kennedy's chief deputy in the Justice Department.

---

[53] Dwight D. Eisenhower, *The White House Years: Mandate for Change, 1953–1956* (New York: New American Library, 1965), pp. 285, 286.

[54] The other eleven justices were Bushrod Washington, Benjamin R. Curtis, John A. Campbell, Noah H. Swayne, Samuel F. Miller, Joseph P. Bradley, Morrison R. Waite, Melville W. Fuller, George Shiras, Pierce Butler (who had been a member of the University of Minnesota Board of Regents), and Owen J. Roberts.

Schmidhauser, "Justices of the Supreme Court," Table 12, p. 37, reports that every member of the Supreme Court except one (George Shiras) had held a political post of some kind prior to his appointment to the higher bench, but Schmidhauser considers judgeships to be political posts and evidently includes brief and irregular association with the government as well as political party offices.

[55] James E. Clayton, *The Making of Justice: The Supreme Court in Action* (New York: E. P. Dutton, 1964), pp. 50, 52.

If these are the ways in which Presidents have sought to put men of their own political stripe on the Supreme Court, it must be said that some Presidents have been less concerned than others with the politics of their justices independent of the circumstances in which appointments have been made. The circumstances that we associated with heightened interest in the political views of candidates were, it will be recalled, the existence of critical national problems, a Presidential policy for coping with these problems, and a Supreme Court that seemed uncertain of, or unfriendly toward, these policies. We must at this point introduce another factor: the conception that Presidents have of the Supreme Court's role and of their relation to the Court. Some Presidents have regarded the Supreme Court more in its legal capacity than have other Presidents and have tended to look upon the selection of justices according to their views as a tampering with the Court's independence and prestige. Herbert Hoover is a good example. Hoover certainly faced a crisis during his Presidency: the Great Depression. If the Court at the time he took office contained a safe conservative majority, Hoover's three appointments served to endanger that safety, for neither Owen J. Roberts nor Benjamin N. Cardozo nor Charles Evans Hughes was of Hoover's political cast. None of these men shared Hoover's economic views (Roberts came closest), and all were part of the post-1936 majority that upheld the New Deal. Hoover seemed genuinely distressed when, during the 1932 Presidential campaign, Franklin D. Roosevelt referred to the Supreme Court as being under the "complete control" of the Republican party. "All appointees to the Supreme Court," Hoover insisted in his reply, "have been chosen solely on the basis of character and mental power," and he asked, correctly as it turned out, if Roosevelt planned, if he won the Presidency, to make the Supreme Court "an instrument of party policy and political action for sustaining such doctrines as he may bring with him?"[56]

Much more than the Democrats, Republicans in the Presidency have acted upon a legal conception of the Supreme

[56] *New York Times*, October 29, 1932, p. 8.

Court. Consider, for example, the matter of political party in appointments to the Court. As we observed earlier, Republican Presidents have, since the two present parties were formed, made all but one of the cross-party appointments to the Court. Or consider the careers of persons appointed during this same period. Republican Presidents have gone most often to the judiciary for their candidates. They chose all but three of the twenty-six justices who were drawn from the state or lower federal courts, and both of the non-judges whose government careers were mainly judicial. Republican Presidents also made most of the appointments of practicing attorneys, having chosen eight of the ten members of the Court after 1857 who had neither been judges nor ex-judges nor had experienced substantial public service in the other branches of government. Democratic Presidents, by contrast, had the distinction of appointing most (seventeen) of the justices who had substantial public service in non-judicial posts (twenty-eight), despite the small portion of appointments that was theirs to make during this period. They held a like advantage in appointments made directly from elective office (four of six).[57] Finally, Democratic Presidents more than Republican (eleven instances to four) found their justices among those whom they had appointed to high administrative offices and whose views, and support, they could presumably depend upon. In brief, the evidence all points to the conclusion that Democrats in the White House have been much more sensitive to the political dimensions of the Supreme Court's activities than have their Republican colleagues. Democrats have been much more willing to select candidates whose orientation to the Court would be, in the larger sense, political: whose views on public questions would be more readily and surely known and in line with those of the appointing Presidents.

Earlier in this chapter we discussed the three groups of officials who appeared to be most influential as Presidential

[57] Joseph A. Schlesinger, *Ambition and Politics: Political Careers in the United States* (Chicago: Rand McNally, 1966), p. 35, shows that the Democratic party also chooses a higher proportion of its Presidential candidates and Cabinet officers from "purely political" offices.

advisers in the selection of Supreme Court justices: attorneys-general, senators, and the justices themselves. Each of these groups, it may be suggested, has a somewhat different orientation from that of the President in regard to the qualifications it emphasizes in judicial candidates. The President is more political than any of the others: He is more concerned than they with the views of candidates on important public questions. The senators are the most concerned with representational qualifications, especially those of geography and, above all, party: they want men of the right party given the reward of high judicial office.[58] The justices seem to be most concerned with the professional qualifications of the men they have supported, although social compatibility in the judicial harness seems also to have influenced some judgments. It is worth observing too that Chief Justice Marshall supported the appointment of Roger B. Taney as an associate justice in 1835 solely on Taney's legal eminence and ability, despite the constitutional gulf that separated the two men.[59] The attorneys-general appear to stand somewhere among these contesting positions and, while sensitive to the desires of their superior, are probably more sensitive than the President to the professional urgings emanating from the bench and the organized bar.[60]

[58] Note the exchange between Theodore Roosevelt and Henry Cabot Lodge in connection with Roosevelt's notion of placing the Democrat Horace H. Lurton on the Court. Roosevelt: "Nothing has been so strongly borne in on me concerning lawyers on the bench as that the *nominal* politics of the man has nothing to do with his actions on the bench. His *real* politics are all important." Lodge: "I am glad that Lurton holds all the opinions that you say he does and that you are so familiar with his views . . . but I do not see why Republicans cannot be found who hold those opinions as well as Democrats." (*Roosevelt–Lodge Correspondence*, Vol. II, pp. 228–229.)

[59] Warren, *Supreme Court in U.S. History*, Vol. I, p. 800.

[60] Franklin Roosevelt, for example, complained to Harold Ickes, his Interior Secretary, that Attorney General Homer Cummings was recommending middle-of-the-road men to him for his crucial first appointment, whereas he felt he had to go further to the political left. Ickes, *Secret Diary*, Vol. II, p. 183.

5

Expectations and Performance

Do Presidents get what they want in the men they appoint to the Supreme Court? How often do they fail to do so? What accounts for the discrepancy between Presidential intention and judicial performance?

In some instances we can relate judicial performance to Presidential expectations with a fair degree of precision, especially when Presidents have indicated, directly or indirectly, what they wanted, or got, in their justices. More often we must make assumptions based upon the general political views of Presidents and on the situations in which they operated. And in some instances, in particular where judicial service was short, we simply cannot say whether Presidents have obtained what they wanted in their justices.

SATISFACTION OF PRESIDENTIAL EXPECTATIONS

Both Washington and John Adams limited their choices of justices to persons who were firm supporters of the Federalist interpretation of the Constitution. They wanted men who would support the broad exercise of power by the national government, especially for the purposes of maintaining public order and encouraging commerce and industry; and who would limit the power of the states to interfere with these and other national purposes. Their appointees hardly ever deviated from these policies, and two of them, John Marshall and Bushrod Washington, espoused them in careers of more than thirty years of service on the Court. In fact, no Federalist dissent was ever recorded against the great Federalist decisions of the first forty years of the Republic. Among these decisions were those which held that a treaty of the United States superseded state law (*Ware* v. *Hylton*, 1796), that the Supreme Court possessed the power to void legislation it judged to be unconstitutional (*Marbury* v. *Madison*, 1803), and that legislative landgrants and corporate charters were contracts that could not be impaired by subsequent legislative enactments (respectively, *Fletcher* v. *Peck*, 1810, and *Dartmouth College* v. *Woodward*, 1819); that upheld the constitutionality of the United States Bank and invalidated a state tax upon this instrumentality (*McCulloch* v. *Maryland*, 1819); and, finally, that construed the national power over commerce in broad terms while striking down a state law for infringing upon that power (*Gibbons* v. *Ogden*, 1824). These decisions were important not only in themselves but in the way in which they influenced future generations to regard and interpret the Constitution. Perhaps the only time that a Federalist-appointed justice departed from a Presidential position in a significant case occurred in 1812 when Samuel Chase sided with the Republican majority on the Court to hold that there were no common-law, but only statute-created, crimes under the national government (*United States* v. *Hudson and Goodwin*).[1]

---

[1] Although Washington and John Adams did not, to this writer's knowledge, express themselves on the question of common-law offenses against the United States, it was general Federalist doctrine that such offenses existed, and Republican doctrine that they did not. Justices appointed by Washington and Adams recognized such offenses in their circuit-court activities. (Chase, incidentally, had once been a Republican.) Although no dissents were

Jefferson and Madison were much less successful than their Federalist predecessors in picking justices who performed according to expectations. The Republican principles of these two men included narrowly construed national and broadly construed state power, especially when state power was directed against commercial wealth. But it should be observed that Madison appears not to have shared Jefferson's great concern with reversing the Federalist doctrines of the Court. He went so far as to place there Joseph Story, a "pseudo-republican" who was "unquestionably a Tory," although it is true that he turned to Story as his fourth choice to fill the New England seat.[2] Story did indeed stand very close to Marshall on the Court, but Jefferson's own appointments also came under Marshall's great influence. No justice appointed by either Jefferson or Madison dissented from the Federalist decisions we have just cited, except for Gabriel Duval (appointed by Madison) in the *Dartmouth College case*. In fact, William Johnson (appointed by Jefferson) wrote a concurring opinion in *Gibbons* v. *Ogden* that went further than Marshall's majority opinion in claiming national control over commerce. In later years Johnson from time to time separated himself from the Federalist positions of Marshall and Story, but he was the only one of the early Republican appointees to do so in important cases (all five Jefferson–Madison appointees were still serving in 1820, and three served beyond 1830). On the other hand, Johnson

registered in the case, it was not unusual for justices to withhold public disagreement with the majority position, and it is known that the other two Federalist-appointed justices, Marshall and Washington, did disagree with that position. See W. W. Crosskey, "Mr. Chief Justice Marshall," in Allison Dunham and Philip E. Kurland, eds., *Mr. Justice*; rev. ed. (Chicago: University of Chicago Press, 1964), p. 11.

[2] The terms were used by Jefferson at the time the appointment was made. See Charles Warren, *The Supreme Court in United States History* (Boston: Little, Brown, 1926), Vol. I, p. 406. Madison was something of a "pseudo-republican" himself. Unlike Jefferson before him or Jackson after, he was willing to accept the judgment of others as to the constitutionality of a United States Bank, and his long letter to Spencer Roane, commenting on the latter's attack on the Bank case (*McCulloch* v. *Maryland*, 1819), nowhere expresses disagreement with the Court's decision. James Madison, *Writings*, ed. by Gaillard Hunt (New York: G. P. Putnam's Sons, 1908), Vol. VIII, 1808–1819, pp. 327, 447–453.

never recanted his broad view of the commerce power, and he joined Marshall in one of their last major decisions, upholding the supremacy of a Cherokee Indian treaty over Georgia law (*Worcester* v. *Georgia*, 1832). When Jefferson indicted the justices in 1820 as constituting "a subtle corps of sappers and miners" made up of a "crafty chief judge" and "lazy or timid associates,"[3] he was passing judgment on a Court four of whose six members had been appointed by himself and Madison.

The election of Andrew Jackson in 1828 opened a new era in American politics. The Republican era had begun with the overthrow of Federalism in the Presidency and Congress, had proceeded to the elimination of the Federalists as a political party, and had ended, in the Presidencies of James Monroe and John Quincy Adams, with the spread of Federalist principles within the ranks of a single Republican party. Given this situation, it is not possible to ascribe an intention to Monroe's appointment of Smith Thompson or to Adams's of Robert Trimble. The Supreme Court had remained the citadel of Federalism during the administrations of Jefferson and Madison, and it was the Court which preserved and then propagated the principles of the defunct Federalist party. Jackson stood for the purification of Jeffersonian principles, and of the two most important Democratic Presidents who succeeded him in the pre-Civil War era, Martin Van Buren was his close ally and James K. Polk his disciple.

As good Jeffersonians, all three Presidents believed in a limited construction of national power (except that of the President as the people's national representative), especially as it concerned assistance to manufacturing and commerce; and all three subscribed to the doctrine of states-rights, especially as it concerned the control of monopolies and of corporate activity generally. But the evidence that would permit us to translate their political beliefs into expectations in the appointment of

[3] Letter to Thomas Ritchie, December 25, 1820, in Thomas Jefferson, *Writings*, ed. by Andrew A. Lipscomb and Albert E. Bergh (Washington: The Thomas Jefferson Memorial Assn., 1903), Vol. XV, pp. 297, 298.

justices is indirect. Even if we assume that these Presidents chose all their justices for the views the justices held, we cannot easily say whether the justices were faithful to the Presidential expectations in a number of the important cases decided during this period. It does appear that in some important cases they were not, as when they joined in the unanimous decision of the —now we may call him—Federalist Story to rule that federal courts may put aside state law in commercial cases in order to define general commercial rules (*Swift* v. *Tyson*, 1842), or when they agreed with their colleagues that the courts could compel Jackson's Postmaster General to perform an act that his superior told him not to perform (*Kendall* v. *United States*, 1838).

We can probably say with some confidence that most of the ten justices appointed by Jackson, Van Buren, and Polk, and the other three justices appointed by later Democratic Presidents in the pre-Civil War period as well, were usually faithful to the states-rights and anti-corporation sentiments of their appointers, and that, among those who served on the Supreme Court during the greater part of this period, Roger B. Taney, John Catron, and Peter V. Daniel (Taney appointed by Jackson and the others by Van Buren) were especially close in their judicial positions.[4] All Democratic justices agreed that the national government's control of commerce did not exclude a state from requiring detailed reports on all immigrants brought by ship to American ports (*New York* v. *Miln*, 1837) and that the issuance of state bank notes, which was made highly expedient by Jackson's action against the Bank of the United States, did not fall under the Constitution's prohibition against state bills of credit (*Briscoe* v. *Kentucky*, 1837). Also, if we can consider McLean's dissent on the question of jurisdiction to have no further intimation, all Democratic justices who addressed themselves to the merits of the case agreed to free state legislatures from the prohibition that Marshall had placed

---

[4] Of the seven justices who served at least most of the period from 1837 to the Civil War, these three paired with each other most often in dissent. John P. Frank, *Mr. Justice Daniel, Dissenting* (Cambridge: Harvard University Press, 1964), p. 237.

on their authority to revoke charters granted by them (*Charles River Bridge* v. *Warren Bridge*, 1837). (Story dissented in all three cases, alone in two of them.)

But three Democratic justices could not be called faithful adherents to the Jacksonian creed: John McLean, Henry Baldwin, and James M. Wayne—all of whom, incidentally, were appointed by Jackson himself. McLean was the most apostate of the group, and he finally gave public acknowledgement to his changed views by joining the Republican party, the successor of the Whigs, two years after its founding in 1854. In the *Kendall case*, the three justices not only believed that the courts could require a Cabinet officer to perform certain acts, but that the Supreme Court had jurisdiction in the particular case to make him do so. They also averred, in opposition to three of their Democratic colleagues, that all state laws regarding fugitive slaves, Southern as well as Northern, were unconstitutional and, moreover, that the states were not obliged to enforce federal fugitive slave legislation or to enact laws of their own to make it effective (*Prigg* v. *Pennsylvania*, 1842). McLean and Wayne supported the ruling that because federal power is exclusive in the realm of foreign relations a state could not return a fugitive from Canadian justice (*Holmes* v. *Jennison*, 1840). These two justices also supported a decision that struck down state laws taxing passengers (most of whom would be immigrants) arriving at American ports (*Passenger cases*, 1849), and dissented from the decision that gave states some concurrent jurisdiction with Congress over national and international commerce (*Cooley* v. *Board of Wardens*, 1851). McLean joined a predominantly Federalist Court in 1832 in declaring that the national government had exclusive jurisdiction over the Cherokee Indians living within Georgia and hence that the state could not legislate over them. This decision went in the face of Jackson's policy of allowing the states east of the Mississippi to deal with their Indians pretty much as they desired. The deviant positions assumed by McLean, Wayne, and Baldwin are further testified to by the fact that Story, the arch-deviator from Jeffersonian doctrine, was alongside them in every one of the mentioned cases decided to 1845, when he retired from the Court.

The first of the Republican Presidents, Abraham Lincoln, got from his five justices what he wanted when he needed it. While the Civil War was raging, his first four appointees, opposed by four of the five justices appointed by his Democratic predecessors, upheld the Union blockade of Southern ports, which had been laid without a declaration of war, and at the same time withheld the status of a belligerent power from the Confederacy (*The Prize cases*, 1863). Joined by their Democratic colleagues, the Lincoln justices also invalidated a state bank tax that would have made the government's financing of the war very difficult (*Bank of Commerce* v. *New York*, 1863) and refused to take jurisdiction of cases challenging legal-tender legislation (*Roosevelt* v. *Meyer*, 1863) and the military arrest and trial of civilians in areas outside the perimeter of war (*Ex parte Vallandigham*, 1864). But after war had ceased, and Lincoln had died, the Court unanimously declared the President to have been without authority to order military trials of civilians (*Ex parte Milligan*, 1866) and, with two of Lincoln's appointees, Salmon P. Chase and Stephen J. Field, joining with three pre-war Democratic justices, ruled legal tenders unconstitutional (*Hepburn* v. *Griswold*, 1870). It should be noted that the other Lincoln appointees—Noah H. Swayne, Samuel F. Miller, and David Davis—stood fast on the legal-tender question and, when Grant added Strong and Bradley to the Court, helped compose the new majority on it (*Knox* v. *Lee*, 1871).

With the exception of the appointments of Joseph P. Bradley and William Strong, we lack clear evidence of Presidential intentions in the selection of Supreme Court justices between the end of the Civil War and the end of the nineteenth century. And while Ulysses S. Grant chose these two men in the expectation they would support the constitutionality of legal tenders, we do not know what other expectations he might have had, nor anything specific about the expectations of his successors in the Presidency. By and large, the post-Civil War Presidents had their hands full finding candidates who would be acceptable to Senates which were usually opposition-controlled or closely divided. Considerations of geography also weighed heavily in their selections. All appointing Presidents did select members of their own party and all, we may surmise, desired in a general way that their appointees share their views in regard to the important issues of their Presidencies. There were two basic issues during the post-Civil War period that were relevant to the judicial function: the scope of the Civil War Amendments, especially as they related to the rights of the enfranchised black man and to state regulation of railroads and other economic activity; and the scope of the national government's authority, especially under the commerce and taxing powers, to regulate economic activity and tax personal wealth.

Inasmuch as President Grant approved the civil rights legislation based on the Civil War Amendments, we may assume that he subscribed to its objectives and believed in its constitutionality. If he expected his justices to support the legislation, he was largely mistaken. Ward Hunt was the only one of four Grant appointees who dissented from a decision which weakened an 1870 act designed to protect Negroes in exercising the right to vote (*United States* v. *Reese*, 1876). None of his appointees dissented from a second weakening decision concerning that right (*United States* v. *Cruikshank*, also in 1876). Finally, neither of two remaining Grant appointees disagreed with decisions holding that the Fourteenth Amendment did not support an 1871 act aimed at the Ku Klux Klan (*United States* v. *Harris*, 1883) and an 1875 act aimed at private discrimination in places serving the public (*Civil Rights cases*, 1883).

The Presidents who came after Grant were more successful in choosing compatible justices on the question of the scope of the Civil War Amendments as they applied to the black man. These Presidents were moderates on the question, in contrast to the Radical Republicans who pushed the laws mentioned through Congress. All their appointees to the Supreme Court, John Marshall Harlan excepted, joined in the two cases decided in 1883 and, Harlan again excepted, in the now-notorious case of *Plessy* v. *Ferguson* (1896), which upheld under the Fourteenth Amendment separate-but-equal railroad accommodations for whites and blacks. Not only was Harlan, appointed by Rutherford B. Hayes, unwilling to accept the moderate consensus on the Civil War Amendments, but he would have used the Amendments to require the states to follow the grand jury procedure used by the national government in bringing persons to trial for serious offenses (*Hurtado* v. *California*, 1884), a step which even the contemporary Supreme Court has not yet taken.[5] No post-Civil War justice, on the other hand, went to the other extreme of believing that the national government had to abandon its efforts on behalf of the freed slaves, and all of them, for example, voted to sustain federal legislation punishing the exclusion of Negroes from juries (*Ex parte Virginia*, 1880) and interference with their right to vote in federal elections (*Ex parte Yarbrough*, 1884).

Inasmuch as the control of corporations and the control of personal wealth did not become salient national issues until the 1880s, it is not possible to ascribe Presidential expectations about them to the justices appointed before that time. Thus, our interest in these questions begins with the eight justices appointed by the two men who shared the Presidency between 1885 and 1897, Grover Cleveland, a Democrat, and Benjamin Harrison, a Republican. Not much distinguishes the views of the two men. Cleveland was perhaps more disposed to the regulation of property: he had called for legal restraints upon corporations and had approved the Interstate Commerce Act; but Harrison had approved the Sherman Anti-Trust Act. Actually, both Presidents were rather conservative in their economic outlooks (Cleveland did not favor a progressive income tax and allowed such a tax to become law without his signature), and so were the men they appointed to the Supreme Court. None of their justices supported the regulation of wealth

[5] But even Harlan had his limits. He joined with the rest of his colleagues to sustain a state law which punished illicit intercourse more severely when committed by persons of different races than when committed by persons of the same race (*Pace* v. *Alabama*, 1882) and in denying that the right to keep and bear arms was a national privilege protected against state interference (*Presser* v. *Illinois*, 1886).

to the same extent as Harlan, appointed by Hayes, but then none opposed it to the same extent as Stephen J. Field, appointed by Lincoln—both of whom served through this period.

There is no clear pattern in the behavior of the Cleveland and Harrison justices in major cases dealing with economic matters. Edward D. White, appointed by Cleveland, and Henry B. Brown, appointed by Harrison, were the most progressive of the six justices who served more than a few years on the Court. Both men dissented from the holding that the national government lacked power to lay a progressive income tax upon personal wealth (*Pollock* v. *Farmer's Loan & Trust Company*, 1895), and both joined in the one that upheld a state eight-hour-day law for workers in mines and smelters (*Holden* v. *Hardy*, 1898). On the other hand, the four other justices, who viewed the Constitution as severely limiting the regulatory authority of both nation and states, were also evenly appointed by the two Presidents. And all six justices joined in the rulings that the Sherman Act did not extend to monopolistic practices in manufacturing (*United States* v. *E. C. Knight Company*, 1895), that Congress could not outlaw anti-union contracts between employers and their employees (*Adair* v. *United States*, 1908), and that a state could not regulate the working hours of bakers (*Lochner* v. *New York*, 1905).

Thus, in a general way, the men Presidents Cleveland and Harrison placed on the Supreme Court met the Presidents' expectations, except that White and Brown probably were close to the limits of these expectations and perhaps went outside them. We must be cautious in our evaluation because neither President appears to have indicated his political intentions in choosing justices for the Court, and neither announced a clear position on most of the issues the Court faced.

From the end of the nineteenth century to the early 1940s, one issue dominated all others in the work of the Supreme Court: the power of the nation and the states to regulate corporate and personal wealth. The issue took different forms, ranging from the regulation of trusts and railroads in the early part of the period to that of labor–management conflict later on; and some questions, such as the regulation of the hours of labor, retained their saliency from beginning to end. The Presidents holding office varied in their efforts to influence the judicial resolution of the issue by means of their Supreme Court appointments. The Presidents who showed the most concern were those who had identified their administrations with policies for dealing with the problem. In this respect three Presidents stand out: Theodore Roosevelt with his Square Deal, Woodrow Wilson with his New Freedom, and Franklin Roosevelt with his New Deal. Both Roosevelts appear also to have been concerned with the Supreme Court's response to questions arising from war.

As we observed in the chapter on appointments, Theodore Roosevelt had fixed notions of what he wanted in his Supreme Court justices. In particular, he sought persons who shared his moderately progressive views on race relations, corporations, and labor. William Moody satisfied him fully, for he was, the President wrote a friend a couple of years after his appointment, "entirely our kind of a judge."[6] Moody's judicial service was, however, short, as ill health forced him to resign from the Court after only four years of service. Oliver Wendell Holmes presents a difficult case. On the one hand, Holmes apparently failed Roosevelt but once on a matter of major concern, an anti-trust action against a railroad merger (*Northern Securities Company* v. *United States*, 1904, which the government won anyway). On the other hand, Roosevelt considered Holmes to be "a bitter disappointment" after four years on the bench, "not because of any one decision but because of his general attitude."[7] If Roosevelt had lived to witness Holmes's libertarianism in cases decided after the First World War (the President had not considered the free-speech issue in making his appointments), his disappointment would have turned to dismay. Roosevelt's third justice, William R. Day, gave much more evidence than Holmes of not living up to his appointer's

[6] Theodore Roosevelt, *Letters*, ed. by Elting E. Morison (Cambridge: Harvard University Press, 1952), Vol. VI, p. 1393.

[7] *Ibid.*, Vol. V, p. 396.

expectations. Day joined majorities which struck down federal legislation protecting union members from discrimination by their railroad employers (*Adair* v. *United States*, 1908) and which freed injured railroad workers from restrictive rules in suing their employers (*Employers Liability cases*, 1908). And he dissented from decisions which upheld Presidential action (by Taft) withdrawing public lands from private economic exploitation (*United States* v. *Midwest Oil Company*, 1914) and eight-hour-day legislation for railroad labor (*Wilson* v. *New*, 1917). Roosevelt was also concerned that the Court might send the Constitution after the flag into the territories gained through the Spanish–American War, that is, apply the provisions of the Constitution fully to those territories, but both Holmes and Day early satisfied him on this question.[8]

Woodrow Wilson appointed three justices to the Supreme Court. He came to feel that he had made a mistake in his selection of one of them, James C. McReynolds. Indeed, McReynolds quickly gave his appointer cause for concern when he sided against the constitutionality of state legislation protecting union members from employer discrimination (*Coppage* v. *Kansas*, 1915) during his first term on the Court, and against the federal eight-hour-day law two years later (*Wilson* v. *New*). In a long judicial career, McReynolds never took a position in accord with Wilson's views on any important regulatory case. On the other hand, Wilson's other appointees, Louis D. Brandeis and John H. Clarke, never took a distinctly anti-Wilsonian position, except for Brandeis's acquiescence in a decision invalidating a national law, enacted in Wilson's administration, which sought to eliminate child labor by taxing its employment (*Bailey* v. *Drexel Furniture Company*, 1922).[9] Although Clarke left the Court after six years, Brandeis con-

[8] *Hawaii* v. *Mankichi* (1903), *Kepner* v. *United States* (1904), *Dorr* v. *United States* (1904), *Trono* v. *United States* (1904).

In the later case of *Balzac* v. *Porto Rico* (1922), however, Holmes was a lone dissenter to an opinion that the constitutional right of jury trial did not extend to that island acquisition.

[9] See Alexander Bickel, *The Unpublished Opinions of Mr. Justice Brandeis* (Cambridge, Mass.: Harvard University Press, 1957), pp. 14–19, for a possible explanation of Brandeis's action.

tinued to dispense the Wilsonian creed until 1939, and McReynolds continued to combat it until 1941.

The third twentieth-century President with a clear policy for the regulation of corporate and personal wealth was Franklin D. Roosevelt. Not one of Roosevelt's justices ever took a position in a case against the New Deal or against a state tax or business regulation on the ground that the state enactment was not permitted by the due process clause of the Fourteenth Amendment. By 1941, with seven Roosevelt justices on the Court, Roosevelt's domestic objectives were, for all practical purposes, fully achieved when the Court upheld the national government's authority, under the commerce power, to regulate child labor and the wages and hours of employment (*United States* v. *Darby Lumber Company*), and that of the states to set maximum rates chargeable by private employment agencies (*Olsen* v. *Nebraska*). Roosevelt's appointees did disagree among themselves on subsidiary questions of economic regulation, such as whether Congress had exclusive authority to regulate certain aspects of commerce or Congressional intent in certain statutory provisions. But the President, it seems safe to say, was not interested in such matters in his selection of justices.

We may impute two other political intentions to Franklin Roosevelt in his appointments to the Supreme Court. First, he wished, in a general way, his justices to be liberal in matters relating to personal freedom and civil equality; and all of them were acceptably so. Some were more liberal than others, but it would be most difficult in cases where they disagreed among themselves to say which justices were unfaithful to their appointer's expectation. Consider, for example, two cases that involved local regulations providing for the pledge of allegiance by school children to the American flag. The issue was whether the pledge could be required of children who asserted their religious beliefs as a barrier to giving it. In the first case, decided in 1940, all five of Roosevelt's justices took the position that the pledge could be required (*Minersville School District* v. *Gobitis*). In the second case, decided three years later, only Felix Frankfurter and Stanley Reed adhered to their original position while Hugo L. Black, William O. Douglas, and Frank Murphy switched theirs and, aided by Roosevelt's two most recent appointees, Robert H. Jackson and Wiley B. Rutledge, helped to shift the Court against the compulsory flag salute (*West Virginia State Board of Education* v. *Barnette*). Which position was in accord with Roosevelt's own view? Without knowing Roosevelt's mind on the matter, one can only guess.[10]

In the second place, we may assume that after 1939 Roosevelt selected his justices with an eye to getting favorable Supreme Court decisions on his actions in preparing the nation against the Axis threat and then in directing it against that threat. Omitting James F. Byrnes, who served only one term on the Court, the objects of this assumed Presidential concern were Frank Murphy, appointed in 1940, Robert H. Jackson, appointed in 1941, and Wiley B. Rutledge, appointed in 1943. It turned out that these justices gave the government the least support of any of Roosevelt's appointees in cases arising under wartime circumstances. They did help to constitute a unanimous Court in the two cases in which Roosevelt was probably most concerned, those dealing with the government's right to try by military tribunal eight saboteurs who entered the United States from German submarines (*Ex parte Quirin*, 1942) and the military order underlying the policy of removing native and foreign-born Japanese–Americans from the West Coast as a security measure (*Hirabayashi* v. *United States*, 1943); but they opposed the government in other cases, and Murphy, who did not participate in the *Saboteur case*, supported the government only once in fourteen war-related cases.

What of those justices appointed by the other Presidents who held office between the end of the nineteenth century and the start of the New Deal? In most cases, it is difficult clearly to relate judicial performance to the expectations of the appointing

---

[10] As it happens, we do know Roosevelt's mind on the flag salute question, if information furnished by Justice Frankfurter is to be credited. According to the justice, Roosevelt expressed a view at an intimate social gathering following the first Court decision "that was an exact statement of Frankfurter's own position" (while Mrs. Roosevelt sided with Chief Justice Stone's lone dissent in the case). *Roosevelt and Frankfurter: Their Correspondence, 1928–1945*, annot. by Max Freedman (Boston: Little, Brown, 1967), p. 701; see also p. 699.

Presidents, and we must be content with asking whether the overall performance of a justice in the more important economic cases seems to have been distinctly out of line with the general political position of the person who placed him on the supreme bench.

William McKinley's single appointment, Joseph McKenna, passes this test. McKenna supported legislation regulating corporations and assisting labor more often than he opposed it, and to about the same extent as William R. Day (appointed by Theodore Roosevelt) during the two decades both men served together on the Court. If Day was more progressive in concurring in the assertion of state power regulating labor and business (*Lochner* v. *New York*, 1905, and *Coppage* v. *Kansas*, 1915), McKenna was more so in regard to the assertion of national power (*Adair* v. *United States*, 1908, *Wilson* v. *New*, 1917, and *Hammer* v. *Dagenhart*, 1917). It seems doubtful that McKinley would have found McKenna's performance unexpectedly disturbing, since he himself was rather sympathetic toward organized labor and maintained good relations with its leaders while in the White House.

William Howard Taft presents a more difficult case because he combined a progressive Republican tendency, emphasized by his close association with Theodore Roosevelt, with an orthodox tendency, and because his justices reflect both tendencies. The difficulty is illustrated in the action Taft took in 1909, before he made any Supreme Court designations, withdrawing from private exploitation public lands which Congress had by law opened to such exploitation. When the action came before the Supreme Court several years later, three of Taft's appointees upheld it and two of them opposed it (*United States* v. *Midwest Oil Company*, 1915). Still later Taft revealed he had "very considerable doubt" as to his power so to withdraw public lands but had conformed to the views of his conservationist predecessor.[11] Charles Evans Hughes, who was one of the justices upholding the case, went somewhat beyond the range of Taft's

[11] William Howard Taft, *Our Chief Magistrate and His Powers* (New York: Columbia University Press, 1916), p. 136.

mild progressivism, as he never seems to have opposed national or state regulation of corporate and personal wealth in his six years as a Taft justice; and perhaps Mahlon Pitney, one of the opposing justices, went somewhat beyond Taft's conservative limits, as he rejected most governmental economic regulation in the ten years of his service. Hughes was the only Taft appointee who thought a state could prohibit discriminatory labor contracts (*Coppage* v. *Kansas*, 1915) and was one of two (but Pitney was the other!) who supported the decision according the states' broad power to regulate insurance rates (*German Alliance Insurance Company* v. *Kansas*, 1914). Pitney's conservative view of constitutional power was indicated in his opposition to the Interstate Commerce Commission's regulation of intrastate railroad rates when they affected interstate commerce (*Shreveport case*, 1914) and in his opposition to a national tax on stock dividends (*Eisner* v. *Macomber*, 1920).

Warren G. Harding appointed five justices to the Supreme Court, including the increasingly conservative William Howard Taft, and none of them appears to have moved beyond Harding's general conservatism in economic matters. In fact, the variations among the Harding justices were not substantial, except for Edward T. Sanford's limited tendency to uphold legislation which most of his colleagues found unconstitutional. Only Sanford and Taft, among Harding's appointees, considered that Congress had the authority to prescribe minimum wages for women in the District of Columbia (*Adkins* v. *Children's Hospital*, 1923), and Sanford alone thought that New York state could prescribe the price at which agencies sold theater tickets (*Tyson* v. *Banton*, 1927). But in most of the significant economic decisions, Sanford and Taft acted as a unit with Harding's two other appointees, George Sutherland and Pierce Butler, and such unity seems to have characterized their behavior on the Court generally.[12]

----

[12] For example, in the eleven railroad-rate and valuation cases decided between 1923 and 1930 (Taft and Sanford ended their service on the Court in the latter year), the Harding justices disagreed among themselves only once. See David J. Danelski, *A Supreme Court Justice Is Appointed* (New York: Random House, 1964), p. 188, table.

There is no problem in determining the relationship of Harlan F. Stone's actions on the Supreme Court to the general expectations of Calvin Coolidge. However much Coolidge might have thought about the appointment, he could not have meant to place on the Court a justice who would join with Holmes and Brandeis to form a liberal bloc in opposition to the Court's majority in questions of economic regulation; who would constitute a similar bloc with Brandeis and Cardozo after Cardozo replaced Holmes; and would be so diligent a supporter of New Deal measures, both before and after the Court-reform fight, that Franklin Roosevelt would promote him to the position of Chief Justice, in 1941. Stone first advertised his liberal views on the constitutionality of economic regulation one year after his appointment to the Court in a case dealing with a state law which prohibited the use of cheap wool as a bedding material on the ground that it was unwholesome (*Weaver* v. *Palmer Brothers*, 1926). With Holmes and Brandeis, Stone dissented from the Court's invalidation of the law, and only rarely thereafter did he oppose national or state regulatory legislation.

Herbert Hoover's justices were Charles Evans Hughes, Owen J. Roberts, and Benjamin N. Cardozo. Hoover could not have thought Cardozo was in general agreement with him concerning the regulation of economic activity, for Cardozo, a Democrat, was known to be progressive on such questions and Hoover was not. Cardozo was selected because of his eminence as a legal scholar and because there was strong pressure from a closely divided Senate for his appointment. Hughes and Roberts seem more in the Hoover pattern: not only were they eminent in their profession, but both were highly successful corporation counsels and both were moderate Republicans. Until the Court crisis of early 1937, Hughes and Roberts assumed a moderate position on economic issues, adhering to neither of the blocs into which the Court was divided. Both men, along with Cardozo, helped uphold the constitutionality of state legislation fixing the price of milk (*Nebbia* v. *New York*, 1934) and protecting debtors from the loss of mortgaged properties (*Home Building & Loan Association* v. *Blaisdell*, 1935), and national government action reducing the gold content of the dollar (*Norman* v. *Baltimore & Ohio Railroad Company*, 1935); and both men, in opposition to Cardozo, held that the government could not regulate agricultural production (*United States* v. *Butler*, 1936) or labor relations in the coal industry (*Carter* v. *Carter Coal Company*, 1936). It is true that Hughes and Roberts swung to full acceptance of the New Deal, and its state counterparts, in 1937, and rarely took a position against the validity of economic regulation after that, but we should probably withhold the conclusion that the two justices departed from Hoover's general expectations of their behavior at the time he appointed them. In addition to the extraordinary circumstances in which the Court found itself, threatened as it was by Franklin Roosevelt's reform proposal, the economic activity of the government that came before the Court after 1936 was by-and-large more scrupulous of constitutional forms than was some of the legislation that the Court had invalidated up to that time. Placed in their position, can one be quite sure of what Hoover himself would have done?

Government regulation of corporate and personal wealth has not been a salient issue in Supreme Court litigation since Franklin Roosevelt's second term nor, in consequence, has it been a salient concern of Presidents in making Court appointments. By the time Harry Truman assumed office, the welfare state had been established. It is hard to say what sort of policy considerations Truman had in mind, if any, in his first two appointments, of Harold Burton (a Republican and former Senate colleague) in 1945 and Fred M. Vinson in 1946. At most, he probably hoped that they would generally support the actions of the welfare state, and perhaps he had the emerging issue of civil rights in mind, too. In his subsequent appointments, of Tom C. Clark and Sherman Minton, in 1949, Truman probably added another concern: judicial support for the Administration's security and anti-Communist programs. By these standards, it does not appear that any of Truman's four justices disappointed him. They were liberal in cases dealing with economic regulation and civil rights and conservative in those dealing with internal security. In the internal security cases decided in Truman's last year, neither Clark nor Minton —nor, for that matter, Vinson or, with one exception, Burton— failed to support the government's position, even though the Court as a whole was sharply divided. They helped constitute Court majorities in cases dealing with Congressional investigations into subversion (for example, *United States* v. *Bryan*, 1950), the requirement of non-Communist loyalty oaths by labor officials (*American Communications Association* v. *Douds*, 1950), advocacy of the overthrow of the government by force and violence (*Dennis* v. *United States*, 1951), and the deportation of persons for former Communist party membership (*Harisiades* v. *Schaughnessy*, 1952). The government's only defeat in a security case in this period involved the arbitrary listing of organizations as subversive for the purpose of determining public employment (*Joint Anti-Fascist Refugee Committee* v. *McGrath*, 1951, in which Burton opposed the government position and Clark did not participate).

Dwight Eisenhower indirectly communicated his feelings about the way his Supreme Court appointments turned out. The key is in what he said about his first appointment, Earl Warren, in his autobiography published in 1963. As we have already noted, Eisenhower stated that he appointed Warren only after he and Attorney General Herbert J. Brownell had satisfied themselves as to Warren's views through personal conversations with the California Governor. Eisenhower did not say that he came to regret the appointment, but a couple of pages later in the autobiography he did say that he subsequently told Brownell that he would thereafter appoint to the Court only persons who had served on a lower federal or a state supreme court. "My thought was that this criterion would ensure that there would then be available to us a record of the decisions for which the prospective candidate had been responsible. These would provide an inkling of his philosophy."[13]

---

[13] Dwight D. Eisenhower, *The White House Years: Mandate for Change, 1953–1956* (New York: New American Library, 1965), p. 287.

The inkling to his "philosophy" which Warren provided after his selection early marked him as a non-Eisenhower liberal in matters involving economic regulation and claims to personal freedom or rights. In cases decided during his first term when the Court was divided, Warren generally sided with the liberal position. These cases included decisions which set aside, as too severe a punishment, the permanent disbarment for trial misconduct of an attorney who had defended Communist party leaders against government prosecution (*Sacher* v. *United States*, 1954), reversed a draft conviction on the ground that the accused had been wrongfully denied exemption as a minister (*Dickinson* v. *United States*, 1953), and reversed a murder conviction on the ground that the obtained confession had been coerced (*Leyra* v. *Denno*, 1954).[14] Warren's liberalism on the bench only increased after that.

If Warren's performance on the Supreme Court was disappointing to Eisenhower, then that of William J. Brennan, named to the Court in 1956, was equally or, in view of the lesson Eisenhower hoped he had learned from the Warren appointment, more so, for Brennan and Warren have been closely aligned in the Court's controversial decisions. Eisenhower may have had some early doubts about John M. Harlan (appointed in 1955) also, for Harlan was associated with the libertarian justices in a spate of end-of-term decisions in June, 1957. These decisions included ones which placed restrictions on investigations into communism by Congressional committees (*Watkins* v. *United States*), as well as those at the state level (*Sweezy* v. *New Hampshire*); overruled a trial judge's refusal to examine FBI files in a case involving a labor official convicted of falsely subscribing to a non-Communist oath required by federal law (*Jencks* v. *United States*); and reversed the conviction of Communist officials accused of conspiring to

[14] In the non-unanimous decisions of the Court in the 1953–1954 terms, Warren ranked third (after Black and Douglas) among the eight justices who participated in both terms in cases dealing with economic matters, and he ranked fourth (after Douglas, Black, and Frankfurter) in cases in which, broadly speaking, claims of personal freedom and rights were raised. Based on data in Glendon Schubert, *The Judicial Mind* (Evanston, Ill.: Northwestern University Press, 1965), pp. 107–108 and 133–134.

overthrow the government (*Yates* v. *United States*). "Possibly in their latest decisions," the President had been provoked to remark, "there are some that each of us has very great trouble understanding."[15]

But Harlan soon moved from this limited association with Warren and Brennan to a position more in keeping with Eisenhower's moderate Republicanism; and Charles E. Whittaker and Potter Stewart, Eisenhower's last appointees to the Court, were usually joined with him there, particularly in cases dealing with internal security and the rights of criminal defendants. Thus Harlan, Whittaker, and Stewart were all on the side of authority, and Warren and Brennan were opposed to them, in cases dealing with legislative investigations into Communism (for example, *Barenblatt* v. *United States*, 1959, and *Wilkinson* v. *United States*, 1961), into the registration of the Communist party as a subversive organization (*Communist Party* v. *Subversive Activities Control Board*, 1961), and, with Whittaker no longer a member of the Court, into an accused person's right to counsel prior to indictment (*Escobedo* v. *Illinois*, 1964). If Stewart has been, overall, somewhat more liberal than Harlan and Whittaker, he has still remained within the Eisenhower fold.

With the Kennedy and Johnson appointments we conclude our inquiry into the relation between Presidential expectation and the judicial performance of Supreme Court justices. (Nixon's justices had not, at this writing, sat long enough on the Court to be evaluated.) Neither President indicated why he chose the men he did for the Court, but both, we may assume, wanted justices who shared their general political views, particularly in the salient areas of civil rights and personal freedom. Of their four justices, only Byron R. White may be said not to be in his appointer's image, although we had in mid-1970 a record of only three terms for evaluating Thurgood Marshall. Our evaluation of White must be tentative. Certainly he has been substantially less solicitous of claims raised on

[15] Cited in Walter F. Murphy, *Congress and the Court* (Chicago: University of Chicago Press, Phoenix Books, 1962), p. 117.

behalf of criminal defendants and personal liberty than has Arthur J. Goldberg who, like White, was appointed by Kennedy, and much less so than was Abe Fortas, appointed by Johnson, or the long-standing libertarian bloc of Douglas, Black, Warren, and Brennan. White supported the governmental position in cases involving a criminal suspect's pre-indictment right to counsel (*Escobedo* v. *Illinois*, 1964), loyalty oaths for teachers (*Keyishian* v. *Board of Regents*, 1967), and the deprivation of citizenship for participation in foreign elections (*Afroyim* v. *Rusk*, 1967), in none of which, incidentally, was he on the prevailing side. But White has been far from reactionary in cases involving government authority,[16] and one may question how far President Kennedy wanted him to be libertarian in such matters—especially where the authority involved was that of the national government. Moreover, he seems closely to have reflected the Kennedy administration's position in cases concerning reapportionment (for example, *Wesberry* v. *Sanders* and *Reynolds* v. *Sims*, 1964), civil rights (*Heart of Atlanta Motel* v. *United States* and *Katzenbach* v. *McClung*, 1964), and separation of church and state (*School District of Abington Township* v. *Schempp*, 1963). On the other hand, White joined Harlan and Black in dissenting from a series of important decisions in 1964 dealing with Negro challenges to acts of private discrimination in lunch counters and other places, in all of which President Kennedy had approved the government's entry as *amicus curiae* on the side of the challengers (for example, *Griffin* v. *Maryland* and *Barr* v. *City of Columbia*).

The conclusion of our survey is that about three-fourths of those justices for whom an evaluation could be made conformed to the expectations of the Presidents who appointed them to the Supreme Court. This estimate must be approximate, for we have had to make inferences from scattered and frequently indirect evidence about a President's interest in the views held by judicial candidates on questions in which he would be

---

[16] Schubert, *The Judicial Mind*, pp. 111–112, provides data which show White as having supported claims based on personal freedom, civil equality, criminal rights, and the like (what Schubert calls "civil liberties") twenty-eight out of fifty-one times in the (combined) 1961 and 1962 terms of the Court.

interested; and we have had to make judgments as to whether justices lived up to the imputed purposes for which they were chosen. We have, to be sure, supported our assumptions and judgments with evidence and arguments. We directed our attention to the major purposes of appointments and sought not to tax Presidents with judicial behavior which they could not reasonably have taken into account at the time of appointment. We did not, for example, ask whether Lincoln's justices conformed to his position on the Negro question for the sufficient reason that the constitutional provisions under which the question was primarily decided were not in existence when Lincoln chose them for the Court. Nor did we ask what Theodore Roosevelt would have thought about Holmes's tolerance for seditious speech, although we might easily guess, because there is no evidence that when he appointed Holmes Roosevelt had in mind the speech problems that made their way to the Court after the First World War and during the 1920s.

We cannot be sure that we have evaluated every justice correctly, but we can be quite firm in our general conclusion that about one justice in four whose performance could be evaluated did not conform to the expectations of his appointer in important matters that came before the Supreme Court. If anything, we may have understated the extent of judicial deviation, for the burden was placed upon showing that the justices did not conform to expectations. Our conclusion is an important one in that it indicates limitations upon the ability of Presidents to influence the policies of the Court through appointments and assures us, retrospectively at least, of a certain, but crucial, measure of judicial independence from Presidential attempts to bring the Court closely into line with the executive branch of the government. Justice Frankfurter is wrong in believing that "the expectation of Presidents regarding the outlook of their appointees on matters of great moment that may come before the Court tell next to nothing about how the justices will actually decide cases,"[17] but so are those who believe

[17] Felix Frankfurter, "The Supreme Court in the Mirror of Justices," *University of Pennsylvania Law Review*, **105** (April, 1957), 796.

that Presidents have with only a few exceptions obtained the justices they have wanted.[18]

PARTISAN AND PERSONAL INFLUENCES ON DECISIONS

Because the Supreme Court's decisions on important constitutional questions have such far-reaching consequences, Presidents cannot, in selecting the men who will, under permanent tenure, be making these decisions, be blind to the views they hold on basic issues that may come before the Court. To assure themselves that the proper persons will be appointed, Presidents typically look to their own political party for candidates, and often to persons within their own circle of personal or political friends. There is nothing shocking in the fact that Presidents generally appoint persons they believe share, by-and-large, their own views on important constitutional questions. Nor is it surprising that most justices, most of the time, live up to Presidential expectations. Mature men are usually quite settled in their views.

Given these circumstances, one is tempted to ask whether either partisan attachment or a sense of personal obligation to an appointing President does not sometimes operate to influence the behavior of Supreme Court justices. Indeed, how often has either of these non-judicial influences in fact been present in the decisions of the Court? Obviously this is a difficult question, but we can offer a partial answer to it and, in doing so, illumine the problem in executive–judicial relations that gives rise to it. Let us take up each influence in turn.

As we have seen, not only have most Supreme Court justices been taken from the same party as the Presidents who selected them, but most were engaged in partisan politics at

[18] John P. Frank, "The Appointment of Supreme Court Justices: Prestige, Principles, and Politics," *Wisconsin Law Review* (July, 1941), p. 488; Daniel S. McHargue, *Appointments to the Supreme Court of the United States: The Factors That Have Affected Appointments, 1789–1932* (Doctoral dissertation, Political Science Department, University of California at Los Angeles, 1949), p. 630.

some time in their pre-Court careers. In a number of cases, partisan feeling has accompanied them to the Court. Some have conducted what one historian has called "underground campaigns" to obtain Presidential nominations.[19] Of these, excluding Charles Evans Hughes, who received the Republican nomination in 1916 unsolicited, only David Davis succeeded, in 1872, and then for only a minor party (although he did get sent to the Senate by the Democratic legislature of Illinois in 1877). The problem of political ambitions on the Court of the 1940s was serious enough for the American Bar Association, abetted by former Justice Owen J. Roberts, to urge the adoption of a constitutional amendment which would render Supreme Court justices ineligible for the Presidency and Vice Presidency for a period of five years after their service on the supreme bench. Some justices have shown partisan feeling by seeking to resign their offices when Presidents of their own party were in power. (Nathaniel Clifford, a Democrat, resolved to hold on to his position after the Republican Grant gained office in 1873, but he was outlasted by Republican success and finally relinquished it through death in 1881.) Probably most justices have, like their fellow citizens, taken satisfaction in the Presidential victories of their party, but some have been quite carried away by partisanship—as, for example, the Democratic Roger B. Taney, when he wrote of James K. Polk's election in 1844 that "We have passed through no contest for the Presidency more important than the one just over, nor have I seen any one before in which so many dangerous influences were combined together as were united in support of [Polk's Whig opponent] Mr. Clay";[20] or, in more recent times, Felix Frankfurter, when he called Wendell Willkie, after the 1940 election, "a bad man—being a man with appetites and without convictions—who needs not only to be defeated but to be destroyed."[21]

It is evident that partisan fires do continue to glow, if for the most part subduedly, in judicial breasts, and are rekindled

[19] Charles A. Beard, *The Republic: Conversations on Fundamentals* (New York: Viking Press, 1943), p. 233.

[20] Carl B. Swisher, *Roger B. Taney* (New York: Macmillan, 1935) ,p. 435.

[21] *Roosevelt and Frankfurter*, p. 551.

under special circumstances. It is not unreasonable to assume that these fires sometimes influence the actions of justices and, in important cases, that the influence has often been in the direction of the expectations of appointing Presidents. We are not referring to those partisan feelings that led justices to associate with one political party or the other in their pre-Court days or influenced their views on public questions then, but rather those that may be allowed to guide a justice's judgment of a case.

How often has partisan feeling led to partisan justice on the Supreme Court? This is hard to say. It seems clearly to have been present in the *Dred Scott case*, at least in the position that the majority took in opening United States territories to slavery. Lincoln certainly believed so when he charged "Stephen [A. Douglas] and Franklin [Pierce] and Roger [B. Taney] and James [Buchanan]," all Democrats, with having "all worked upon a common plan or draft" to nationalize slavery, and he emphasized that the *Dred Scott decision*, which was Taney's contribution to the plan, had been rendered by a Court all, or nearly all, of whose members were Democrats.[22] And we now know that President-elect Buchanan had a conduit to the Court in Justice Catron. Catron kept Buchanan fully informed as to what was happening in the *Dred Scott case*, told him how he could make political capital from it in his inaugural address (to be given prior to the announcement of the decision), and urged him to get Justice Grier to go the full way with his Democratic colleagues, all of which advice Buchanan followed.[23] Theodore Roosevelt also believed that partisanship entered into judicial decisions, but, in what he regarded as the "higher" sense, properly so. He thought that a justice should keep constantly in mind "his relations with his fellow statesmen who in other branches of the government are striving in cooperation with

---

[22] Lincoln first made the charge in his Springfield speech, June 16, 1858, accepting the Republican nomination for United States senator, and repeated it throughout his subsequent debates with Douglas. The quoted remarks are found in his *Complete Works*, ed. by John G. Nicolay and John Hay (New York: Lamb Publ. Co., 1894), Vol. III, p. 10; and the reference to the partisan composition of the Court, from the Speech at Freeport, August 27, 1858, is at p. 286.

[23] Swisher, *Taney*, pp. 496–502.

him to advance the ends of government." What Roosevelt had
particularly in mind was a series of cases dealing with the
application of the Constitution to territories gained through the
Spanish–American War (the most significant of which were
DeLima v. *Bidwell, Dooley* v. *United States,* and *Downes* v. *Bidwell,*
all 1901). He praised the Court's majority who had, "although
without satisfactory unanimity, upheld the policies of President
McKinley and the Republican party in Congress," while the
minority "stood for . . . reactionary folly. . . ."[24] Roosevelt's im-
putation of partisan motivation in the cases is less than persuasive. There is no evidence that the justices were so
motivated; and not only did the Court's five-member majority
include one Democrat, but its four-member minority contained
three Republicans. But then Roosevelt was not one to allow
party affiliation to stand in the way of partisanship.

The *Dred Scott decision* apart, it is more than a little difficult
to cite instances where members of the Supreme Court have
acted from clearly partisan motives. There is the suspicion that
such motives were in play in decisions which found the justices
sharply divided along party lines. Partisan divisions upon the
Court appear to have occurred most often, in major cases, in
decisions relating to the Civil War and its direct consequences.
Several arose from wartime actions,[25] and others from Reconstruction acts directed against those who had participated in
the rebellion[26] or aimed at protecting civil rights, especially of

---

[24] *Roosevelt–Lodge Correspondence,* Vol. I, p. 518.

[25] In *The Prize Cases,* 2 Black 635 (1863), the Court's three Republicans held that
    Lincoln had authority to order a blockade of Southern ports, while its five
    Democrats divided on the question, with two of them (one a Lincoln ap-
    pointee) siding with the Republicans. In *Ex parte Milligan,* 4 Wall. 2 (1866),
    the lines were less closely drawn, but still four Democrats and one Republican
    (Davis, who was to change parties) ruled that neither the President nor
    Congress could have civilians tried by military tribunals where the civil
    courts were functioning, while three Republicans and one Democrat would
    have granted such authority to Congress. Finally, in the *Legal Tender Cases—
    Hepburn* v. *Griswold,* 8 Wall. 603 (1870), and *Knox* v. *Lee,* 12 Wall. 457 (1871)
    —the Court's three Democrats, abetted by Chase, first outvoted three
    Republicans (*Hepburn*) and then were outvoted (*Knox*) when President Grant
    added two Republicans to its membership.

[26] In *Cummings* v. *Missouri,* 4 Wall. 277 (1867) and *Ex parte Garland,* 4 Wall. 333
    (1867), the Court's five Democrats and four Republicans divided cleanly. In
    the first, the Court voided a state constitutional provision requiring as a

the freedmen.[27] If partisanship influenced the judgments of at least some of the justices in these and other cases when the Court was sharply split along party lines—and we do not know that it did—we should keep in mind that in the great majority of its significant decisions the Court has not been so divided. On the other hand, it seems quite likely that partisanship has influenced the judgments of justices in some cases which do not bear the tell-tale evidence of sharp party cleavage.

The second non-judicial influence we wish to examine is the sense of personal obligation that may be involved in appointments. All justices are susceptible to this influence. "They are appointed by the President," as Charles Pinckney observed in a Senate debate in 1800, "and if the moment after they receive their commissions, they were really so independent as to be completely out of his reach—that no hope of additional favor, no attempt to caress could be reasonably expected to influence their opinions, yet it is impossible for them ever to forget from whom they have received their present elevation."[28] We do not know how many justices have in fact been influenced in their decisions by the recollection of their benefactor. We do know that justices have on a number of occasions reached decisions which directly repudiated the actions of the Presidents who appointed them. We have in mind, for example, Justice William Johnson's decision, while on circuit duty in South Carolina, that the embargo instructions issued by Jefferson to his port collectors were invalid (*Ex parte Gilchrist*, 1807).[29] There

precondition to pursuing a calling an oath that a person had not supported the Confederate cause, and in the second it voided a federal law requiring the same thing of attorneys practicing before federal courts.

[27] *Strauder* v. *West Virginia*, 100 U.S. 303 (1880) and *Ex parte Virginia*, 100 U.S. 339 (1880) deal with the exclusion of Negroes from jury service in state courts, and *Ex parte Siebold*, 100 U.S. 371 (1880) with ballot-stuffing in federal elections. The Court's two Democrats dissented from decisions sustaining the application of civil rights legislation.

[28] *History of Congress*, March 5, 1800, p. 101. But note *Federalist 51* (Alexander Hamilton, James Madison, and John Jay, *The Federalist*, ed. by Max Beloff [Oxford: Basil Blackwell, 1948], p. 264): "The permanent tenure by which the appointments are held in the [judiciary], must soon destroy all sense of dependence on the authority conferring them."

[29] That decision apparently had the result of severing contact between the two men for well over a decade. See Donald G. Morgan, *Justice William Johnson: The*

is also the position taken by all five of Lincoln's justices (one year after his death) that Lincoln lacked authority to establish military tribunals for the trial of civilians (*Ex parte Milligan*, 1866). And that taken by two of Truman's appointees (two took a contrary position) that their President's action imposing government control upon a strike-threatened steel industry during the Korean War was authorized neither by the Constitution nor by statute (*Youngstown Sheet & Tube Company* v. *Sawyer*, 1952). And, finally, the unanimity among all five of Eisenhower's Supreme Court members that Eisenhower had acted improperly in removing a War Claims Commissioner from office (*Wiener* v. *United States*, 1958).[30]

The susceptibility of justices to Presidential influence appears to be greater for justices who are personal or political friends of appointing Presidents than for those who are not. The appointment of friends to public office has the mark of a favor, while that of strangers seems to be based on the recognition of merit; and favors rendered to friends are debts to be discharged. Perhaps this is what Harold L. Ickes had in mind when he assured Franklin Roosevelt that "if Frankfurter were named [to the Supreme Court], it [the Court] would be the President's long years after he had retired from office"; and when he said of himself that, if Roosevelt appointed him, "I believe he would trust my loyalty and good sense."[31]

We earlier (in Chapter 4) made the estimate that Presidents have personally known about three-fifths of the persons they have selected for the Supreme Court. Many of the personally known candidates seem to have been personal or political friends as well, and thus the question of judicial objectivity in regard to the Presidency has arisen in a more acute form in a large portion of the appointments to the Court. The question was raised directly with one pre-appointment friend of a

First Dissenter (Columbia: University of South Carolina Press, 1954), pp. 73–74.

[30] Warren, *Supreme Court in U.S. History*, Vol. I, pp. 21–22, discusses a number of instances in which justices opposed the actions of Presidents who appointed them.

[31] Ickes, *Secret Diary*, Vol. II, pp. 551, 486.

President, Abe Fortas, by a member of the Senate Judiciary
Committee when Fortas's nomination as associate justice was
being considered by the Senate in 1965. "Is there anything in
your relationship with the President," Fortas was asked, "that
would militate in any way against your being able to sit on that
bench and pass judgment on cases that come along and thus
affect your ability to function in the true judicial fashion and
tradition?" Fortas acknowledged the problem of Presidential
influence over a justice who had been a close associate in his
reply that his activity as a Presidential adviser had been "vastly
exaggerated."[32] And President Truman seemed to answer the
question when he referred to his old friend Fred M. Vinson,
whom he had made Chief Justice, as "a devoted and undemon-
strative patriot who could also consistently practice personal and
party loyalty."[33]

Speaking generally, the only offices superior to that of a
Supreme Court justice are the Presidency, the Vice Presidency,
and, of course, the chief justiceship. Thus if a President were to
hold the "hope of additional favor"—to use Pinckney's term—
before a justice, it would most likely be to one of these places. It
appears that the dangling of such Presidential favors before the
eyes of justices has been, at the most, rare. Franklin Roosevelt
let it be known that William O. Douglas was acceptable to him
as a Vice-Presidential running-mate in 1944 (one source close
to the President thought Douglas was his first choice), and

---

[32] United States Senate, Committee on the Judiciary, *Nomination of Abe Fortas*,
Hearings, August 5, 1965, 89th Congress, 1st Session, 1965, p. 50. Contrast
Fortas's disavowal with what Theodore H. White, in *The Making of the
President, 1964* (New York: Atheneum, 1965) says of some of the assistance
which Johnson got from "his old friend and companion of the New Deal"
(p. 46) during Johnson's initial year in office: Fortas helped prepare Johnson's first message to Congress following President Kennedy's assassination
(*ibid.*); was one of only three men on the President's 1964 election campaign
staff whom the President could trust with his "inner ruminative thinking"
(p. 262); was one of the (same three) persons consulted by Johnson when a
special White House assistant was arrested on a morals charge (p. 349);
and tried to get the Washington, D.C., papers not to print the story of the
scandal (p. 368) and, when this failed, went to the assistant, at the President's
request, in order to obtain his resignation before the story was published
(p. 369).

[33] Harry S. Truman, *Memoirs: Years of Trial and Hope* (Garden City, N.Y.: Doubleday, 1956), Vol. II, p. 490.

Truman told Chief Justice Vinson as early as the summer of 1950 that he wanted Vinson to be his successor in the Presidency.[34] But we do not know how long Douglas had the possibility of the Vice Presidency held before him, and we do know that Vinson declined Truman's efforts to have him seek the Presidential nomination. Two justices have been raised to the office of Chief Justice: Edward D. White, in 1910, and Harlan F. Stone, in 1941. Although both men had supported the positions of the Presidents who promoted them, in neither case is there evidence that the promotion had come as a promised reward.[35] One justice, at least, did have the chief justiceship held out to him. When he went on the Supreme Court in 1941, Robert H. Jackson was ambitious to fill the Chief Justice vacancy, and Roosevelt, in giving it to Stone, told Jackson that he would like to move Jackson to that post when Stone, then 68, retired.[36] Jackson's record of opposing the government in a number of wartime cases furnishes proof that the attraction of higher office did not curb his exercise of independent judgment.

If very few Presidents have held allurements before the men they have placed on the Supreme Court, not a few have maintained cordial relations with them. As we have noted elsewhere, such relations appear to be confined to Presidents and justices who knew each other personally at the time of appointment. We don't know how many justices might have felt in their social relations with Presidents what Pinckney, in our quoted statement, referred to as a Presidential "caress," but a number of them appear to have been rendered susceptible to Presidential influence through their contacts. Carried beyond a certain point, personal relations between a justice and a President cannot help but keep warm, and strengthen the memory

[34] Harold L. Ickes, *Secret Diary* (New York: Simon and Schuster, 1954), Vol. III, p. 229; Truman, *Memoirs: Years of Trial and Hope*, Vol. II, p. 490.

[35] In *Our Chief Magistrate and His Powers*, pp. 102–103, however, Taft intimated that he chose White because of his opinion in a case of special importance to Taft. According to his biographer, Alpheus T. Mason, *Harlan Fiske Stone: Pillar of the Law* (New York: Viking Press, 1956), pp. 277–283, Stone had been regarded, and regarded himself, as a candidate for the chief justiceship at the time Hughes got the office in 1930.

[36] Eugene C. Gerhart, *America's Advocate: Robert H. Jackson* (Indianapolis: Bobbs-Merrill, 1958), p. 231.

of the benefaction bestowed by appointment, and indeed they may entangle the justice in a web of new obligations. This is particularly true when, as has tended to happen, close social relations assume a political cast and justices become political confidants of Presidents. Even if a justice can preserve his impartiality under such circumstances, he cannot, if the fact becomes known, preserve either his or the Court's reputation for impartiality.

The following justices seem to have been at least fairly active political advisers in this century to the Presidents who appointed them to the Supreme Court: Louis D. Brandeis, Felix Frankfurter, James F. Byrnes, Fred M. Vinson, Abe Fortas, and perhaps William O. Douglas. As with all Presidential advisers, these men sometimes gave their assistance directly to their Presidents and sometimes through Presidential subordinates. All of them had been close political associates of their Presidents before going on the Court, and all shared the general political perspective of their appointers. Of course, minds do not necessarily run in identical grooves, and the Supreme Court and the Presidency tend to give their occupants somewhat varying perspectives on public issues which enter the judicial process. And yet none of the justices we have named deviated from the positions of their appointers on any important judicial issue while their appointing Presidents were alive. We do not maintain that the close association of justices with the executive branch has ever necessarily impaired judicial impartiality, but it must at times have placed strains upon it. Could adviser–justices separate one role from the other? Could they avoid feeling a sense of obligation to those who not only elevated them to the Court but depended upon them for help after their appointments? Could they face with equanimity the prospect of tension in their liaison with the President, or perhaps the loss of Presidential favor, should they reach a decision contrary to the views of their benefactors? We doubt it.

Fortunately, not many justices have penetrated deeply into the court of advisers that surrounds Presidents, although we should keep in mind that other justices may have had their judicial impartiality affected by less intense relations with the executive branch. Fortunately, too, as we noted in Chapter 3, both justices and Presidents have usually been conscious of the proprieties in their liaisons. Finally, relations between Presidents and their advisers seem inevitably to weaken after appointment to the Court, because of judicial proprieties or demands of the Court, or both. Becoming a member of the Supreme Court has seemed to loosen the bonds between Presidents and their advisers on the supreme bench.

THE LIMITS OF PRESIDENTIAL INFLUENCE

If our estimate is correct, one justice in four has turned out to be quite different from what his appointer wanted. In addition, other justices have failed to live up to expectations in particular cases. Why have these discrepancies between Presidential expectation and judicial performance occurred as often as they have? This is the most interesting question arising from our examination of judicial voting records.

One obvious answer is that some Presidents think that their judicial candidates hold different views than they actually do. This happens for several reasons, the most common of which is that these Presidents insufficiently probe the doctrinal positions of persons they appoint to the Court, relying heavily instead upon party affiliation or other indicators of views. Other Presidents assume that they know how a man would act generally from their knowledge of his position on certain matters. President Wilson, for example, assumed that James C. McReynolds would be a liberal generally because he was a liberal in anti-trust policy. It is, of course, always difficult to comprehend the full range of another man's mind, even if he is a friend or has had a substantial public career. How much more difficult it must be when a President appoints someone from private life or someone who is not known personally to him or to a trusted adviser. There are, furthermore, limits set by propriety as to how far a President may go in probing into the views of his candidates, and it is ironic that two Presidents who appear to have probed quite far, Theodore Roosevelt and Dwight D. Eisenhower, both should have expressed disappointment in the men they subjected to scrutiny.

In the second place, Presidents may fail in their quest for doctrinally compatible justices because men's minds sometimes change, even in mature adulthood. Change of mind seems to have happened, for instance, to several of the Republican justices who came under Marshall's influence. Or consider Chief Justice Salmon P. Chase's reason for invalidating the legal-tender policy he had supported as Secretary of the Treasury: "Not a few who [during the Civil War] insisted upon [the] necessity [of making government notes legal tender], or acquiesced in that view, have, since the return of peace, and under the influence of calmer time, reconsidered their conclusions, and now concur in those which we have just announced."[37] A third reason for Presidential failure is that the actions of some Presidents have been influenced largely by other considerations. In appointing John McLean to the Court, for example, Jackson was anxious to get a troublesome person out of his Cabinet. And in appointing Edward D. White, Cleveland was anxious to find someone whom the Senate would approve (after having had his first two nominations rejected by it).

Finally, Presidents have missed their mark in Supreme Court appointments because of what we may call the effect of the judicial obligation. The obligation, simply put, requires justices to decide cases in accordance with the Constitution and laws, not in accordance with views not supported by such sources or by passion or interest. Judges are not the only public officials who take an oath to support the Constitution, but, as John Marshall has noted, the oath "applies in an especial manner to their conduct,"[38] for it is peculiarly a judicial responsibility to say what the law is. If selected with care, justices should, by ability, by training, and by temperament, be better able to perform this responsibility than most other persons in public life. In addition, the Constitution frees them, as it

---

[37] *Hepburn* v. *Griswold*, at 625–626.
[38] *Marbury* v. *Madison*, 1 Cranch 137 (1803), at 180.

does not the President and Congress, from the influences of
ambition and interest, in the performance of their obligation. It
gives them high honor, high responsibility, and guaranteed
tenure and salary, so that they need neither seek higher office
nor worry about retaining the one they have. These conditions,
at once emancipating and greatly demanding, result in judicial
behavior which may not conform either to Presidential expectations or to the views that the justices expressed before joining the
Court.

Justice Robert H. Jackson furnishes an excellent example
of what we are discussing. As Franklin Roosevelt's Attorney
General in 1941, Jackson justified his superior's seizure, without
statutory authorization, of a strike-bound aircraft plant while
the United States was still technically at peace. The seizure was
not tested in the courts. In 1952, as a Supreme Court justice, he
was required to determine the legality of President Truman's
seizure, without authorizing legislation, of steel companies
threatened by a strike while the United States was, again, still
technically at peace. (In both cases, the country was actually
engaged in limited but undeclared hostilities.) Government
counsel in the *Steel Seizure case* recalled to Jackson his earlier
position of justification, and Jackson, in an opinion which
rejected Truman's action, replied: "A judge cannot accept
self-serving press statements of the attorney for one of the
interested parties [in the aircraft-plant seizure] as authority in
answering a constitutional question, even if the advocate was
himself"; and, changing to the personal pronoun: "I should not
bind present judicial judgment by earlier partisan advocacy."[39]
In this statement Jackson clearly demonstrated the effect that
the judicial obligation can have on a justice, and the contrast
between the necessities of political partisanship and the opportunities of judicial independence.

What can a President do to a justice who fails him? In
ordinary times, little—unless the justice has in some way become
obligated to or dependent upon him beyond the minimal

[39] Concurring, *Youngstown Sheet and Tube Company* v. *Sawyer*, 343 U.S. 579 (1952), at
647 n. and 649 n.

feeling of gratitude that may accompany an appointment. The President may threaten to exclude a justice from his social calendar, as Theodore Roosevelt threatened to do in reaction to Holmes's decision in the *Northern Securities Anti-Trust case*, but this was in Holmes's estimation a laughable threat. But if a justice seeks favors which the President alone can give, or derives strong satisfaction from moving within the radiance of the Presidency, or in other ways becomes closely connected with the President, that justice's judicial objectivity and independence are impaired. It is then that he fails in his judicial obligation.

6

The Executive in Court

LAWYER FOR THE EXECUTIVE BRANCH

In examining the role of the executive branch as litigant in the Supreme Court, our attention should be set not upon the President, for he is not directly involved in this aspect of the executive–judicial relationship, but upon the lawyer for the executive in the Supreme Court: the Solicitor General. The Solicitor General is appointed by the President with the consent of the Senate. The President usually takes a substantial interest in the person selected for the position; he may even do his own selecting, as Lyndon B. Johnson did in choosing Thurgood Marshall in 1965. More importantly, the Solicitor General usually decides which judicial decisions lost by the executive branch will be appealed to the federal courts of appeal and to the Supreme Court, and he generally defends the government against appeals from lower court decisions it has won. In addition, he decides whether the executive, as *amicus curiae*, will enter Supreme Court cases in which it is not a party, in order to inform the Court how it thinks other people's disputes should be settled, and he is called upon to give his permission to those who wish to act as *amicus curiae* in cases in which the government is a party. The only parts of the executive branch which do not come under the full control of the Solicitor General are the regulatory agencies, but they do not come under the full control of the President, either.

The Solicitor General and his staff serve the President specifically by coordinating the litigation of the executive branch at the levels of the courts of appeals, but especially in the Supreme Court, and they serve both him and the executive branch generally by directing, when they do not conduct, the government's campaigns in the Supreme Court. The Solicitor General also serves the Court itself, for the justices depend upon him to screen out undeserving litigation and to furnish them with an agenda of those government cases that deserve serious consideration. As we shall see, the Supreme Court has come to expect even more from the Solicitor General's Office, but it is enough now to say that the Solicitor General has succeeded in linking his services to both the executive and judicial branches and, as a consequence, in placing himself in the difficult, if challenging, position of trying to serve two masters.

The Solicitor General's role in the executive branch is not unique. The Director of the Budget, too, performs services which draw him into relationships with the President, the executive agencies, and another branch of government—in this instance Congress. The Budget Director has general charge of requests by executive agencies for appropriations and legislation. He serves the President by deciding which requests for legislation will be incorporated into the legislative program which the President submits to Congress or which will otherwise be given Presidential approval, and the levels at which appropriations requests will be incorporated into the budget that the President submits. The executive agencies are aided in their dealings with Congress by having their budgetary and legislative proposals given the Presidential imprimatur, and

Congress is aided by having both a draft budget to use as a basis for its deliberations and an annotated guide to those bills, among the many hundreds affecting the executive branch which are introduced each year, that the President thinks ought to be given serious consideration.

There are some important differences in the ways in which the Solicitor General and the Budget Director perform their services. In general, the Budget Director enjoys a much closer relationship to the President than does the Solicitor General. His appointment lies exclusively with the chief executive. Whereas the Bureau of the Budget is part of the Executive Office of the President (until 1939 it had been a unit of the Treasury Department), the Office of the Solicitor General is within the Justice Department, and its leading officials see a good deal more of the President and of officials in the Presidency who speak directly for him. In about 95 per cent of the government's adjudication connected with the Supreme Court, the Solicitor General reaches his decisions without outside consultation. In the other cases he will consult with the Attorney General, and in perhaps three or four cases a year he and the Attorney General will find it necessary to clear matters with the White House.[1] In contrast, the Budget Director and his staff must clear scores of matters with the White House, although it needs to be added that the executive branch conducts a great deal more business with Congress than it does with the Supreme Court. Symbolic of the autonomy possessed by the Solicitor General, although rarely executed, is his refusal to participate in a government case before the Court when he feels, in opposition to his superiors, that the government's position is wrong. It is hard to conceive of the Budget Director's acting in this way and, in fact, he willingly allows the President and his assistants to shape Bureau policy in matters of legislation and budget.

If the Solicitor General is freer of Presidential control than is the Budget Director, the executive agencies are considerably

[1] Interview with Mr. Ralph S. Spritzer, then First Assistant to the Solicitor General, March 7, 1967.

less free of his control than they are of that of the Budget
Bureau. With few exceptions, the Solicitor General determines
whether the executive branch appeals cases to the Supreme
Court. Only the Interstate Commerce, Federal Communications, Federal Maritime, and Atomic Energy Commissions,
and, in certain kinds of cases, the Department of Agriculture,
have the statutory authority to decide for themselves whether
lower-court defeats should be appealed, and only the Interstate
Commerce Commission has made more than rare use of its
authority. The Commerce Commission, it may be added, has
serious trouble getting into the Court when it goes there without
the support of the Solicitor General. The executive agencies, on
the other hand, may take their requests for legislation to
Congress when denied the Budget Bureau's stamp of approval,
and one of them—the Interstate Commerce Commission—at no
discernible disadvantage, even refuses to proffer its legislative
business to the Bureau for inspection. The Budget Bureau has
its greatest influence over the agencies in the presentation of
appropriations requests to Congress, for these requests can be
presented only in the amounts approved by it (and by the
President), but the agencies can, and not infrequently do,
get restored sums which the Bureau has decreased or eliminated.

   The Solicitor General's control over executive litigation
extends to the conduct of cases in the Supreme Court. His
Office not only authorizes all litigation in the Court, with the
exceptions noted, but sets down the position the government
will take and frequently writes or substantially revises the
briefs. And in about half of all cases involving executive agencies,
whether carried to the Court by the government or by opposing
parties, the Solicitor General or members of his staff present the
government's argument. By way of contrast, the Budget Bureau has a very minor part to play in the conduct of executive
business with Congress. Its officers will make the general case
for the President's budget, answer Congressional requests for
comments on legislation, and coordinate the written comments
of executive agencies, but the active prosecution of executive

interests in the legislative process is conducted by the agencies themselves and by the White House staff.

Finally, in the point of differences, the Solicitor General enjoys a relationship with the Supreme Court which the Budget Director does not with Congress. It is true that these two agencies both assist their non-executive colleagues in the government by sifting through the executive business submitted to them and in providing an agenda and priorities for judicial and legislative action. But the Budget Director is not trusted by Congress as the Solicitor General is by the Supreme Court, despite the fact that his agency was intended by law to serve the budgetary needs of the legislative branch. The reason is clear: The Budget Bureau operates within the Executive Office of the President and in close and subordinate relationship to the Presidency, whereas the Solicitor General's Office operates for the most part in seeming isolation even of the Justice Department. It thus assures the Supreme Court of its independence and impartiality by refusing to appeal to the Court most cases which the executive branch has lost in lower federal courts and by occasionally confessing to the Court that the executive branch did not deserve certain victories it attained in these courts. To put the difference between the Budget Director and the Solicitor General in legal terms, the Budget Director is viewed by Congress as acting *ex parte* President, and the Solicitor General tends to be viewed by the Supreme Court as acting *amicus curiae*.

The position of Solicitor General was established when the Department of Justice was, in 1870. Congress's plan to centralize all legal activities within the new Department was only partly successful (legal counsel operating throughout the government, for example, managed to keep their agency attachments), but Congress did succeed in giving the Department control of nearly all executive litigation before the Supreme Court. This control has never been seriously weakened, despite the subsequent rise of the independent regulatory commissions and of other agencies engaged in formal administrative adjudication. The Justice Department would, naturally, be opposed to a decentralization of control, but the Supreme Court, too, strongly desires to have a single voice speak for the government.[2] Most of the some three dozen solicitors-general who have filled the office since its creation have been distinguished in their professions, and several went on to higher public honor: William Howard Taft to the Presidency and the Supreme Court; John W. Davis to the Democratic nomination for the Presidency; and Stanley Reed, Robert H. Jackson, and Thurgood Marshall to the Supreme Court.[3]

The Solicitor General is assisted by a staff of lawyers which in 1970 numbered only ten. We have already indicated the scope and importance of the work which this small group does. We shall now examine that work in some detail: in controlling executive litigation, in getting into the Supreme Court, and in winning Court cases. Finally, we shall offer some reasons why the government is as successful as it is in Supreme Court litigation.

CONTROL OF EXECUTIVE LITIGATION

The United States is involved in a great and constantly growing number of cases handled by the federal courts. It is now a party to about 6,000 cases tried in the district courts (about two-thirds of all trials) and in about 2,500 cases decided in the courts of appeals (about half the total).[4] This litigation could, in theory, all end up in the Supreme Court, but very little of it does. In 1968 the government was a party to only

[2] See Carl B. Swisher, "Federal Organization of Legal Functions," *American Political Science Review*, **33** (December, 1939), esp. 996–997.

[3] Not all solicitors general have graced the Office with distinction. The one initially entrusted with defending the New Deal in the Supreme Court was "an estimable but ineffectual old gentleman" who "showed his unfitness for the responsibility [by] losing ten of seventeen cases in his first five months." (Arthur M. Schlesinger, Jr., *The Age of Roosevelt: The Politics of Upheaval* [Boston: Houghton Mifflin, 1957], Vol. III, p. 261.)

[4] See *The Annual Report of the Director of the Administrative Office of the United States Courts* (Washington: Government Printing Office), Tables C4 and C7, recent issues.

about 180 cases decided by that Court on the merits.[5] Whether appeals will be taken to higher courts depends on the losing party, except that the United States cannot, of course, appeal its trial defeats in criminal cases.

As with any other unit of government, the United States has the right to enter other litigants' cases in the capacity of *amicus curiae*.[6] It may thus participate in every case that goes before the Supreme Court if it wishes. Private parties, on the other hand, must obtain the consent of either the litigants or the Court. Since the government is a party in about half the cases decided by the Court, it controls a great deal of the *amicus* activity there. The Solicitor General decides whether the government will act as *amicus* or permit others to do so in the government's litigation. His Office states—correctly, it appears —that its permission does not hinge upon the positions taken by *amicus* applicants but upon the Court's wishes.[7] The Supreme Court seemed briefly after 1949 to want the Solicitor General to be more stringent in passing upon *amicus* requests, and he responded (or perhaps overreacted) by denying a large number of them. Contrariwise, in recent years his decisions have reflected the desire of a majority of the justices that consent be freely given. The Solicitor General now denies few *amicus* requests, especially when they are presented by organized groups, and the government's adversaries in litigation generally give their consent when the Solicitor General has done so. Should consent by either side be withheld, the Court is likely to grant it anyway. Thus has the Court through its *amicus curiae* policy encouraged interest groups to operate in the judicial process.

[5] *Annual Report of the Attorney General of the United States, Fiscal Year 1968* (Washington: Department of Justice, n.d.), Table X, p. 102. The table reports the government to have participated in 200 cases. On the basis of data reported in Table IX, pp. 100–101, about twenty of these participations were as *amicus curiae* and not as a party to litigation.

[6] On the development of the *amicus curiae*, see Samuel Krislov, "The *Amicus Curiae* Brief: From Friendship to Advocacy," *Yale Law Journal*, 52 (March, 1963), 694–721.

[7] "Statement of Policy and Practice Regarding Applications to the Solicitor General for Consent to File *Amicus Curiae* Briefs in the Supreme Court" (Washington: Office of the Solicitor General, May, 1957), mimeographed.

The Solicitor General has little to say about the trial of cases in the district courts. His opinion as to how the Supreme Court might decide a case on appeal sometimes influences the Justice Department's judgment on initiating a prosecution or suit in the first place, but his participation in the judicial process really starts after this stage. He decides whether the government should appeal the defeats it sustains there and in the appellate courts. In practice, he concerns himself almost exclusively with those government-lost cases which the Justice Department divisions and the agencies have recommended for appeal. When they do not so recommend, the Solicitor General practically never decides otherwise, and in the great majority of instances his staff probably does not even review the case records. (Many defeats are simply not appropriate for review: for example, where a court of appeals reverses a criminal conviction for lack of evidence to support the jury verdict.) Thus, the Solicitor General's Office deals with relatively little of the mass of litigation coming out of the district courts and courts of appeal.

In the 1968 fiscal year (which began on July 1, 1967), the government lost 892 cases in the district courts that might have been appealed to the courts of appeal. These consisted of cases handled by the Justice Department divisions, such as the Criminal, the Civil, and the Antitrust divisions. We do not know in how many of the cases the divisions recommended appeal, but the Solicitor General authorized it in 264 cases, or 30 per cent of the total number of defeats.[8] Since parties have a right to review in the courts of appeal, all of the appeals authorized by the Solicitor General were considered there. In the same fiscal year, the government sustained 379 defeats in the courts of appeals and 35 defeats in the district courts directly appealable to the Supreme Court. These consisted of cases handled by the regulatory agencies, such as the Federal Communications Commission, the Federal Trade Commission, and the National Labor Relations Board, as well as by the Justice Department. Again, we do not know in how many cases appeal was

[8] Data provided by the Office of the Solicitor General, July 15, 1969.

recommended to the Solicitor General, but he sanctioned review by the Supreme Court in forty-three, or one-tenth, of these defeats.[9] We do know that between 1952 and 1961 the Department and agencies recommended an average of sixty appeals a term to the Supreme Court, and that the Solicitor General authorized appeal in about three-fifths of these cases.[10]

At each stage of the appellate process, therefore, most of the litigation under the government's control is kept from rising to a higher level, thus relieving the Supreme Court of a potentially tremendous burden of case work.

The government's adversaries are not nearly as reluctant as the government to carry their lower-court defeats to higher levels. To consider only their appeals from the courts of appeals to the Supreme Court, in the 1967 term of the Court (running from October, 1967, to the following June), they appealed no fewer than 936 cases, or nearly half of those which they might have.[11] The government appealed only 36 of 379 appeals courts defeats in fiscal 1968. How do we explain the different rates of appeal? The government is at least as able as its adversaries to pay the costs of Supreme Court litigation. The answer clearly is that it is much more selective in the issues it chooses to take to the Court. This is so for two reasons. In the first place, lower-court defeats usually mean much less to the United States than they do to other parties. It may not matter very much to the government if a court of appeals rules that the product of a small food canner is not too stringy for easy eating, but it probably matters a great deal to the canner. In the second place, the government has, as private litigants do not, an

---

[9] *Ibid.*

[10] William E. Brigman, "The Office of the Solicitor General of the United States" (Doctoral dissertation, Political Science Department, University of North Carolina, 1966), pp. 35, 37.

[11] The *Annual Report of Attorney General, 1968*, Table IX, pp. 66–67, gives the number of certiorari petitions and appeal writs sought by the government's adversaries in the 1967 term; data provided by the Office of the Solicitor General have the government losing 379 cases in the courts of appeals in fiscal 1968; and the *Annual Report of Administrative Office, 1968*, Table B1, p. 174, indicates that the government was a party to 2,478 cases in these courts in the same fiscal year.

independent source of restraint upon the desire to litigate further. The Solicitor General is not associated with cases before they go to the Supreme Court and hence is able to look at them in a detached manner. He thus has neither the passion nor the interest to appeal lower-court defeats which are inconsequential, not likely to be reversed, or, to his mind, deserved. More than this, he feels a responsibility, as one occupant of the Office has expressed it, "not to swamp the Supreme Court with more business than it can handle . . . to assist the Court to function efficiently and expeditiously as a vital segment of our governmental structure."[12] One could not blame him if he were also moved by a desire to cultivate the good will of the Court for the litigation which does matter to him.

We have noted that the Solicitor General approved about 60 per cent of the agency recommendations made to him in a recent ten-year period. This figure, we may suggest, is a statistical approximation of the point of equilibrium between the agencies seeking too few and seeking too many approvals, on one side, and the Solicitor General granting too few and granting too many approvals, on the other. When the agencies substantially increase their recommendations to the Solicitor General, he reacts by increasing his disapprovals. As we shall see, the Solicitor General's relationship to the Supreme Court in the matter of getting appeals accepted is remarkably similar to that of the agencies to him.

Not all cases recommended to the Solicitor General for appeal to the Supreme Court stand the same chance of success. If a case falls within the Court's so-called non-discretionary jurisdiction, it has a better-than-even chance of being approved by him; but if it falls within the Court's certiorari jurisdiction, it has about one chance in ten. The subject-matter of the appeal often determines its disposition: recommendations in antitrust and civil rights cases receive much more favorable treatment than other recommendations. Furthermore, whether by design

---

[12] Philip B. Perlman, "The Work of the Office of the Solicitor General of the United States" (Address before the Fifty-fourth Annual Meeting of the Maryland State Bar Association, July 2, 1949), mimeographed, p. 4.

or not, government defeats have a much better chance of entering the Solicitor General's approved list if the court of appeals was divided or if there was disagreement between the court of appeals and the district court. Also, the recommending agency seems important. The Labor Department, for instance, gets about three times as many of its recommendations accepted as the Agriculture, Defense, or Treasury Departments. The interested divisions of the Justice Department may comment on recommendations made by a number of executive agencies, and when they support appeals the Solicitor General is more likely to act favorably than when they oppose appeals.[13]

The Solicitor General exerts only somewhat less supervision over litigation handled by the regulatory agencies than over that handled by the Justice Department divisions.[14] These agencies, as we have noted, enjoy substantial autonomy within the executive branch. The deference accorded them depends partly upon the person who is Solicitor General. For example, Archibald Cox, who served under Kennedy, was a specialist in administrative law and supervised the regulatory agencies quite closely. He even reminded them on one public occasion that they had a "prime responsibility" for the government's policy in their areas and that their recommendations in cases would not be "automatically" approved.[15] It is indicative of the Solicitor General's power over the regulatory agencies that two of them possessing a legal right of appeal, the Federal Communications Commission and the Federal Maritime Commission, appear to

[13] Brigman, "Office of Solicitor General," p. 75. The Department of Health, Education and Welfare had none of its recommendations accepted in the ten-year period under study (1952–1961), but its cases generally raised factual and not legal issues and thus were not considered appropriate grist for the Court. Other departments had fewer than ten cases before the Solicitor General and have been omitted from consideration.

Brigman is also our source on the relationship between lower-court conflict and appeal authorizations (pp. 71, 79–80) and the influence of the Justice Department divisions on authorization requests of other agencies (pp. 76, 129).

[14] See, for example, Robert L. Stern, "The Solicitor General's Office and Administrative Agency Litigation," *American Bar Association Journal*, **41** (February, 1960), 155; and, by the same author, "'Inconsistency' in Government Litigation," *Harvard Law Review*, **54** (March, 1951), 768.

[15] Quoted in the *Washington Star*, September 23, 1965.

have asserted it on only one and a few occasions, respectively, and then without success. The statistics do not suggest a greater latitude in appeals for the regulatory agencies than for the Justice Department divisions. The percentage of cases carried to the Supreme Court on certiorari by these agencies, excluding the Interstate Commerce Commission, in a recent five-year period was the same as that carried by the divisions, and so was the percentage of requests for certiorari that was authorized by the Solicitor General.[16] The regulatory agencies do not have any greater latitude than the rest of the government in composing their briefs, and some of them even have most, if not all, of their cases now argued by lawyers from the Solicitor General's Office or from elsewhere in the Justice Department.

The Solicitor General's role in carrying appeals to the Supreme Court does not end with the approval of recommendations. His Office supervises the preparation of the briefs that argue why the Court should accept the government's cases and is thereby involved in revising or writing the Justice Department or agency briefs. The Office is similarly involved in preparing nearly all government briefs opposing the granting of certiorari or the noting of jurisdiction in the appeals of the government's adversaries. Thus, the Solicitor General not only determines whether the executive branch goes to the Supreme Court, but what it will say there.

What can government agencies do about the Solicitor General's refusal to take their appeals to the Supreme Court? Usually, not much. The Justice Department divisions and most other agencies must accept the Solicitor General's decision, unless they can get the Attorney General or the Presidency to overrule it. Considering the volume of cases involved, they cannot carry their disagreements beyond the Solicitor General's Office very often, and when they do they generally lose. Only rarely is the Solicitor General overruled by his superiors.[17] Those agencies that possess statutory authority to appeal cases to the

---

[16] Brigman, "Office of Solicitor General," pp. 120–121, gives data on regulatory agency certiorari appeals for the period 1957–1962.

[17] Spritzer interview.

Supreme Court are in a somewhat different situation. They can go to the Court without the Solicitor General's blessing, but in doing so they incur risks the gravity of which depends upon the extent of his disagreement with them. By simply withholding his name from an agency brief, the Solicitor General notifies the Court that he does not concur in the appeal. Or he may oppose the appeal or permit some other agency to oppose it, or submit a brief to the Court giving the arguments favoring and opposing the acceptance of a case in which he may or may not take a position himself. The above steps are taken very seldom. More often, the Solicitor General supports an appeal in exchange for modifications in the agency's statement of the issues.

Even where the Solicitor General can forbid agencies to carry appeals to the Supreme Court, he may authorize the appeals under any of the conditions just mentioned. In imposing such conditions, whatever the government unit involved, the Solicitor General and his staff do more than control the movement of litigation to the Supreme Court. They are also engaged in coordinating judicial policy, resolving conflicts among agencies, determining which positions will prevail before the Court, and shaping the policies the Court will be asked to rule upon. The Office of the Solicitor General thus influences not only the actions of the Supreme Court but also the policies of the executive branch.

GETTING INTO COURT

Why do the Justice Department divisions and the regulatory agencies generally accept the decisions and advice of the Solicitor General regarding appeals to the Supreme Court? It is not enough to speak of his power to deny them access to the Court. For one thing, he lacks that power over several agencies, and yet they generally accept his position. Moreover, the other parts of government very seldom appeal his judgments to the Attorney General or to the Presidency. Most significantly, governmental litigants hesitate to take appeals to the Court when he authorizes them to do so but refuses to associate himself with their briefs or threatens to oppose them. In short, the Solicitor General's influence over the Justice Department and agencies is based upon more than power. It derives also from the discretionary nature of the Supreme Court's jurisdiction: the Court is free, in effect, to accept or reject nearly all appeals that come to it, regardless of whether they come under the writ of certiorari, in which it has statutory discretion in taking cases, or under direct appeal, in which appellants have a legal "right" to seek review.[18] The Solicitor General has been able to persuade his governmental colleagues that he knows which cases the Court is likely to accept and to persuade the Court, most of the time, that it should accept the cases he supports. His ability to persuade the Court is reflected in the government's record of getting cases into it, and this success in turn has enabled him to deal authoritatively with the executive branch.

The Solicitor General has been remarkably successful in getting the government into the Supreme Court. In ten recent terms (through June, 1968), the Court accepted 72 per cent of its appeals and only 9 per cent of those of its adversaries.[19] (The rates vary somewhat among terms.) Not only that, but he

[18] Nearly all appeals to the Supreme Court, by whatever party and from whatever court, are carried there by these two procedures. A direct appeal is used where special three-judge district courts have acted on injunctions relating to the constitutionality of federal or state laws, where district or appellate courts have declared such laws unconstitutional in other proceedings, and in certain antitrust and other actions brought in district court by the government. The writ of certiorari is used where district or appellate courts have upheld the constitutionality of federal or state laws and where the issue concerns the interpretation of the Constitution or a federal statute. The Supreme Court in fact exercises discretion in both certiorari and appeal cases. When the writ of certiorari is sought, the losing party in the court below must file a petition in the form of a brief arguing why the Court should take the case, which the winning party answers with another brief; and when an appeal is taken, the losing party must file a jurisdictional statement in the form of a brief, which the winning party answers, in which the same issue is argued in the guise of the question whether the Court should "note jurisdiction" of the case. For our purposes, the major difference between cases carried to the Supreme Court under certiorari and under appeal is that the former are many times more numerous and the latter stand a much better chance of being accepted by the Court for consideration.

[19] In the 1958–1967 terms, the Court accepted 232 of 330 government petitions for certiorari and noted jurisdiction in 83 of 106 of its appeals. The comparable

helped the government's adversaries to get a number of their cases accepted. In one term, a third of their successful certiorari appeals (most cases are appealed under that writ) were made with government support.[20]

In selecting cases to appeal, the Solicitor General appears to enter into a sort of reciprocal relationship with the Supreme Court similar to that which the Justice Department divisions and other agencies enter into with him. If he presses too many cases upon it, the Court reacts by increasing its rejection rate and he then cuts back; when he does so, the rejection rate goes down and, spurred by the feeling that he is not pressing enough (and probably by agency remonstrations as well), he increases his activity. The range of movement in certiorari petitions appears to be between 60 and 80 per cent, with the point of equilibrium about 70 per cent.

We still do not have a full picture of the government's success in getting into the Supreme Court for we have not yet considered its efforts in the capacity of *amicus curiae*. These efforts are directed toward persuading the Court to accept or reject litigation in which the government is not a party. The government may enter any case as *amicus curiae*, but before the 1940s, neither it nor other *amici* had given much attention to this preliminary stage of the Court's proceedings. In the 1923–1924 terms, for example, the Solicitor General intervened only twice as *amicus curiae* in the consideration of appeals, and all other parties only three times. But this restraint no longer exists, and in the 1963–1964 terms, the government alone appeared as *amicus* forty-two times to support or oppose appeals by parties to get their cases into Court.[21] We need hardly add that the government's *amicus* activity constitutes a substantial

figures for the government's adversaries are 530 of 6,640 petitions and 61 of 260 appeals. Data derived from *Annual Report of Attorney General*, 1968, Table IX, pp. 99–100.

[20] Perlman, "Work of Solicitor General," p. 5, reports that the Court granted 13 per cent of the petitions filed by the government's opponents in the 1948 term, of which only 8 per cent were accepted over the government's objections.

[21] The data for the 1923–1924 terms were compiled from the Court reports. The 1963–1964 data were furnished by the Solicitor General's office and reveal

part of its efforts to get favored cases into the Supreme Court, and we should emphasize that the direction of government activity is toward greater involvement.

In appeals to the Supreme Court the Solicitor General has had an even more impressive record as *amicus curiae* than as direct party. When he supported attempts by others to get into the Court in the 1958–1967 terms, the Court granted certiorari 82 per cent of the time (as compared to 70 per cent on the government's own petitions). Where the government was neither a party nor an *amicus*, incidentally, the Court in these terms granted certiorari only 7 per cent of the time. In the less frequent instances when the Solicitor General has as *amicus curiae* opposed attempts by others to get into the Court, their acceptance rate has been 24 per cent.[22] Unless we are to assume that the *amicus* action of the Solicitor General actually helps disfavored litigants get into the Supreme Court, it must be that he opposes the granting of certiorari in non-government litigation only when he feels that the chances would otherwise be abnormally good. From this viewpoint, the Solicitor General has probably achieved considerable success in helping to keep the rate of acceptance for disfavored litigants to one case in seven.

We shall say more later about the government's *amicus* interventions, but will now take time only to summarize the Solicitor General's success in the Supreme Court's consideration of cases on appeal. Whether he seeks to get the government into Court, or to keep its adversaries out of it, or to advise the Court on other people's litigation, the Solicitor General is clearly a

more government *amicus* participation at the acceptance stage than the *Annual Report of Attorney General, 1966*, Table II, pp. 50–51.

[22] The government supported the petitioner as *amicus curiae* in sixty-five cases in the 1958–1967 terms, with the Court granting certiorari fifty-three times. It opposed the petitioner as *amicus curiae* in forty-six cases during this time, with the Court denying certiorari thirty-five times. In this period, the Court accepted 914 and rejected 13,289 certiorari petitions in cases in which the government was neither a party nor an *amicus*. *Annual Report of Attorney General, 1968*, Table IX, p. 99.

The government was an *amicus* in thirty-one cases which went to the Court under direct appeal, but the Attorney General's figures permit us to say only that the parties it supported were successful in between eighteen and twenty-five instances.

persuasive party in the Supreme Court, and his success there helps explain the acceptance by executive agencies of his control over their appeals.

The Solicitor General is not only a favored party in the cases the Supreme Court accepts for decision, but the dominant one as well. In ten recent terms, the government has, as direct party or *amicus curiae*, participated in 57 per cent of all cases argued in the Court.[23] There is, of course, a difference between getting one's case before the Court for decision and achieving success there, but for the government, as we shall presently see, getting into the Supreme Court is winning half the battle, and then some.

WINNING CASES

Throughout its history the United States has won most of its cases in the Supreme Court, and at a level of success which has not varied by very much from one period to another. An examination of the Court's opinions, chosen at ten-year intervals starting at 1800, shows that the government won 62 per cent of its litigation there during the nineteenth century, and so far has won 64 per cent of it during this century.[24]

We might expect the government to win most of the cases

---

[23] *Annual Report of Attorney General, 1968*, Table X, p. 102. The government participated in 819 of 1,432 argued cases in the 1958–1967 terms of the Court.

[24] In the sampled years, the government won 81 of 130 cases decided between 1800 and 1890, and 254 of 399 cases decided between 1900 and 1950. Data were compiled from the Court reports.

The government won 221 of 345 cases in the 1961–1967 terms. The data were obtained from the following reports on "The Supreme Court Term" in the *Harvard Law Review*: **76** (November, 1962), Table III, between pp. 80 and 81; **77** (November, 1963), Table III, between pp. 84 and 85; **78** (November, 1964), Table III, between pp. 180 and 181; **79** (November, 1965), Table II, between pp. 106 and 107; **80** (November, 1966), Table II, between pp. 144 and 145; **81** (November, 1967), Table II, between pp. 128 and 129; **82** (November, 1968), Table II, pp. 304–305.

Since the 1950s the Court has increasingly made use of summary judgments, but this practice has apparently not affected the ratio of government victories. When all decisions, both with and without opinion, were examined in the 1964–1966 terms, the government won 64 per cent (179) of the 278 cases in which it was a party. Data collected from Court reports.

which it has carried to the Court in recent decades. The Court favors the appealing party whoever he may be. In fact, taken as a group, the initiators of appeals have been victorious about two-thirds of the time in the contemporary Court. The reason seems clear. Since the Supreme Court was given discretion over most of its caseload in 1925 it has, increasingly over the years, tended to accept those cases it has tentatively suspected of being wrongly decided in the state or lower federal courts. But this does not tell the full story of the government's success. When it has been the initiator of action by the Court it has done substantially better than other parties, winning about 70 per cent of the cases decided with opinion in a sampling of decades between 1930 and 1960, and winning 78 per cent of all cases decided on the merits (both with and without opinion) in the 1964–1966 terms. What sets the government apart from other litigants is that it does quite well when its adversary has carried the appeal to the Court. In the 1930–1960 period, its record as respondent (or appellee) was as good as that as petitioner (or appellant), and in the 1964–1966 period it still managed to win 56 per cent of its cases.[25] Its achievement in this position underscores the superiority of the government over other litigants in the Supreme Court.

It is instructive to compare the record of the United States as a Supreme Court litigant with that of the state and local governments. The Court is strikingly disposed toward the national government and away from the states and localities. No matter how cases are selected, the national government comes out well and the others poorly. Consider, for example, cases decided with opinions in the 1961–1967 terms: The states (and localities) won one-fourth of their litigation while the United States won nearly two-thirds. Compare this with all cases decided in the 1964–1966 terms, by summary judgment as well as with opinions: The states won one-third of their cases and the United States won two-thirds.[26] The states have not, to

[25] In the 1930, 1940, 1950, and 1960 terms, the United States won 64 of 92 cases as petitioner (or appellant); in the 1964–1966 terms, 82 of 105 cases.

[26] The states and localities won 57 (31 per cent) of 242 cases decided with opinions

be sure, always lagged behind the national government. Throughout the nineteenth century, according to our sample of terms, they and the national government were equally successful in the Supreme Court, and in the first three decades of this century the states actually did better than the United States. Even as recently as the 1940–1960 period the states lagged behind the national government by only a very few percentage points.[27] But today they lag seriously behind and, moreover, they have much more trouble than the national government in getting into Court and in keeping their adversaries out of it. While the national government was getting four-fifths of its appeals accepted in the 1964–1966 terms, the states succeeded with only one-third of theirs. While the former's adversaries got only one case in seven accepted by the Court, the latter's adversaries got one case in four accepted.[28]

Finally, we must examine the *amicus curiae* activity of the United States in cases decided by the Supreme Court. When we considered the Court's acceptance of cases for decision, we pointed out that the United States has greatly increased its *amicus* participations, that the parties it has supported have done extremely well in acceptances, and that the parties it has opposed have done very poorly. Indeed, the government has an even better record as *amicus curiae* than as a direct party in litigation. All these factors apply with equal force to the government's *amicus* interventions at the decisional stage, except that it is yet more active here.

The government appears more often as *amicus curiae* than

in the 1961–1967 terms ("The Supreme Court Term," *Harvard Law Review*), and 57 (33 per cent) of 175 cases decided on the merits in the 1964–1966 terms.

[27] In 11 sampled terms during the nineteenth century, beginning with 1800, the states won 23 (61 per cent) of 38 cases, and in six sampled terms during this century, between 1900 and 1950, they won 111 (72 per cent) of 154 cases. It will be recalled that the national government won 62 and 64 per cent of its cases, respectively, in these periods.

[28] The states and localities had 36 (35 per cent) of 102 appeals accepted by the Court in the 1964–1966 terms, as compared with 137 (23 per cent) of 616 appeals for their adversaries. The comparable figures for the national government were 105 (81 per cent) of 129 appeals, and for its adversaries, 173 (14 per cent) of 1,235 appeals.

any other party in cases which the Supreme Court decides on
the merits. In recent terms it has averaged seventeen *amicus*
briefs a term, about one-fifth of all such participations and a
marked contrast to the three suits it entered a term in the 1920s.[29]
Part of the explanation lies with the Court itself, for it has in
recent years considerably expanded its invitations to the
Solicitor General to file *amicus* briefs in cases. The government
as *amicus curiae* is nearly always aligned with the winning party
in the Court, and in several post-Second World War terms
sampled, its ratio of success was 87 per cent, substantially
greater than its success as a direct litigant and far greater than
that of other *amici*, taken as a group.[30]

We now have a full picture of the government's record in
Supreme Court decisions in recent terms: In the 1958–1967
terms, the government, as direct party and *amicus curiae*, was
successful in 71 per cent of the cases in which it participated.
The figure looms even bigger when we observe that the government during this period was involved in half the cases argued
before the Court.[31]

It is understandable that the United States has become an
increasingly frequent litigant in the Supreme Court. The
national government is now greatly involved in matters that
once concerned the state and local governments or private
person's and involvement naturally produces conflict which in
turn produces litigation. For example, economic matters were
of practically no concern to the national government in the
mid-nineteenth century and still were of little concern by the
end of the century. But today the government participates in
nearly every important part of the country's economic life. It is
not surprising therefore that the largest part of the Court's
business should now consist of cases dealing with federal

[29] In the 1963–1967 terms, the government participated as *amicus* in eighty-four
 argued cases and in the 1923–1924 terms in six cases. (*Annual Report of
 Attorney General*: for 1923, p. 6; for 1924, p. 10; for 1968, Table X, p. 102.)
[30] In an examination of cases decided in the 1943, 1944, 1963, and 1965 terms, the
 government sided with the winning party in 87 per cent (54) of 62 cases, and
 other *amici* did so in 57 per cent (120) of 209 cases.
[31] Based on *Annual Report of Attorney General*, Table X, p. 102, for the 1958–1967
 terms.

economic regulation, whereas there were only a few such cases around 1900, and none at all fifty years earlier.[32] Similarly, the national government has expanded its participation as *amicus curiae* in the Supreme Court as the legal quarrels of other parties have increasingly impinged upon the responsibilities of executive agencies. An illustration is the Solicitor General's recent intervention, at the invitation of the Court, in a state labor case in which he informed the Court that the national government did not consider national laws to preclude the states from regulating labor disputes involving supervisory personnel.[33]

When all explanations are made, there is still cause for concern in the extent of the national government's activity in the Supreme Court. The government is necessarily a major litigant there, but should it fill up the Court's docket as it does? Should it seek to influence the outcome of so many cases in which it is not a party? In particular, should the government enter other parties' litigation when it does not have a concrete and substantial interest in the outcmoe, for example, in cases dealing with legislative apportionment? It is true that the use of the *amicus curiae* brief generally has become common in the Supreme Court—an average of about eighty *amicus* briefs have been filed on the merits in recent Court terms,[34] but it does not seem fair for the government to lend its great prestige to one of the litigants in other people's controversies. It seems especially unfair for the government to try to get favored litigants into the Court or, above all, to try to block other litigants from getting there. This behavior smacks too much of partisanship; it subjects the Solicitor General to strong pressures from organizations and individual litigants who are encouraged to believe that the government might be bent to their assistance; and, having no limits set upon it, it could dangerously change the

[32] For the major categories of litigation involved in the 1854–1855, 1904–1905, and 1954–1955 Court terms, see Felix Frankfurter, "The Supreme Court in the Mirror of Justices," *University of Pennsylvania Law Review*, **105** (April, 1957), 792–793.

[33] *Hanna Mining Company* v. *District 2, Marine Engineers Beneficial Association*, summary of government brief, 15 L. ed. 2d 939–940 (1965).

[34] Krislov, "The *Amicus Curiae* Brief," p. 716, n. 119.

adversary nature of proceedings in the Supreme Court. The government's signal achievements in an *amicus* capacity do not lighten our concern.

REASONS FOR SUCCESS

Why is the United States so successful in the Supreme Court? Why does it win as often as it does there, whether as appellant or appellee or as *amicus curiae*? Why has it consistently come out ahead in its litigation during the course of American history? We can suggest one general and three specific reasons.

The general reason has to do with the relationship between the executive and judicial branches. We have in previous chapters noted certain factors which tend to draw the two branches toward each other; the consequence of this tendency is to incline the Supreme Court somewhat toward the position of the executive in litigation which comes before it. The two branches share, for example, a rather similar governmental perspective, in that the power they exercise is generally concerned with the execution or enforcement of law. They also tend to share a similar doctrinal perspective, in that Presidents usually have a fairly free hand in appointing persons to the Court and usually seek persons whose views on important issues are more-or-less like theirs. Thus justices reflect the doctrinal perspective of the Presidency more than they do that of the Senate, and least of all that of the House of Representatives. Of course, when Presidential perspectives change sharply, there is discordance between the two branches until new appointments draw them together again.

The specific reasons for the government's success in the Supreme Court are the expertise of the Solicitor General's Office, the credit which the Solicitor General has developed with the Court, and the government's agreement with the Court on doctrinal position.

The expertise of the Solicitor General's Office certainly

helps the government win its cases in the Supreme Court. The Office attracts highly capable persons, most of whom come to it from private practice, and its members are able to outmatch in ability the average counsel arrayed against them. In addition, the Office has more experience with the Supreme Court than any law firm in the country. It is in some way involved in over half the cases argued in a normal term of the Court. No other lawyers specialize to the same extent in Supreme Court litigation, and most lawyers who appear before the Court have had little, if any, previous experience there. All government briefs to the Court are first approved, and usually revised, by the Solicitor General's Office, and the Office's staff argues about half the government's cases in the Court; most of the rest are handled by Court-experienced attorneys in the Justice Department divisions or in the independent agencies. Not only do the government attorneys generally know how to construct able written and oral presentations, but they know the men who receive the presentations better than most of their adversaries do and, in consequence, they know which style and substance of argument may be most influential in different circumstances. One informed estimate is that oral argument in the Court has some influence on the Court's decision in about three-quarters of the cases, and a decisive influence in about one case in ten.[35] Those government attorneys who have handled much litigation in the Supreme Court are probably so attuned to its mood that they know pretty well how individual justices will react to their arguments and most of the time know how their cases will be decided when argument has been completed. In fact, they have a fairly good idea of the outcome of some cases even before they enter the Court.[36]

The government's success in the Supreme Court seems to owe something also to the credit which the Solicitor General's Office has built up with the Court. The Solicitor General has done this, in the first place, by helping the Court manage its great and

---

[35] Interview with Mr. John W. Davis, Clerk of the Supreme Court, March 7, 1967.
[36] Spritzer interview.

growing burden of casework. The Court had nearly 3,600 cases on its dockets in the 1967 term, an increase of about 1,500 cases from a decade earlier. To assist them the justices are allotted only two law clerks (the Chief Justice, three) who generally come directly from law school and serve but one or two terms. In this situation the Solicitor General's ministrations to the Supreme Court are most valuable. He holds to a trickle what could be a deluge of government appeals; he sometimes tells the Court when the government's adversaries have deserving appeals; and he also offers his advice as *amicus curiae* in other people's litigation. The Solicitor General helps the Court, in the second place, by ensuring that the government's legal work is competently done, so much so that when the justices or their clerks want to extract the key issues in a complicated case quickly, they turn, according to common report, to the government brief.[37] The Solicitor General gains further credit with the Supreme Court by his demonstrations of impartiality and independence from the executive branch. He does so, of course, in refusing to appeal the government's lower-court defeats to it and by supporting the appeals of the government's adversaries. He does so, too, in those relatively rare instances when he opposes an independent agency before the Court or when he refuses to associate himself with the government's position.

The most dramatic demonstration of impartiality and independence by the Solicitor General occurs when he goes into the Supreme Court to confess error. He does this only when the government has won in the court below, for when he thinks the government's position was wrong in cases it lost he need do nothing more than refuse to authorize appeal. Usually when he refuses authorization, the case was handled by the Justice Department's lawyers, for in cases handled by the independent agencies his practice has been to side with the non-government party when he thinks the government is wrong. It was Frederick W. Lehman, the Solicitor General under Taft, who gave strong

---

[37] Joseph Tanenhaus *et al.*, "The Supreme Court's Certiorari Jurisdiction: Cue Theory," in Glendon Schubert, ed., *Judicial Decision-Making* (New York: The Free Press, 1963), p. 122.

impetus to the notion that the Solicitor General is more than a partisan advocate and who, according to one of his successors in the Office, took "delight" in confessing error to the Supreme Court.[38] Confessions are usually made in criminal and other cases where severe penalties might be imposed on individuals. The Solicitor General usually confesses error in one to three cases a term.[39]

Finally, the government owes much of its success in Supreme Court litigation to its doctrinal position in cases: whether it has favored the claims made in the name of personal liberty, civil equality, and the rights of criminal defendants; the claims of employees, unions, and consumers against business; and small business against large business. Using the terms in their common meaning, we can say that the government's position is liberal when it favors these claims and is conservative when it does not favor them.

The influence of doctrinal factors upon the government's record of success in the Supreme Court not only completes our explanation of that success but places it in proper perspective. Doctrinal factors probably have had more to do with the extraordinary success of the government than has the expertise of its lawyers or its credit with the Court, at least in contemporary times. Two considerations are relevant to an examination of the impact of doctrine upon success: the government's record of liberal versus conservative positions in cases, and the proportion of cases in which it acts in each position.

Since 1937, in those cases that can be so classified, the government has done much better in the Supreme Court when its doctrinal position has been liberal than when it has been conservative. In the 1964 and 1965 terms of the Court, for

---

[38] Simon E. Sobeloff, "Lawyer for the Government" (Address at the Annual Dinner of the New York University Law School Alumni Association, New York City, March 15, 1955), mimeographed, pp. 4–5.

[39] Brigman, "Office of Solicitor General," pp. 104–105, counted twenty-eight government confessions in the six terms running from October, 1957, to June, 1962, including motions to remand which were tantamount to confessions. But a number of these confessions were not such within our meaning, since the government was seeking to remove from the Court's docket cases in which its position had just been rendered defective by decisions of the Court.

example, the government won nine out of ten cases when it assumed a liberal position and only about one out of four cases when it took a conservative position.[40] Other evidence indicates that the government has been similarly, if not as overwhelmingly, successful in Court in other years after 1937. We learn from one study that the government in the 1941–1946 period won two-thirds of the cases involving the Fair Labor Standards Act in which it held, presumably, the liberal position and just under half the cases in which it held the conservative position of opposing civil liberty and criminal defendant claims.[41] And in the 1953–1959 terms, according to another researcher, the government won four-fifths of the time when its position was liberal in cases dealing with business, and only one-fourth of the time when its position was conservative; the corresponding figures in labor union cases (involving the National Labor Relations Board) rise to about nine cases in ten and one case in three.[42] Furthermore, the government appears more often in the liberal than in the conservative position before the Court. In

[40] The author's data. There were eighty-three decisions with opinions in these terms in which the government's position could be clearly ascribed as liberal or conservative. The government won forty-eight and lost five cases in the first capacity and won eight and lost twenty-two in the second capacity.

[41] C. Herman Pritchett, *The Roosevelt Court: A Study in Judicial Politics and Values, 1937–1947* (New York: Macmillan, 1948), reports that the government won fourteen of twenty-one decisions under the Fair Labor Standards Act in these terms (pp. 207–208) and twenty-three of forty-eight decisions involving civil liberty and criminal defendant claims (Table XXIII, p. 254). Furthermore, it was the winner in fifty-five of fifty-nine cases involving the National Labor Relations Board (p. 199), but it probably held the conservative position in some of these victories.

[42] The government was a liberal winner in 80 per cent of all business regulation cases and a conservative winner in 26 per cent of them. The percentages are given by Harold J. Spaeth, "Warren Court Attitudes toward Business: The 'B' Scale," in Schubert, ed., *Judicial Decision-Making*, p. 96. Spaeth is also the source of our information on the government's success in labor cases: it won 88 per cent of the time (fifteen of seventeen cases) when its position was liberal and 36 per cent of the time (five of fourteen cases) when its position was conservative. ("An Analysis of Judicial Attitudes in the Labor Relations Decisions of the Warren Court," *Journal of Politics*, 25 (May, 1963), 307, n. 26.
    We could have made our points in a somewhat different way. The justices of the Supreme Court cast 446 votes in 52 non-unanimously decided union and business regulation cases involving the government in the 1953–1959 terms, with the government obtaining 66 per cent of them when it held the liberal position and 52 per cent of them when it held the conservative

the 1964–1965 terms, its liberalism dominated by nearly a two-to-one margin. Evidence from earlier terms in the post-1937 period indicates a similar, though less strong, tendency toward liberalism.[43]

If the United States has usually been a liberal litigant in the Supreme Court in recent decades, and if it has usually done much better there when it has been liberal than when it has been conservative, then it seems to follow that the Court itself has been strongly liberal during this period. This has indeed been true. Not only has the government done well as a liberal litigant in the Court since 1937, but so have all parties on the liberal side of cases. In the litigation decided during the 1964 and 1965 terms in which the United States was not a party and which raised the liberal–conservative issue, the Court favored the liberal litigant 84 per cent of the time.[44] In cases relating to economic matters only, the Court, during the longer period from 1953 to 1965, favored the liberal litigant 71 per cent of the time.[45] When the Court's treatment of litigants is viewed over an even longer period, since the 1946 term, we can see that it not only has favored the liberal position but has done so increasingly through the period.[46] What makes the Court's liberal predisposition so significant is that so much of its

position. The votes were tallied from Tables VII and VIII in Spaeth, "The Judicial Restraint of Mr. Justice Frankfurter—Myth or Reality?", *Midwest Journal of Political Science*, **8** (February, 1964), 35, 36. If unanimously decided cases had been included, the liberal percentage would have been higher and the conservative percentage lower, for such cases are generally decided for the liberal litigant and this is usually the government.

[43] See notes 41 and 42.

[44] The numerical figures are ninety-two wins for the liberal litigant and eighteen wins for the conservative.

[45] Harold J. Spaeth, *The Warren Court: Cases and Commentary* (San Francisco: Chandler, 1966), p. 35.

[46] Using the data provided by Glendon Schubert, *The Judicial Mind: The Attitudes and Ideologies of Supreme Court Justices, 1946–1963* (Evanston, Ill.: Northwestern University Press, 1965), pp. 104–112 and 130–138 (but excluding evenly divided cases), we find that the Court, where it could be classified, was liberal 51 per cent of the time (in 559 of 1,093 cases) in non-unanimous decisions during the 1946–1962 terms. It was liberal 38 per cent of the time (in 186 of 485 cases) during the 1946–1954 terms and 61 per cent of the time (in 373 of 608 cases) during the later terms. These percentages considerably understate the extent of the Court's liberalism for they do not include those cases, constituting roughly half the total number, in which the Court was

business today contains liberal–conservative claims. According to one source, 66 per cent of the cases decided between 1946 and 1962 contained such claims, and according to another, 80 per cent of the cases decided between 1953 and 1965 did so.[47] Indeed, the Court's liberalism extends to the accepting of cases for decision in addition to the deciding of cases. When the United States is not a party in an appeal under certiorari, the Court is much more likely to grant review if a civil liberty or civil rights issue is involved than if other issues are involved.[48]

The government's doctrinal record in the contemporary Supreme Court may be contrasted with that in the pre-1937 Court. It is well known that the earlier Court tended to be conservative in its constitutional and statutory interpretations. In liability suits between railroad workers and their employers, to cite one published study, the Court favored the worker only 18 per cent of the time between 1921 and 1937 whereas it favored the railroad by an even smaller percentage in the period from 1938 to 1948.[49] Our own research into the government's record in the 1923 and 1924 terms of the Court bears out this contrast. When the government took the liberal position in those terms, in cases which could be classified in this way, it was successful less than half the time, but when it was in the conservative position it was successful in seven cases out of ten.

unanimous, and the Court is liberal most of the time in its unanimous decisions. For example, Spaeth, "An Analysis of Judicial Attitudes," p. 294, reports that the Court was liberal about half the time in labor union cases when it was divided and liberal four-fifths of the time when it was unanimous. What the percentages do reveal is the great increase in the Court's liberalism after 1954.

[47] Schubert, *The Judicial Mind*, p. 97; Spaeth, *The Warren Court*, p. 21.
[48] Tanenhaus *et al.*, "The Supreme Court's Certiorari Jurisdiction," pp. 111–132. In a sample of 2,631 certiorari petitions filed in the 1947–1958 terms of the Court it was found that, in cases not involving the government, the Court granted certiorari 33 per cent of the time when the issue was an economic one; and 13 per cent of the time when there was disagreement in the lower court or between two or more courts and agencies in a given case (but when neither a civil liberty–rights issue or an economic issue was present). In all other cases not involving the government the rate of granting certiorari was 6 per cent.
[49] Glendon Schubert, "Policy without Law: An Extension of the Certiorari Game," *Stanford Law Review*, 14 (March, 1962), 294. Workers won seven and lost thirty-one cases in the first period and won twenty-five and lost four cases in the second period.

The government's liberalism was confined to cases dealing with economic subjects; in no case involving personal rights or civil equality did it appear on the liberal side. Inasmuch as the government was liberal more often than it was conservative before the Court in these two earlier terms, its success in cases having doctrinal overtones was modest—certainly so by the standards of the 1950s and 1960s, amounting to no more than 57 per cent.[50]

We may summarize by saying that the United States government tended to win its cases in the conservative position in the 1920s and to lose them in the 1960s, and conversely in the liberal position; that the Court tended to favor the government when it assumed the liberal position in the later period; and that the government tended to win a majority of its ideologically-tinted cases in each period because it held the position favored by the Court most of the time.[51] But we cannot end our summary without two further observations. First, the Supreme Court appears to have been much more liberal in the 1960s than it was conservative in the 1920s. Second, the government and the Court were much more closely aligned ideologically in the 1960s than in the 1920s. The first observation leads one to ask whether the shifts in, and the extremity of, the Court's ideological partiality comport with either the requirements of individual justice or fidelity to the intention of the Constitution and statutes it construes; but such questions appear to lie outside the scope of this study.[52] We are, however, interested in questions raised by the observation concerning the ideological compatibility between the government and the Court.

[50] The government was liberal in sixty-seven cases and conservative in forty-six cases decided in the 1923–1924 terms. It won thirty-two cases in the liberal position and thirty-three cases in the conservative position, or 48 and 72 per cent of its cases, respectively. It won 65 of the 113 doctrinal cases in which it was involved, and won 32 of the 42 personal liberty–civil equality cases in which it defended the conservative position.

[51] References to the 1920s and 1960s are specifically to the 1923–1924 and 1964–1965 terms of the Court.

[52] For a recent consideration of these questions, the reader is referred to Thomas S. Schrock, "The Liberal Court, the Conservative Court, and Constitutional Jurisprudence," in Robert A. Goldwin, ed., *Left, Right, and Center* (Chicago: Rand McNally, 1965), pp. 87–120.

Can the government's success in the liberal Court be wholly explained by ideological congruence? Do expertise and standing with the Court contribute nothing substantial to that success? Apparently ideology is not the only factor in success. If it were, the government should do no better in the liberal position that its adversaries do when they are in that position; do no better in either the liberal or the conservative position than litigants in cases in which the government is not involved; and do no better than other litigants in cases lacking ideological dimensions. But none of these things is true. The government, as we have shown, wins overwhelmingly when it is liberal and, inasmuch as it does fairly well when it is conservative, its adversaries must trail behind it by a considerable margin when they are liberal. In the 1964–1965 terms, for example, it won 91 per cent of its cases in the liberal position and 27 per cent of its cases in the conservative position (and so its adversaries won 9 per cent of their cases in the conservative position and 73 per cent in the liberal position).[53] The government in these terms did not do much better in the liberal position than liberal contestants in cases where it was not a party, but it did far better than conservative contestants in such cases: the Court there ruled in favor of the liberal contestants 84 per cent of the time.[54] Finally, the government does better than average in the Supreme Court in cases which seem to lack an ideological cast. In the 1923–1924 terms, it won 56 per cent of these cases, and in the 1964–1965 terms 75 per cent of them. We have argued that the government wins many cases in the Supreme Court partly because of its expertise and its credit with the Court. We can infer from the figures just cited that the government's expertise and credit were considerably greater in the more recent than in the earlier terms. When we recall that the government won seven out of ten cases in the 1923–1924 terms

[53] See the data presented in note 40.

[54] The court favored the liberal contestant ninety-two times and the conservative contestant eighteen times in cases not involving the government in these terms. Pritchett, *Roosevelt Court*, p. 162, reports that the Court decided for the national government in sixteen (48 per cent) of thirty-three cases and for the state governments in only five (28 per cent) of eighteen cases involving criminal defendant claims in the 1941–1946 terms.

and nine out of ten cases in the 1964–1965 terms when it held the Court-favored ideological position, we are tempted to say that ideological compatibility contributed in these terms roughly 15 percentage points to the government's record of success in the Supreme Court.[55]

Thus, doctrinal compatibility appears to be a major factor in the success of the United States government in the Supreme Court, but it is not the only important factor. The government's success owes something, too, to advantages which accrue to it as a highly competent and respected party in litigation, and doctrinal compatibility and respect are themselves related to the special relationship which exists between the judicial and executive branches. The government has owed more to the ideological predisposition of a majority of the justices during the present era of the liberal Court than it did during the earlier era of the conservative Court, and government and Court appear to have been in closest ideological harmony in the most recent terms of the Court.

The Supreme Court's generally liberal course over the past few decades is widely known. The government's successful record in the Court is less so, and overlooked by nearly all scholars is the connection between the Court's liberalism and the government's success. Since the Solicitor General's Office controls the government's litigation in the Court, we are led to wonder whether the Solicitor General and his staff tend to be guided by the Court's ideological predilections in carrying litigation to the Court. It would seem that they are. As we have seen, the Solicitor General's staff follows the practice of appealing those defeats in lower courts that it thinks the Supreme Court is likely to accept, and the Court tends to accept appeals in those cases that it believes were wrongly decided below; and thus the government's lawyers must, consciously or not, favor those requests for appeal where the government's position is liberal

[55] But we must be cautious: this suggestion is based on fifty-four non-ideological cases decided in the 1923–1924 terms, and twenty-eight such cases decided in the 1964–1965 terms; and, further, some ideological influence, at least, must have been present in non-ideological cases which comprised in large part patent and tax disputes and monetary claims against the government.

and disfavor those requests in which its position is conservative. There is support for this inference in the fact that the Solicitor General in 1964 and 1965 authorized appeals in 42 per cent of the cases in which the government's position was liberal and in but 2 per cent of the cases in which it was conservative.[56] There is further support in the Solicitor General's confessions of error, which appear to take place predominantly when the government's position is conservative, and in his opposition in Court to the Interstate Commerce Commission, which appears to occur when the Commission's position is conservative.

Finally, the Solicitor General reveals the government's alignment with the Court's liberal inclinations in cases in which the government appears not as a litigant but as *amicus curiae*. In such instances the Solicitor General is not conducting litigation initiated elsewhere by others in the executive branch. In some instances, to be sure, such non-government litigation impinges so directly upon some part of the executive branch that the Solicitor General's position in approving intervention as *amicus* is little different from that in approving an appeal to the Court; but in many other instances he appears to act upon either his own (or his Office's) political inclinations or those of the Attorney General and Presidency.

We have shown that the United States has had phenomenal success as *amicus curiae* in the Supreme Court. The question is: why? There is no reason to believe that the Solicitor General's Office performs more ably as *amicus* than as a party in litigation. The Court does appear to regard the government somewhat more favorably when it acts in the first

---

[56] *Annual Report of Attorney General*, for 1965 and 1966, Table V, p. 42, and Table V, p. 54, respectively. We have assumed that the government held the liberal position in the appeal requests and in authorizations dealing with antitrust, civil rights, labor, and the regulatory agencies; and the conservative position in those dealing with criminal prosecutions and internal security. In these cases, the Solicitor General authorized 37 appeals and rejected 52 when the government was liberal, and authorized 10 appeals and rejected 215 when it was conservative. A definitive assessment of the government's doctrinal position in appeal requests and authorizations would require an examination of the cases themselves, as well as an examination and classification of the government's lower-court defeats for which the Justice Department divisions and the agencies did not request appeals.

capacity. We have noted that the Solicitor General has gained credit with the Court as a party in cases by demonstrating impartiality on occasion. He appears to gain even more credit as *amicus curiae*. According to one Court source, the justices look upon the government as having no axe to grind when it approaches them as *amicus*, but rather as sharing their own concern with seeing that justice is done.[57]

The government's success as *amicus curiae* is closely related to its doctrinal position in that role. Since 1937, as we have seen, the government has usually won its cases in Court when it has held the liberal position, and its usual position has been a liberal one. As *amicus* it has done even better. In the first place, it has chosen to align itself overwhelmingly with the liberal party in litigation. It supported the liberal position sixty-two times in terms sampled during this period and the conservative position only eight times. Secondly, the government won over 90 per cent of the time when it backed the liberal party. This record was substantially better than its record when it acted as a direct party in litigation.[58]

Why is the government more often in a liberal position today when it acts as *amicus curiae* in the Supreme Court than when it acts as a direct party in litigation? One reason is that it is not involved in defending its successful criminal prosecutions in federal district courts, for the government necessarily occupies the conservative position in arguing against defendants' claims in such proceedings. It seems clear, in addition, that the Solicitor General's Office has been entering a number of cases in the liberal position where no immediate governmental interest is involved. It has done so mostly when the subject under litigation concerns civil liberty or equality. When it enters someone else's litigation concerning economic regulation, the government usually has a tangible interest as *amicus curiae*: the National Labor Relations Board may wish the Solicitor General to enter a suit arising under national labor legislation

---

[57] Davis interview.
[58] The sampled terms were 1943–1945 and 1963–1965. Liberal litigants supported by the government won fifty-seven times and lost five times, and conservative litigants supported by it won six times and lost two times.

brought by union members against union officials, or the Anti-
trust Division of the Justice Department may wish him to enter
a suit brought by one business against another under antitrust
legislation—although parties in these and other economic
disputes at times seek to draw the government in as an amical
ally. But the Solicitor General's entry into cases concerning
civil liberty and equality generally have not come about as a
result of pressures from government agencies with statutory
responsibilities in the controversies. Rather they have come
about at the initiative of the Solicitor General or, more usually,
the Attorney General or the Presidency, often as a result of
pressures from non-governmental organizations. These interventions most clearly reveal the government's political predilections. In the six terms since the 1940s that we have
examined, one-fourth of the *amicus* actions by the government
concerned civil liberty and equality. It is striking that the
government should have supported the winning—that is, the
liberal—side in every instance, and no less striking that nearly
all of the *amicus* interventions occurred in the most recent Court
terms studied.[59] Hence, the government is lending its weight to
liberal contestants—really broad interests—in political and
racial conflicts which make their appearance in the Supreme
Court. Since the Supreme Court's 1954 *School Segregation case*,
the government has received considerable, and apparently
growing, pressure to enter important civil rights and liberties
cases;[60] and it appears to be responding to them.

The government probably first gave its *amicus* support in a
major case involving civil liberties or rights in 1948, when it
entered the *Restrictive Covenant cases* at the request of the
National Association for the Advancement of Colored People.[61]
During the Kennedy administration, it was decided that the

---

[59] In the 1943–1945 terms only two of the government's thirty-two *amicus* inter-
       ventions involved civil liberty–equality matters, and in the 1963–1965 terms
       sixteen of thirty-six interventions involved such matters.
[60] Spritzer interview.
[61] The NAACP's effort to gain the Attorney General's *amicus* support is told in
       Clement E. Vose, *Caucasians Only* (Berkeley and Los Angeles: University of
       California Press, 1959), pp. 169–170, 173.

Solicitor General should support efforts to bring about Congressional redistricting and state legislative reapportionment, and desegregation in Southern schools, and eliminate discrimination in privately-owned places serving the public.[62] These activities were continued in the Johnson administration, though at a considerably reduced tempo, and involved the government in judicial attacks upon the use of residence certificates and poll taxes in state elections.[63]

There is one *amicus curiae* which wins about as often as the government does in that capacity. This is the American Civil Liberties Union, which often represents the forward margin of liberalism in cases dealing with claims of individual liberty, civil equality, and criminal defendants. In the 1963–1964 terms, the Civil Liberties Union appeared as *amicus* in twenty-three cases and, of those decided on the merits, was aligned with the successful party in twelve cases, and the unsuccessful party in two. These included some momentous and bitterly contested suits, including two cases in which the Civil Liberties Union opposed the government and emerged victorious.[64] The ACLU has not always done this well nor been this active as *amicus curiae*. In the 1943–1944 terms it was aligned with the winner in seven cases and with the loser in four cases decided on the merits, and twenty years earlier it was not involved in any cases handled by the Supreme Court.[65] The recent figures on the ACLU's *amicus* participation in the Court do not tell the full story of that organization's activity there, for the ACLU has been shifting increasingly from *amicus* to direct support of litigation. By its own count, the ACLU in early 1967 had eleven *amicus curiae* and thirty direct party actions before the Supreme Court in one stage or another of the Court's proceedings.[66]

[62] Spritzer interview. See, for example: *Baker* v. *Carr*, 369 U.S. 186 (1962), *Wesberry* v. *Sanders*, 376 U.S. 1 (1964), and *Reynolds* v. *Sims*, 377 U.S. 533 (1964) [redistricting and reapportionment]; *Griffin* v. *Prince Edward County*, 377 U.S. 218 (1964) [segregation]; *Bell* v. *Maryland*, 378 U.S. 226 (1964) and *Bouie* v. *Columbia*, 378 U.S. 347 (1964) [private discrimination].
[63] *Harman* v. *Forssenius*, 380 U.S. 528 (1965), *Harper* v. *Virginia*, 383 U.S. 663 (1966).
[64] *Aptheker* v. *Secretary of State*, 377 U.S. 500 (1964) and *Schneider* v. *Rusk*, 377 U.S. 163 (1964).   [65] Data compiled from Court reports.
[66] "Consolidated Docket of the American Civil Liberties Union and its Affiliates

SUMMARY

The Solicitor General has a dual responsibility in the American political system. One is to the President through the Attorney General, and the other is to the Supreme Court. The President expects him to coordinate the activities of executive agencies in the judicial realm, and to win cases there. The Court expects him to hold down the amount of executive litigation appealed to it, and to be generally candid with it. The Solicitor General and his staff serve both superiors to a remarkable degree, but it is to the executive branch that he owes his more fundamental loyalty.

The executive branch is the Supreme Court's major client. It is involved, one way or another, in over a third of the cases appealed to the Court and in half of those decided by it. The executive is also a very successful client. Most of its appeals get accepted for decision and most decisions where it is a party are in its favor. The government's success does not depend essentially upon the capacity in which it appears before the Court. It wins most of the cases it carries there and, though not to the same extent, most of the cases its adversaries carry; and it wins overwhelmingly when it intervenes in other people's litigation as *amicus curiae*.

There are four reasons why the government wins as often as it does in the Supreme Court. First, the general relationship between the two branches tends to draw them together. Second, the Solicitor General and his staff of able lawyers have great experience in dealing with the Court. Third, the Solicitor General has built up considerable credit with the Court. Fourth and, at least today, most significant, the government and the Court more often than not share a common ideological perspective in much litigation in which the government is involved, especially where it appears as *amicus curiae*.

and the Civil Liberties Defense and Education Fund and Its Roger Baldwin Projects," dated March 1, 1967, mimeographed. See also the *New York Times*, January 21, 1968, IV, p. E13.

7

Conclusion

THE SPECIAL RELATIONSHIP

This book has not dealt with the Supreme Court or the Presidency as separate entities, nor with the judicial doctrine of the executive, but with relations between the two institutions. Its thesis is that the two branches have had a special relationship to each other that neither has had to Congress. This is so for several reasons. In the first place, there is an affinity in the basic powers given to the Supreme Court and the Presidency. As Madison observed in the Constitutional Convention,[1] both are concerned with the execution and the expounding of the law. This common concern tends to give them, we have suggested, a common perspective on the broad problems of government. Secondly, the Constitutional framers strengthened the judicial and executive branches relative to Congress in order to offset the power of Congress. The legislative branch, they

[1] See his remarks quoted at p. 4.

believed, posed the greatest danger to a system of separate—but equal—powers. It was assumed that the judiciary and the executive would act together to keep from being absorbed into the legislative vortex, and thus would individual liberty be protected from the threat of government tyranny. Finally, in vesting the appointive power as they did, the framers intended that the Supreme Court should share the constitutional and, broadly speaking, political perspective of the Presidency and, to a lesser extent, of the Senate; and this perspective was seen to be different from that of the House of Representatives. The House was clearly the most democratic of the institutions formed by the Constitution, elected as it was by the same voters eligible to vote for the generally democratic lower chambers of the state legislatures. The President was at least once removed from the people, for he was to be chosen, in secrecy, by small groups of electors who were themselves to be selected in a manner prescribed by the state legislatures. These legislatures, whose upper chambers were generally elected by substantially restricted electorates, were also given the power of electing the Senate. To mitigate further popular influence upon them, the President, senators, and, of course, judges were all given longer terms of office than representatives. The framers intended the democratic impulse to find its most favorable outlet through the House of Representatives; the Presidency, Supreme Court, and Senate should be, to varying degrees, more receptive to the claims of property and to the virtues they saw arising from that foundation.

What emerged from the Constitutional Convention was not a formal alliance between the Supreme Court and the Presidency (with the Senate a weaker adherent). That would have happened if the proposal of a Council of Revision had been adopted, to bring together the executive branch and members of the Court to pass upon the constitutionality and policy of both Congressional and state legislative acts before they took effect. What did emerge was, for limited purposes, an informal alliance formed by the considerations that we have set forth. Because of this perceived special relationship between the two branches George Washington, always sensitive to the constitutional boundaries of his power, saw nothing wrong in appointing Chief Justice Jay to serve simultaneously as Minister Plenipotentiary to Great Britain, or in asking Jay, along with his department heads, for advice on policy matters and for ideas for proposed legislation. It was also because of this perceived relationship that Washington was willing to ask the Court if he might have its advice on legal questions arising from hostilities between Great Britain and France. Likewise, Congress considered it proper to have circuit courts assist the Secretary of War in deciding upon invalid pension claims by having them, in effect, recommend action to that official on them.

The Supreme Court was not, of course, intended to be a satellite of the Presidency. Its members were to be eminent and independent men, not hirelings, and their term of office and protected salary were to permit them to retain their independence beyond the terms of any President. There was, moreover, a difference in the power given to the Court and to the Presidency. In the Madison remarks to which we have referred concerning the similarity between the judicial and executive branches, two differences were also noted. The chief executive has much more to do with the collective interest and security of the nation, and much greater latitude of opinion and discretion in administering his branch than does the Court. This is essentially what Hamilton and Marshall taken together meant, when Hamilton stated in *Federalist 78* that the judiciary exercises judgment, not force or will, and Marshall stated as a member of Congress that the President was the sole organ of the nation in foreign affairs.[2]

The Supreme Court exercises its judgment in deciding cases, and here it acts both as a law court and as a constitutional court. In the first capacity it resolves disputes between particular parties, including the executive; and in the other it interprets the Constitution, including those provisions dealing with the powers of the governmental branches. In both capacities

[2] See pp. 4–5, 18.

the Court's obligation is to the Constitution and to justice, and not to the President. The obligation is twofold and relates to the great purposes of the principle of separation of powers. These purposes, it will be recalled, are, first, and mainly, to safeguard popular liberty against the actions of government and, secondly, to prevent either of the two main classes in society from politically dominating the other. Now in the view of the framers it was Congress, especially the House of Representatives, which posed the most serious danger to the constitutional system of separation of powers, and thus the Court was expected to be usually—but not always—aligned against Congress, and alongside the Presidency, in constitutional conflicts. It is in this sense that the Constitution established a limited alliance between the judicial and executive branches.

The Supreme Court has in fact been closer to the Presidency than to Congress. Presidents have had the dominant part in appointing its members. Their extra-curiam relations with justices have been more numerous. They have probably been less affronted than Congress by judicial invalidations of legislation—except during the New Deal. Perhaps two dozen laws of some significance were voided to 1933, nearly all of which had been enacted without significant executive backing. Some invalidations could not have perturbed the chief executive at all (for example, *Pollock* v. *Farmers Loan & Trust Company*, 1895, invalidating the federal income tax of 1894, which had become law without President Cleveland's signature). A few were clearly welcome (for example, *Myers* v. *United States*, 1926, which ruled that Congress had no power to restrict the President's power to remove executive officials). An even more remarkable pattern is formed by the invalidations since the 1937 reorientation of the Supreme Court. The prediction made about then—that the Court would no longer attempt to obstruct Congressional law-making—has proved singularly wrong. National legislation had been declared unconstitutional in at least twenty-two cases decided through the middle of 1970, and nearly all of the invalidations occurred during the era of the Warren Court. In every instance the legislation restrained some claimed personal liberty or criminal right, and in most instances it had been shaped by Congress and not the Presidency—despite the fact that most public legislation since the time of Franklin Roosevelt has borne the executive imprimatur.

The Supreme Court has, of course, struck down Presidential actions as not being authorized by either the Constitution or statute. But this has not happened often.[3] Moreover, in only a few decisions of consequence was the authority of the Presidency directly at stake.[4] In one of these cases (*Marbury* v. *Madison*, 1803), the Court told the President that he had acted improperly, but it ruled a provision of law, and not his action, to be outside the Constitution; and in another (*Ex parte Milligan*, 1866), its ruling affected Congress as much as the Presidency.[5] The President's authority was indirectly involved in one other consequential Court decision (*Little* v. *Barreme*, 1804),[6] not to overlook the case of *Ex parte Merryman* (1861), in which Chief Justice Taney, and not the Court, administered a rebuke to the exercise of a claimed executive power.[7] Matched against these decisions are a greater number of important cases in which the assertion of the constitutional power of the

[3] Glendon Schubert, *The Presidency in the Courts* (Minneapolis: University of Minnesota Press, 1957), Appendix A, pp. 361–366, lists sixteen Supreme Court decisions in which it happened with respect to Presidential orders down to 1956.

[4] These were *Ex parte Milligan*, 4 Wall. 2 (1866), concerning the trial of a civilian by court-martial outside the theater of the Civil War; *Youngstown Sheet and Tube Company* v. *Sawyer*, 343 U.S. 579 (1952), concerning the seizure of the strike-bound steel industry; and *Rathbun* v. *United States*, 295 U.S. 602 (1935) and *Wiener* v. *United States*, 357 U.S. 349 (1958), dealing with the removal without cause of members of agencies vested with quasi-judicial or quasi-legislative functions; and *Marbury* v. *Madison*, 1 Cranch 137 (1803), involving a private suit to compel Secretary of State James Madison to deliver a commission of office to a minor judicial officer appointed under the preceding Adams administration.

[5] Five of the nine justices declared Congress, as well as the President, to be without authority to authorize courts-martial under the conditions mentioned.

[6] 2 Cranch 170 (1804), a private suit in which the Court ruled that the President could not empower the seizure of American ships bound from French ports since Congress had authorized such action only when such ships were bound for that country's ports, although the President might have had the constitutional power in the absence of Congressional regulation.

[7] 17 Fed. Cases 144 (No. 9487) (1861).

President was upheld by the Supreme Court, often in broad and affirmative terms.[8]

The Supreme Court's relations with Congress and the Presidency may be considered from the standpoint of efforts to overturn judicial decisions. Such efforts have been initiated by the legislative branch more often than by the executive branch. This was true of the Eleventh Amendment, which prohibited suits in federal courts by private parties or foreign governments against the states, without their consent; of the Fourteenth Amendment, which overruled the Supreme Court in extending citizenship to all persons born in the United States; and of the amendment proposed, but not ratified, in the 1920s, to give Congress power over the use of child labor. Recent serious attempts to overrule the Court through the amendment process have had their support in Congress but not in the executive branch—proposals, for example, to limit the President's power to make treaties and executive agreements, to allow prayers in public schools, and to permit states to reapportion one legislative chamber on some basis other than population. Indeed, in probably all of these instances, the chief executive either was opposed or gave no encouragement. The same has been the case with statutory actions aimed at overturning Supreme Court interpretations of federal law. These actions have been taken mainly at the initiative of Congress, stung by what it has considered improper judicial interpretations of its enactments, and the President either has supported the Court, or remained neutral. In recent decades successful Congressional overturnings have ranged from the Labor–Management Relations Act of

[8] Presidential actions carried out without Congressional authorization: *The Prize Cases*, 2 Black 635 (1863) (blockade of Southern ports); *In re Neagle*, 135 U.S. 1 (1890) (assigning protection to a Supreme Court justice); and *In re Debs*, 158 U.S. 564 (1895) (use of court injunction to prevent forcible obstruction of the mails). Presidential actions carried out in opposition to Congressional legislation: *U.S.* v. *Midwest Oil Co.*, 236 U.S. 459 (1915) (suspending private exploitation of public lands); and *Myers* v. *U.S.*, 272 U.S. 52 (1926) (removal of postmaster without cause). Other important Presidential actions: *Ex parte Grossman*, 267 U.S. 87 (1925) (pardoning a person punished by a court for contempt); *Biddle* v. *Perovich*, 274 U.S. 480 (1927) (commutation of a prison sentence regardless of the recipient's wishes); and *Ex parte Quirin*, 317 U.S. 1 (1942) (trial of accused German saboteurs by special military tribunal).

1947 to the Crime Control Act of 1948, both of which contained provisions directed against Supreme Court decisions. One study reports that there were twenty-one legislative overrulings of Court decisions in the twelve years from 1945 to 1957, not counting tax-law reversals.[9] But this rate is probably atypically high, for Congress was stronger in its relations with both the judicial and executive branches in that period than in the twelve years that preceded or have followed it.

Finally, most actions directed against the jurisdiction and independence of the Supreme Court have been Congressionally inspired. It is true that Jefferson spurred the Republicans in Congress to repeal the Judiciary Act of 1801 and to launch impeachment proceedings against Justice Samuel Chase, and that Franklin Roosevelt initiated the attempt to increase the size of the Court. More often it has been the legislative branch that has leveled the threats. To be sure, only once did threats against the Court's jurisdiction or independence result in legislation: when Congress deprived the Supreme Court of habeas corpus jurisdiction shortly after the Civil War and thereby prevented it from rendering judgment in a case before it which challenged Reconstruction legislation (*Ex parte McCardle*, 1869). In the 1820s and early 1830s, however, there was constant agitation in Congress to take away the Court's jurisdiction over state judicial decisions; and in the 1950s a strong threat developed to remove its jurisdiction over several categories of cases, relating mainly to internal security. No President joined in the early criticism, Andrew Johnson vetoed the habeas corpus act (only to have it re-passed), and Dwight Eisenhower lent his weight to keep the last effort from being enacted.[10]

THE DEMOCRATIC IMPACT

The balance among the three branches of government has been seriously affected by the democratization of American life.

[9] "Congressional Reversal of the Supreme Court, 1945–1957," *Harvard Law Review*, **71** (May, 1958), 1324–1327.

[10] See Walter F. Murphy, *Congress and the Court* (Chicago: University of Chicago

This trend, which began almost at the very start of our constitutional history, was checked by the aggressive spirit of
property in the latter part of the nineteenth century, but has,
with some pauses, been extending itself with increasing rapidity
during the present century. This trend has increased the power
of the Presidency more than that of the Senate, the House of
Representatives, or the states. More than any other institution,
the modern Presidency has articulated the democratic aspirations of liberty and, with marked emphasis in recent decades,
equality; and his office has in return received the support of the
mass of the people. To the power that has thus accrued to him
as the tribune of the people, the President has added the
awesome authority given to him by the Constitution in times
of international and domestic conflict. And as he has gained
strength in relation to Congress, so too, it appears, has his ally,
the Supreme Court. No longer is Congress the branch against
which protection is needed in the balance of powers. It is easy
today to agree with Woodrow Wilson's judgment, written in
1884, that "the central government is constantly becoming
stronger and more active," but who would concur in the rest of
the sentence: "and Congress is establishing itself as the one
sovereign authority in that government"?[11] Indeed, the great
power that Congress possessed during much of the nineteenth
century was about at its peak when the sentence was composed,
and the start of its gradual decline was not far off. Even the
Supreme Court, operating generally within the protective
shadow of the Presidency, has been emboldened in recent decades to make incursions upon the legislative power, imposing
its will in place of that of Congress through loose statutory
construction, imposing it where Congress has chosen not to act,
and curtailing the exercise of Congress's discretion in matters
once considered to fall within the prerogative of the legislative
branch. The Court's decisions on Congressional districting
(*Wesberry* v. *Sanders*, 1964) and on Congressional power to

Press, Phoenix Books, 1962), and C. Herman Pritchett, *Congress versus the
Supreme Court*, 1957–1960 (Minneapolis: University of Minnesota Press, 1961).
[11] Woodrow Wilson, *Congressional Government: A Study in American Politics* (Boston:
Houghton Mifflin, 1885, 1925), p. 316.

exclude persons elected to it (*Powell* v. *McCormack*, 1969) are perhaps the two most striking instances. This is what is meant by an activist Supreme Court.

The democratic aspirations which the President and the Supreme Court, more than Congress, espouse today take the doctrinal form of contemporary liberalism, which we have briefly described in its judicial setting in the preceding chapter. This doctrine puts great emphasis upon freedom from governmental restraint, except when economic freedom or egalitarian claims are involved. It sympathizes with the claims of criminal defendants against the state; employees, unions, and consumers against business; small business against large business; and, most of all, equality against privilege and often much else besides. Since Democratic Presidents have been more liberal than has Congress in the contemporary period of the Court, and since they have held office during most of this period, it is not surprising that the Supreme Court has also been more liberal than Congress. The Supreme Court since 1937 has been sharply different than it was in any preceding period. No earlier Court was as democratic in terms of the common origins of its members. No earlier Court pressed the constitutional rights of property as far as the present Court has pressed those of personal liberty and civic equality. No earlier Court was ever so charmed by any political principle contained in the Constitution as the present Court has been by democracy.

The democratizing of the Presidency has also affected relations between that institution and the Supreme Court. It has, we may suggest, contributed to strains in their relations, especially to those that have on several occasions resulted in open conflict: during the Presidencies of Jefferson, Jackson, Lincoln, and Franklin Roosevelt. Theodore Roosevelt would be on this list except that his irritation with the Supreme Court never quite reached the point of his taking action against it other than occasionally to criticize it quite sharply. Each President was a major one whose election inaugurated a new political era, which meant that each in taking office confronted a Supreme Court that represented the orientation of the era just ended. The framers probably did not anticipate much friction between the two branches, because they did not anticipate wide shifts in the political outlook of the Presidency, The President, it must be repeated, was to be chosen by a select body of electors, and not through partisan nomination and popular election. The electors would be the distinguished members of their communities, excluding congressmen and other federal officeholders; and, if chosen by the people, would not be nominated or controlled by the people in their voting, which would be done secretly. The framers seem to have assumed that "the system of checks and balances [would] preserve *the factual distribution of power* which then existed in American society between the few and the many."[12] Thus they must have expected considerable continuity in the policies and general outlook of the Presidency and, to a lesser extent, the Senate, and so contemplated greater harmony between the judicial and executive branches than has in fact existed.

In the process of becoming democratized, the Presidency was exposed to the varying currents and coalitions of the electorate. Since its members hold their positions for life, the Supreme Court has responded to new Presidential courses only as quickly as the appointive process, aided perhaps by external pressure, could produce new majorities. The process of judicial adaptation might be aided by the presence of older justices with constitutional perspectives "ahead of their time," as happened in the New Deal; but it might be impeded or largely prevented by the conversion of new justices to the older perspectives, as tended to happen to the men appointed by Jefferson and Madison.

The last significant conflict between the Supreme Court and the Presidency occurred over three decades ago. Since the New Deal, relations between the two have been generally amicable, undisturbed by the outbursts that have characterized the Court's relations with Congress. A powerful, democratic

---

[12] Paul Eidelberg, *The Philosophy of the American Constitution* (New York: The Free Press, 1968), p. 252. See also his discussion of the original conception of the electoral college, pp. 169–191.

Presidency has had its impact upon the Court. The Court now shares the executive branch's democratic aspirations. The executive has become a dominant participant in it, as litigant and as *amicus curiae*. The Court is greatly dependent upon the Solicitor General for assistance in coping with its ever-mounting flow of cases, and grateful. Since the turn of the century, and especially since the New Deal, justices have, much more than in the past, been attracted by the power of the Presidential domain, and a number of them have entered into it as social companions, administrative helpers, and political advisers. In their contemporary relationship, the Presidency has gained considerable influence over the Supreme Court.

Yet the President cannot be said to dominate the Court. If the Court treats him well when he comes before it in support of egalitarian or libertarian positions, so does it, if not quite so fully, treat all other parties in those positions. If it generally rules against other parties supporting non-liberal positions (in the contemporary context), so does it, if not quite so often, rule against the government in those circumstances. The Court in this way helps to shape the doctrinal cast of the litigation that the Solicitor General brings to it, for he tends to appeal those losses in lower federal courts in which the government occupies the liberal position and not to appeal those in which it occupies the non-liberal one. Thus, the flow of influence between Court and Presidency moves in two directions.

Tension continues to exist between the two institutions. If nothing else, the interests and ambitions of justices and Presidents cannot be the same. We must remember that the framers gave the members of the three branches not only "the necessary constitutional means," but also "personal motives, to resist encroachments of the others."[13] Hence rivalry must permeate judicial–executive relations to at least some extent. But neither can the doctrinal perspectives of the two branches coincide. A President cannot be sure that he is getting what he thinks he is getting in his appointments, a person may change his views

---

[13] *Federalist 51*, in Alexander Hamilton, John Jay, and James Madison, *The Federalist*, ed. by Max Beloff (Oxford: Basil Blackwell, 1948), p. 265.

after joining the Court, and the judicial obligation calls upon a justice to heed the Constitution and the laws, and not Presidential positions. On the other hand, even an executive strongly dedicated to libertarian goals must preserve public order, and thus he must restrain some assertions of personal liberty. Moreover, the doctrinal perspective of the Presidency may shift sharply once more—in the direction of a greater balance of classes, or in some other direction: a President dedicated to equality need not be dedicated to personal liberty. In either instance, the two branches of government could again confront each other across a doctrinal chasm.

However it comes about, if it should, a new conflict between the Supreme Court and the Presidency might find the Court much less able to defend itself than in the past. We should not overestimate the Court's strength on the basis of its ability to encroach upon Congress without significant retaliation. Congress is not easy to stir into action on controversial matters, and the Court has doctrinal allies there, as well as many who hold the Court, if not necessarily certain of its members, in high respect. In addition, some attempts to move against the Court have needed a two-thirds majority vote. And we should not forget that the contemporary Court has enjoyed the support, or at least the benevolent neutrality, of the Presidency. What would happen if the Court, in a situation of heightened tension, discovered that the arm of wrath had been raised by the President, or by a Congress undeterred by the President? To whom could the Court turn for help? The bar and the people generally? On what ground? That it is the agent of the democratic will? But the President and Congress would be much better able to claim that role than would nine men holding their positions for life, not popularly chosen but appointed, probably some time in the past, hatching their decisions in a conclave of secrecy. That is not democracy, the President or Congress could say, but rather, echoing Jefferson and Lincoln, judicial despotism. Or would the Court appeal to the people on the ground that it acts in the traditional role of guardian of the Constitution, exercising judgment and not will, its decisions untainted by ideological partiality? If it did. would it be believed? Is it possible that an activist Court, engaged in making judicial policy, operating as part of the regular political process, could convince the people that it still occupies that elevated constitutional position that has justified the peculiar power which the Supreme Court has enjoyed in the American political system?

Appendix: Appointments to the Supreme Court

This is a listing of persons who accepted appointments to which the Senate had given its consent. Several persons declined such appointments: Robert H. Harrison (1789), William Cushing (from associate justice to Chief Justice, 1796), John Jay (1801), Levi Lincoln (1811), John Quincy Adams (1811), and William Smith (1837). John Randolph served briefly in an interim appointment (1795), but the Senate rejected his nomination to a regular one.

Party affiliations are abbreviated as follows: Fed.= Federalist; Rep.= Republican; Dem.= Democrat; Ind.= Independent.

The number in the far right column indicates the Court position to which the appointment was made.

Footnote citations (1–4) are explained at the conclusion of the Appendix.

George Washington (1789–1797)

John Jay (Ch. Jus.)	N. Y.	Fed.	Sept. 1789	June 1795	1
John Rutledge	S. C.	Fed.	Sept. 1789	Mar. 1791	2
William Cushing	Mass.	Fed.	Sept. 1789	Sept. 1810	3
James Wilson	Pa.	Fed.	Sept. 1789	Aug. 1798	4
John Blair	Va.	Fed.	Sept. 1789	Jan. 1796	5
James Iredell	N. C.	Fed.	Feb. 1790	Oct. 1799	6
Thomas Johnson	Md.	Fed.	Aug. 1791[1] Nov. 1791	Mar. 1793	2
William Paterson	N. J.	Fed.	Mar. 1793	Sept. 1806	2
Samuel Chase	Md.	Fed.	Jan. 1796	June 1811	5
Oliver Ellsworth (Ch. Jus.)	Conn.	Fed.	Mar. 1796	Sept. 1800	1

John Adams (*1797–1801*)

Bushrod Washington	Va.	Fed.	Sept. 1798[1] Dec. 1798	Nov. 1829	4
Alfred Moore	N. C.	Fed.	Dec. 1799	Mar. 1804	6
John Marshall (Ch. Jus.)	Va.	Fed.	Jan. 1801	July 1835	1

Thomas Jefferson (*1801–1809*)

William Johnson	S. C.	Rep.	Mar. 1804	Aug. 1834	6
Brockholst Livingston	N. Y.	Rep.	Nov. 1806[1] Dec. 1806	Mar. 1823	2
Thomas Todd	Ky.	Rep.	Mar. 1807	Feb. 1826	7

James Madison (*1809–1817*)

Gabriel Duval	Md.	Rep.	Nov. 1811	Jan. 1835	5
Joseph Story	Mass.	Rep.	Nov. 1811	Sept. 1845	3

James Monroe (*1817–1825*)

Smith Thompson	N. Y.	Rep.	Sept. 1823[1] Dec. 1823	Dec. 1843	2

John Quincy Adams (*1825–1829*)

Robert Trimble	Ky.	Rep.	May 1826	Aug. 1828	7

Andrew Jackson (*1829–1837*)

John McLean	Ohio	Dem.	Mar. 1829	Apr. 1861	7
Henry Baldwin	Pa.	Dem.	Jan. 1830	Apr. 1844	4
James M. Wayne	Ga.	Dem.	Jan. 1835	July 1867	6
Philip P. Barbour	Va.	Dem.	Mar. 1836	Feb. 1841	5
Roger B. Taney (Ch. Jus.)	Md.	Dem.	Mar. 1836	Oct. 1864	1

Martin Van Buren (*1837–1841*)

John Catron	Tenn.	Dem.	Mar. 1837	May 1865	8
John McKinley	Ky.	Dem.	Apr. 1837[1] Sept. 1837	July 1852	9
Peter V. Daniel	Va.	Dem.	Mar. 1841	May 1860	5

John Tyler (*1841–1845*)

Samuel Nelson	N. Y.	Dem.	Feb. 1845	Dec. 1873	2

James K. Polk (*1845–1849*)

Levi Woodbury	N. H.	Dem.	Sept. 1845[1] Jan. 1846	Dec. 1851	3
Robert C. Grier	Pa.	Dem.	Aug. 1846	Jan. 1870	4

Millard Fillmore (1850–1853)

Benjamin R. Curtis	Mass.	Whig	Sept. 1851[1] Dec. 1851	Sept. 1857	3

Franklin Pierce (1853–1857)

John A. Campbell	Ala.	Dem.	Mar. 1853	May 1861	9

James Buchanan (1857–1861)

Nathan Clifford	Me.	Dem.	Jan. 1858	July 1881	3

Abraham Lincoln (1861–1865)

Noah H. Swayne	Ohio	Rep.	Jan. 1862	Jan. 1881	7
Samuel F. Miller	Iowa	Rep.	July 1862	Oct. 1890	5
David Davis	Ill.	Rep.	Oct. 1862[1] Dec. 1862	Mar. 1877	9
Stephen J. Field	Calif.	Dem.	Mar. 1863	Dec. 1897	10
Salmon P. Chase (Ch. Jus.)	Ohio	Rep.	Dec. 1864	May 1873	1

Ulysses S. Grant (1869–1877)

Edwin M. Stanton	Pa.	Rep.	Dec. 1869	Dec. 1869	4
William Strong	Pa.	Rep.	Feb. 1870	Dec. 1880	4
Joseph P. Bradley	N. J.	Rep.	Mar. 1870	Jan. 1892	6
Ward Hunt	N. Y.	Rep.	Dec. 1872	Jan. 1882	2
Morrison R. Waite (Ch. Jus.)	Ohio	Rep.	Jan. 1874	Mar. 1888	1

Rutherford B. Hayes (1877–1881)

John M. Harlan	Ky.	Rep.	Nov. 1877	Oct. 1911	9
William B. Woods	Ga.	Rep.	Dec. 1880	May 1887	4

James A. Garfield (1881)

Stanley Matthews	Ohio	Rep.	May 1881	Mar. 1889	7

Chester A. Arthur (1881–1885)

Horace Gray	Mass.	Rep.	Dec. 1881	Sept. 1902	3
Samuel Blatchford	N. Y.	Rep.	Mar. 1882	July 1893	2

Grover Cleveland (1885–1889)

Lucius Q. C. Lamar	Miss.	Dem.	Jan. 1888	Jan. 1893	4
Melville W. Fuller (Ch. Jus.)	Ill.	Dem.	July 1888	July 1910	1

Benjamin Harrison (1889–1893)

David J. Brewer	Kans.	Rep.	Dec. 1889	Mar. 1910	7
Henry B. Brown	Mich.	Rep.	Dec. 1890	May 1906	5
George Shiras, Jr.	Pa.	Rep.	July 1892	Feb. 1903	6
Howell E. Jackson	Tenn.	Dem.	Feb. 1893	Aug. 1895	4

Grover Cleveland (1893–1897)

| Edward D. White | La. | Dem. | Feb. 1894 | Dec. 1910² | 2 |
| Rufus W. Peckham | N. Y. | Dem. | Dec. 1895 | Oct. 1909 | 4 |

William McKinley (1897–1901)

| Joseph McKenna | Calif. | Rep. | Jan. 1898 | Jan. 1925 | 1 |
| | | | | | (8)* |

Theodore Roosevelt (1901–1909)

Oliver W. Holmes	Mass.	Rep.	Dec. 1902	Jan. 1932	3
William R. Day	Ohio	Rep.	Feb. 1903	Nov. 1922	6
William H. Moody	Mass.	Rep.	Dec. 1906	Nov. 1910	5

William Howard Taft (1909–1913)

Horace H. Lurton	Tenn.	Dem.	Dec. 1909	July 1914	4
Charles E. Hughes	N. Y.	Rep.	May 1910	June 1916	7
Edward D. White (Ch. Jus.)	La.	Dem.	Dec. 1910	May 1921	1
Joseph R. Lamar	Ga.	Dem.	Dec. 1910	Jan. 1916	5
Willis Van Devanter	Wyo.	Rep.	Dec. 1910	June 1937	2
Mahlon Pitney	N. J.	Rep.	Mar. 1912	Dec. 1922	9

Woodrow Wilson (1913–1921)

James C. McReynolds	Tenn.	Dem.	Aug. 1914	Feb. 1941	4
Louis D. Brandeis	Mass.	Dem.	June 1916	Feb. 1939	5
John H. Clarke	Ohio	Dem.	July 1916	Sept. 1922	7

Warren G. Harding (1921–1923)

William H. Taft (Ch. Jus.)	Ohio	Rep.	June 1921	Feb. 1930	1
George Sutherland	Utah	Rep.	Sept. 1922	Jan. 1938	7
Pierce Butler	Minn.	Dem.	Dec. 1922	Nov. 1939	6
Edward T. Sanford	Tenn.	Rep.	Jan. 1923	Mar. 1930	9

Calvin Coolidge (1923–1929)

| Harlan F. Stone | N. Y. | Rep. | Feb. 1925 | July 1941² | 8 |

Herbert Hoover (1929–1933)

Charles E. Hughes (Ch. Jus.)	N. Y.	Rep.	Feb. 1930	June 1941	1
Owen J. Roberts	Pa.	Rep.	May 1930	July 1945	9
Benjamin N. Cardozo	N. Y.	Dem.	Mar. 1932	July 1938	3

Franklin D. Roosevelt (1933–1945)

Hugo L. Black	Ala.	Dem.	Aug. 1937	—	2
Stanley Reed	Ky.	Dem.	Jan. 1938	Feb. 1957	7
Felix Frankfurter	Mass.	Ind. (Dem.)[4]	Jan. 1939	Feb. 1965	3
William O. Douglas	Conn.	Dem.	Apr. 1939	—	5
Frank Murphy	Mich.	Dem.	Jan. 1940	July 1949	6
James F. Byrnes	S. C.	Dem.	June 1941	Oct. 1942	4
Harlan F. Stone (Ch. Jus.)	N. Y.	Rep.	July 1941	Apr. 1946	1
Robert H. Jackson	N. Y.	Dem.	July 1941	Oct. 1954	8
Wiley B. Rutledge	Iowa	Dem.	Feb. 1943	Sept. 1949	4

Harry S. Truman (1945–1953)

Harold H. Burton	Ohio	Rep.	Sept. 1945	Oct. 1958	9
Fred M. Vinson (Ch. Jus.)	Ky.	Dem.	June 1946	Sept. 1953	1
Tom C. Clark	Tex.	Dem.	Aug. 1949	June 1967	6
Sherman Minton	Ind.	Dem.	Oct. 1949	Oct. 1956	4

Dwight D. Eisenhower (1953–1961)

Earl Warren (Ch. Jus.)	Calif.	Rep.	Oct. 1953[1] Mar. 1954	June 1969	1
John M. Harlan	N. Y.	Rep.	Mar. 1955	—	8
William J. Brennan, Jr.	N. J.	Dem.	Oct. 1956[1] Mar. 1957	—	4
Charles E. Whittaker	Mo.	Rep.	Mar. 1957	Apr. 1962	7
Potter Stewart	Ohio	Rep.	Oct. 1958[1] May 1959	—	9

John F. Kennedy (1961–1963)

Arthur J. Goldberg	Ill.	Dem.	Sept. 1962	July 1965	3
Byron R. White	Colo.	Dem.	Apr. 1962	—	7

Lyndon B. Johnson (1963–1969)

Abe Fortas	Tenn.	Dem.	Aug. 1965	May 1969	3
Thurgood Marshall	N. Y.	Dem.	Aug. 1967	—	6

Richard M. Nixon (1969–   )

Warren E. Burger (Ch. Jus.)	Minn.	Rep.	June 1969	—	1
Harry A. Blackmun	Minn.	Rep.	May 1970	—	3

[1] Interim appointment; date of regular appointment listed below.

[2] Elevated to chief justiceship at this time.

[3] It makes sense to eliminate position ten here and to assign McKenna to the empty position eight. Position ten was established in 1863 when the Court's size was increased to ten members, and Field served in it from then until his retirement in 1897. Strictly speaking, the position was not affected by changes made in the Court's size in 1866 and 1869, to seven members (as vacancies occurred) and to nine members, respectively. Instead, the vacancy created in position eight by Catron's death in 1865 was simply not filled.

[4] At the time of his appointment Frankfurter classified himself as an Independent, but seemed generally aligned with the Democrats.

Select Bibliography

General

Beveridge, Albert J. *The Life of John Marshall.* Boston: Houghton Mifflin, 1916–1919. 4 volumes.

Fairman, Charles. *Mr. Justice Miller and the Supreme Court, 1862–1890.* Cambridge: Harvard University Press, 1939.

Mason, Alpheus T. *Harlan Fiske Stone: Pillar of the Law.* New York: Viking Press, 1956.

Roosevelt and Frankfurter: Their Correspondence, 1928–1945, annot. by Max Freedman. Boston: Little, Brown, 1967.

Swisher, Carl B. *American Constitutional Development,* 2nd ed. Boston: Houghton Mifflin, 1954.

Warren, Charles. *The Supreme Court in United States History.* Boston: Little, Brown, 1926. 2 volumes.

Separation of Powers

Beard, Charles A. *The Supreme Court and the Constitution.* New York: Macmillan, 1912.

Corwin, Edward S. *The Doctrine of Judicial Review: Its Legal and Historical Basis and Other Essays.* Princeton: Princeton University Press, 1914.

Fairlie, John A. "The Separation of Powers," *Michigan Law Review*, **21** (February, 1923), 393–436.

Farrand, Max, ed. *The Records of the Federal Convention of 1787*; rev. ed. New Haven: Yale University Press, 1937. 4 volumes.

Hamilton, Alexander, John Jay, and James Madison. *The Federalist*, ed. by Max Beloff. Oxford: Basil Blackford, 1948.

Kolstad, William A. "The Presidents and Judicial Review." Doctoral dissertation, Political Science Department, University of Texas, 1964.

Meigs, William. *The Relation of the Judiciary to the Constitution.* New York: Neale Publ. Co., 1919.

Locke, John. *Two Treatises on Civil Government.* London: George Routledge and Sons, 1884. Book II.

Montesquieu, Baron de. *The Spirit of the Laws*, trans. by Thomas Nugent. New York: Hafner Publ. Co., 1949. Book XI.

Parker, Reginald. "The Historic Basis of Administrative Law: Separation of Powers and Judicial Supremacy," *Rutgers Law Review*, **12** (Spring, 1958), 449–481.

Powell, Thomas R. "Separation of Powers: Administrative Exercise of Legislative and Judicial Power," *Political Science Quarterly*, **27** (June, 1912), 215–238.

Appointments

Abraham, Henry J., and Edward M. Goldberg. "A Note on the Appointment of Justices of the Supreme Court of the United States," *American Bar Association Journal*, **46** (February, 1960), 147–150, 219–222.

Danelski, David J. *A Supreme Court Justice Is Appointed.* New York: Random House, 1964.

Ewing, Cortez A. M. *The Judges of the Supreme Court, 1789–1937: A Study of Their Qualifications.* Minneapolis: University of Minnesota Press, c. 1938.

Frank, John P. "The Appointment of Supreme Court Justices: Prestige, Principles, and Politics," *Wisconsin Law Review* (March, 1941), 172–210; (May, 1941), 343–379; (July, 1941), 461–512.

Frankfurter, Felix. "The Supreme Court in the Mirror of Justices," *University of Pennsylvania Law Review*, **105** (April, 1957), 781–796.

Grossman, Joel B. *Lawyers and Judges: The ABA and the Politics of Judicial Selection.* New York: John Wiley, 1965.

McHargue, Daniel S. "Appointments to the Supreme Court of the United States: The Factors that Have Affected Appointments, 1789–1932." Doctoral dissertation, Political Science Department, University of California at Los Angeles, 1949.

Schmidhauser, John R. "The Justices of the Supreme Court: A Collective Portrait," *Midwest Journal of Political Science*, **3** (February, 1959), 1–57.

Conflict

Alsop, Joseph, and Turner Catledge. *The 168 Days*. Garden City, N.Y.: Doubleday, Doran, 1938.

Fisher, Sidney G. "The Suspension of Habeas Corpus during the War of the Rebellion," *Political Science Quarterly*, 3 (September, 1888), 454–485.

Hart, Henry M., Jr. "The Power of Congress to Limit the Jurisdiction of Federal Courts," *Harvard Law Review*, 66 (June, 1953), 1362–1402.

Longaker, Richard P. "Andrew Jackson and the Judiciary," *Political Science Quarterly*, 71 (March, 1956), 341–364.

Pollitt, Daniel H. "The Executive Enforcement of Judicial Decrees," *American Bar Association Journal*, 45 (June, 1959), 600–603, 606.

Randall, James G. *Constitutional Problems under Lincoln*; rev. ed. Urbana: University of Illinois Press, 1951.

Rossiter, Clinton. *The Supreme Court and the Commander in Chief*. Ithaca: Cornell University Press, 1951.

Schweppe, Alfred J. "Enforcement of Federal Court Decrees: A 'Recurrence to Fundamental Principles,'" *American Bar Association Journal*, 44 (February, 1958), 113–116, 187–190, 192.

Van Buren, Martin. *Inquiry into the Origin and Course of Political Parties in the United States*. New York: Hurd and Houghton, 1867.

The War of the Rebellion: A Compilation of the Official Records of the Union and Confederate Armies. Washington: Government Printing Office, 1897.

Out-of-Court Relations

"The Association and the Supreme Court," *American Bar Association Journal*, 32 (December, 1946), 862–863.

"Independence of Judges: Should They Be Used for Non-Judicial Work?", *American Bar Association Journal*, 33 (August, 1947), 792–796.

McCloy, John J. "Owen J. Roberts' Extra Curiam Activities," *University of Pennsylvania Law Review*, 104 (December, 1955), 350–353.

Murphy, Walter F. *Elements of Judicial Strategy*. Chicago: University of Chicago Press, 1964.

Senate Committee on the Judiciary, Nominations of Abe Fortas and Homer Thornberry, Hearings, July 11, 12, 16, 17, 18, 19, 20, 22, and 23, 1968, 90th Congress, 2nd Session, 1968. Washington: Government Printing Office, 1968.

See also "*General*" bibliographic references at start of Select Bibliography.

Expectations and Performance

Decisions of the Supreme Court. Published in three places: (1) *United States Reports*. Washington: Government Printing Office; (2) *Supreme Court Reporter*. St. Paul: West Publ. Co.; and (3) *United States Supreme Court*

Reports, Lawyers' Edition. Rochester, N.Y.: Lawyers Cooperative Publ. Co.

See also "General" bibliographic references at start of Select Bibliography.

The Executive in Court

Annual Report of the Attorney General of the United States. Washington: Department of Justice (published at end of each fiscal year).

Brigman, William E. "The Office of the Solicitor General of the United States." Doctoral dissertation, Political Science Department, University of North Carolina, 1966.

Klonoski, James R. "The Influence of Government Counsel on Supreme Court Decisions involving the Commerce Power." Doctoral dissertation, Political Science Department, University of Michigan, 1958.

Krislov, Samuel. "The *Amicus Curiae* Brief: From Friendship to Advocacy," *Yale Law Journal,* **72** (March, 1963), 694–721.

Perlman, Philip B. "The Work of the Office of the Solicitor General of the United States." Address before the Fifty-fourth Annual Meeting of the Maryland State Bar Association, July 2, 1949. Mimeographed.

Sobeloff, Simon E. "Lawyer for the Government." Address at the Annual Dinner of the New York University Law School Alumni Association, New York City, March 15, 1955. Mimeographed. Published, in revised form, as "Attorney for the Government," *American Bar Association Journal,* **41** (March, 1955), 229–232.

"Statement of Policy and Practice regarding Applications to the Solicitor General for Consent to File *Amicus Curiae* Briefs in the Supreme Court." Washington: Office of the Solicitor General, May, 1957. Mimeographed.

Stern, Robert L. "'Inconsistency' in Government Litigation," *Harvard Law Review,* **64** (March, 1951), 759–769.

Stern, Robert L. "The Solicitor General's Office and Administrative Agency Litigation," *American Bar Association Journal,* **46** (February, 1960), 154–158, 217–218.

Swisher, Carl B. "Federal Organization of Legal Functions," *American Political Science Review,* **33** (December, 1939), 973–1000.

INDEX

INDEX

Abraham, Henry J.: on senatorial courtesy, 102

Adams, John:
and assignment of Ellsworth to executive duty, 67
and expectations in appointments, 125–26
on government powers, 4

Adams, John Q.: and expectations in appointments, 128

Advising Presidents:
Council of State, 61–62
judicial advice, 65–66
legal advice, 63–64
political advice: general, 68–69; minor and unsolicited, 69; more than minimal, 70–78; restraints upon giving, 83–84

American Bar Association: role in appointments, 92–93

Appointments:
advising the President: general, 88–89, 93; Attorney General, 89–90; senators, 90–91; justices, 91; others, 91–93
frequency, 86
importance of chief justiceship, 87
number of justices appointed, 86; and length of Presidential service, 86–87
(*See also* Presidential control of appointments; *and* specific names of justices and Presidents)

Baldwin, Justice Henry: and Presidential expectations, 130

Bickel, Alexander: on Brandeis's position in *Bailey case,* 136

Black, Justice Hugo L.:
early political association, 106
opposition to R. Jackson, 91
political advice to F. Roosevelt, report, 73; unsolicited, 69

223